Foreign Accents

The International Studies in Shakespeare and His Contemporaries
Jay L. Halio, General Editor

Editorial Advisory Committee

Jay L. Halio, Chair
University of Delaware

Professor J. Leeds Barroll III
University of Maryland

Professor Stanley Wells
The Shakespeare Institute
University of Birmingham

Professor Yoshiko Kawachi
Kyorin University

Professor Arthur F. Kinney
University of Massachusetts

Professor Jerzy Limon
University of Gdansk

Dr. Barbara Mowat
Folger Shakespeare Library

Professor Werner Habicht
Institüt for Englische Philologie
University of Würzburg

Professor George Watson Williams
Duke University

1993
Shakespeare and His Contemporaries: Eastern and Central European Studies, eds. Jerzy Limon and Jay L. Halio

1995
French Essays on Shakespeare and His Contemporaries, eds. J. M. Maguin and Michèle Willems

1998
Redefining Shakespeare: Literary Theory and Theater Practice in the German Democratic Repubic, eds. J. Lawrence Guntner and Andrew M. McLean

Japanese Studies in Shakespeare and His Contemporaries, ed. Yoshiko Kawachi

Russian Essays in Shakespeare, eds. Alexandr Parfenov and Joseph Price

Strands Afar Remote: Israeli Essays on Shakespeare and His Contemporaries, ed. Avraham Oz

1999
Italian Studies in Shakespeare and His Contemporaries, eds. Michele Marrapodi and Giorgio Melchiori

2001
Foreign Accents: Brazilian Readings of Shakespeare, ed. Aimara da Cunha Resende

2002
Shakespeare and Scandinavia: A Collection of Nordic Studies, ed. Gunnar Sorelius

Foreign Accents

Brazilian Readings of Shakespeare

Edited by Aimara da Cunha Resende

Language Consultant:
Thomas LaBorie Burns

Newark: University of Delaware Press
London: Associated University Presses

© 2002 by Rosemont Publishing & Printing Corp.

All rights reserved. Authorization to photocopy items for internal or personal use, or the internal or personal use of specific clients, is granted by the copyright owner, provided that a base fee of $10.00, plus eight cents per page, per copy is paid directly to the Copyright Clearance Center, 222 Rosewood Drive, Danvers, Massachusetts 01923. [0-87413-753-5/02 $10.00 + 8¢ pp, pc.]

Other than as indicated in the foregoing, this book may not be reproduced, in whole or in part, in any form (except as permitted by Sections 107 and 108 of the U.S. Copyright Law, and except for brief quotes appearing in reviews in the public press).

Associated University Presses
440 Forsgate Drive
Cranbury, NJ 08512

Associated University Presses
16 Barter Street
London WC1A 2AH, England

Associated University Presses
P.O. Box 338, Port Credit
Mississauga, Ontario
Canada L5G 4L8

The paper used in this publication meets the requirements of the American National Standards for Permanence of Paper for Printed Library Materials Z39.48-1984.

Library of Congress Cataloging-in-Publication Data

Foreign accents : Brazilian readings of Shakespeare / edited by Aimara da Cunha Resende ; language editor, Thomas La Borie Burns.
    p. cm.—(International studies in Shakespeare and his contemporaries)
Includes bibliographical references and index.
ISBN 0-87413-753-5 (alk. paper)
    1. Shakespeare, William, 1564–1616—Appreciation—Brazil.
    2. Shakespeare, William, 1564–1616—Criticism and interpretation.
I. Resende, Aimara da Cunha. II. Burns, Thomas La Borie. III. Series.
PR2971.B7 F67   2002
822.3′3—dc21   2001034696

PRINTED IN THE UNITED STATES OF AMERICA

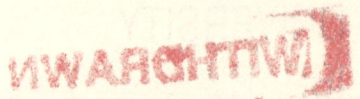

Contents

Acknowledgments	7
Introduction: Brazilian Appropriations of Shakespeare AIMARA DA CUNHA RESENDE	11
Theater for the Oppressed: Augusto Boal's *A Tempestade* MARLENE SOARES DOS SANTOS	42
Shakespeare's Sonnets: A Case of Nontranslation SOLANGE RIBEIRO DE OLIVEIRA	55
Hamletrash: A Brazilian *Hamlet* Made of Scraps ANNA STEGH CAMATI	62
Quotations from *Hamlet* in the Chronicles of Machado de Assis SILVIA MUSSI DA SILVA CLARO	76
Staging Practices in the Elizabethan Theater: *Titus Andronicus* at the Rose MARIA CLARA VERSIANI GALERY	100
Homo/Vir: The State of Man and Nature in *Macbeth* THOMAS LABORIE BURNS	114
The Taming of the Shrew: Shakespeare's Theater of Repetition MARIA LÚCIA MILLÉO MARTINS	126
Shakespeare's *Hamlet,* Salman Rushdie's "Yorick," and the Dilemmas of Tradition ADELAINE LA GUARDIA NOGUEIRA	138
"Uhuru!": Césaire's and Shakespeare's Uncontainable Calibans JOSÉ ROBERTO O'SHEA	154
Intertextuality in Shakespeare's *The Tempest* and Césaire's *Une Tempête* WILLIAM VALENTINE REDMOND	174
Stoppard's and Shakespeare's Views on Metatheater BERNARDINA DA SILVEIRA PINHEIRO	183

Godard: A Contemporary *King Lear* 198
    THAÍS FLORES NOGUEIRA DINIZ
Multiple Texts and Performance in the Final Scene of
Henry V 207
    MARGARIDA GANDARA RAUEN

Contributors 224
Index 228

Acknowledgments

My thanks are due to all those who have made this publication possible. As they are many, their names may not appear here, but they will be remembered with gratitude. Some, though, must be mentioned now. I would like to thank Dr. Jay Halio for his belief in our work and his unfailing support. Dr. Carlos Daghlian has continuously been supportive and in his position as President of ABRAPUI (Brazilian Association of University Teachers of English) he has permanently helped the contributors in this volume in his endeavor to make their research known and in allowing publication of essays found in the Annals of the Association. I would also like to thank CNPq, CAPES and FAPEMIG, funding Institutions in Brazil that have made possible some research the result of which is to be found here. The British Council in Brazil and the Folger Library have also supported some researchers for their stays at the Shakespeare Institute and the Library in Washington. To all those who, though not mentioned here, have contributed with their opinions, agreement and doubts, all my gratitude. Finally, and most deeply, to my husband, Ramiro Resende, for his patient support and enthusiastic encouragement.

Foreign Accents

Introduction: Brazilian Appropriations of Shakespeare

AIMARA DA CUNHA RESENDE

BRAZIL, NINETEENTH CENTURY. IN RIO, BOURGEOIS HOUSES WERE furnished and adorned with porcelain, pictures, and tapestry brought from Europe. Submissive women, considered part of their chauvinist husbands' property, had tea or coffee in the afternoon among social gossip, read romantic novels, including, for instance, José de Alencar's portrait of idealized Eurocentric Indians, or went with their husbands to the theater, where they would see plays imported from Europe, often performed by European companies, such as Ernesto Rossi's and Tomaso Salvini's. As stated by contemporary Latin American thinkers, such as Retamar, Vasconcelos, Rodo, Santiago, Bellei, and masterfully shown by Mário de Andrade in *Macunaíma,* Latin American history, including Brazilian, has been made of abrogation, of continuous loss of identity, traits explained by the center, the "civilized world," as a desirable entrance into this very world.

When the colonizers came to Central and South America, they established here their view of human relationships, a capitalist determination of what was right and wrong. Discriminatory social relationships were essential for the maintenance of profit earned by the strongest, the idea of strength itself being the characteristic ability of the most capable according to their ethos: the capacity to destroy, both physically and intellectually. The natives—"savages," to the Europeans—had to learn how to speak the conqueror's language so as to assimilate his religion and his morals and, most of all, to accept the fact/fiction that theirs was an inferior position, and that they were slaves because they were unable to perform the same violent rituals of destruction or create arts/crafts of the kind found in Europe. Imitation was determined and determinant for the formation of identity of the New World. Caliban should speak Prospero's language to understand what Prospero expected of him. What he expected of Prospero did not count. Loss of language was necessary. So was loss of the natives' faith and their rituals, the ways of expressing that faith. Because they favored experience over speech, the inhabitants of the New World were seen by the center as being exotic, that is, out of place, a place that had been predetermined by a Eurocentric viewpoint. To fill in the void left by the violent extirpation of their own being, their sense of belonging, the people of the New World had to assimilate, little by little, the ways of the foreign metropolis. It was necessary—or unavoidable?—to become a simulacrum, a copy of the only "perfect reality."

With the passing of time, this feeling of not belonging, of having to exist as copies, became more and more ingrained in the minds of these people. Theirs was not the primary language—it was either Spanish or Portuguese; their books, if they had them, as was the case with the Mayas, had been burned, and consequently their religion and their science disappeared. Their totems, live entities they could see and feel, had been substituted by another deity they tried to believe in but whose reality they could never grasp. Their arts had been underestimated and taken to Europe as curiosities. Their gold, silver, and precious stones, elements used to dignify their gods and glorify their tradition through artistic productions, had been defiled and turned into objects of profane exchange, undignified causes of violence. The only alternatives then left the "savages" were either passive submission and lack of identity detectable in a vicarious *modus vivendi,* or reaction against the conqueror and subsequent death. In nineteenth-century Brazil, artists and writers among them did their best to emulate productions from the center. In literature, for instance, José de Alencar produced the Eurocentrically idealized Iracema and Pery, and Álvares de Azevedo offered a naïve copy of Byron. There was no way out. Either the native population agreed to import foreign models or they would remain as curiosities not worth consideration by those controlling political and intellectual life. In this predicament, Brazilian artists and intelligentsia found one only way to survive: mediation. As Sérgio Bellei stated in 1993:

> To talk about the decentering of Brazilian culture, of course, is by now a commonplace, the history of the centers of our culture being the history of a shift from Lisbon in colonial times, to Paris and London in the nineteenth Century, to New York in the twentieth. This decentering and

the resulting necessity to copy has often been associated with the characteristic discomfort of cultures on the frontier, the discomfort produced by the awareness that decentering might well mean non-being and non-existence. . . .

In short, if we are anything, we are a culture and a people ON the frontier, never inside any frontier nor outside of it: a culture and a people ambiguously, uncomfortably, and perhaps dangerously experiencing the reality of the borderland, being neither insiders nor outsiders. (11)

This culture of mediation, often submissive copying, was the one that received Shakespeare's plays. Significantly, in the nineteenth century, *Othello* was one of his most performed plays (*Hamlet* was the other) in this chauvinist society whose main intellectual trait was perhaps the putting on of a mask of culture by discussing and "appreciating" imported art such as the convulsive show of demented jealousy that the Italian Ernesto Rossi was able to offer in 1871, at Teatro Lírico Fluminense, where he performed not only *Othello,* but also *Romeo and Juliet, Hamlet,* and *Macbeth.* The bourgeois Brazilians who applauded Rossi might have never heard of him before, or of Shakespeare, but it was considered elegant to go to the theater, extremely well dressed (or overdressed!) and talk about the performance the next day at an evening party in some rich house. There were other performances, previous to Rossi's, by João Caetano, the founder of Brazilian theater, who, in 1835, performed *Romeo and Juliet, Coriolanus,* and Ducis's adaptation of *Othello.* As the plays by Shakespeare were heretofore poor translations from French texts and adaptations, in 1871 Rossi may have been, as Eugênio Gomes (1961, 17) states, the introducer of the "true Shakespeare in Brazil," though not necessarily the best actor.

Rossi came back in 1879 to be once more warmly applauded by the *nouveaux riches.* These persons' inability to understand the "Bard" was equal to their incapacity to realize the strenuous effort they had to make to keep up appearances and maintain the hegemonic status quo as thousands of people were exploited for the welfare of few. Also in 1871 Tomaso Salvini came over with his *Othello* and *Hamlet,* and this time the intellectuals approved of the performances, which had not been the case with Rossi's interpretation. Not Brazilian culture but culture in Brazil was entirely based on European standards. The native traditions, folkloric as well as religious, the symbiosis of attitudes, rituals, and values, from the

Indians above all, and then from the Africans and Portuguese, were forgotten. As Iuri Lotman (1986) would have it, memory was used to keep what was determined to be valuable by the dominating center, and forgetfulness was encouraged to lull Brazilians into an oblivion of their origins, origins whose low value, according to European standards, was better left lying dormant in the unconscious.

Besides the preference for the "original" *Othello* on the stage, a play was published, in 1861, that was a legitimized copy of this text of Shakespeare's: *Leonor de Mendonça,* by the romantic author Gonçalves Dias. Taking place in Portugal, with a Duke and his wife as the main protagonists, Dias's play deals with the themes of betrayal and revenge, this time creating the appearance of adultery more as a consequence of imprudence on the part of the Duchess than of the devilish machinations of a demented villain. This Duke has nothing of Othello's nobility, but is, on the contrary, hated by all those surrounding him from the very beginning of the action. Irascible, tormented by visions of the past that, according to him, point to his melodramatic final crime, the Duke lacks the Moor's charm.

Leonor de Mendonça is weak drama, a play more to be read than seen on the stage. The author even writes an introduction, which he calls a "prologue," in which he takes pains to demonstrate his moral purpose in writing what he called a drama (which I would call a melodrama, quite in accordance with the taste of the time, when João Caetano's Othello, "roaring like a lion," aroused the enthusiasm of audience after audience).

After the text of the play there is an appendix with the copy of statements taken from Portuguese chronicles about the real facts that had served as sources for *Leonor de Mendonça*. All this care with the written work rather than with the play itself points towards the "discomfort of cultures on the frontier," the borderline situation that Sergio Bellei talks of. Trying to seem original, Gonçalves Dias nevertheless falls into the trap of his own submissiveness to the central product, when he makes his Duke say to the heroine, in a situation that has nothing to do with wars, and in words that do not show his love for her (a love, in any case, that is nonexistent): "I thank you, my fair warrior . . . (1.8). What warrior is this? A woman quite unlike Desdemona, whose main traits are total submission to those who raised her and then to her unloved husband and a generosity more spoken of than evident in her behavior!

While writers like Gonçalves Dias and not very learned audiences created and/or applauded melodramatic performances or appropriations of Shakespeare, the really educated read him in English and were critical of the centripetal recreations often produced here. Machado de Assis, the greatest nineteenth-century Brazilian novelist, parodied his work, carnivalistically subverting the canon and transforming the "essential Bard" into a totemic part of the really Brazilian novel. He, like all great writers, was a forerunner of our contemporary literature, a dazzling example of the Rabelaisian/Shakespearean process of writing. Between Machado and the literature written nowadays, Shakespeare is often stylized and parodied. Still the "Bard," a model received from the center, worshipped, copied, and mostly read and rewritten with stylized reverence. So far, apart from a few writers like Machado, he was treasured by another hegemonic group, the intellectuals, who, almost a century later, would be seen by José Enrique Rodó as Latin Americans upholding the dominant Eurocentric system. Brazil, in the nineteenth and beginning of the twentieth centuries, remained on the borderline.

Ours, then, was a society full of prejudices, materialistic, not sure of its own values, but ostentatiously supported by alien cultures and productions, a society whose upper class members were usually rather uncultured self-made men, either urban public officials and merchants or rude but rich farmers, the *coronéis* (lit. *colonels*), whose sons went to Europe to "complete" their education and whose daughters learned how to speak French, played Chopin on the piano, and used India Company porcelain at dinner. In such a society, talking about Shakespeare, Dante, and Cervantes might be correlated with learning characteristic of people ascending the social and intellectual spheres. This aspiration led to pedantic demonstrations of knowledge among the intellectuals, marveled at by the pseudoeducated. Though our Ariels, that is, artists and intelligentsia kept mediating between the center and this country, the masses remained unaware of Shakespeare's work.

This mediating creative attitude in Brazilian arts continued for some time, not only in literature and theater but in criticism as well. With the advent of modernism and the manifestos by Oswald de Andrade (*Manifesto Pau Brasil* and *Manifesto Antropófago*), written in 1924 and 1928, respectively, the need for a national character in the arts as well as in the behavior of Brazilian intellectuals emerged. The moment had come for Brazilians, like all other Latin American intellectuals and artists, to strive for a new expression, their own, symbiotic but individually marked. With Oswald de Andrade, Mário de Andrade, and their companions, the intelligentsia began trying to define the place of Brazilianity, to establish the sort of identification indicated by Silviano Santiago (1978, 11–28) when he said:

> Latin America has instituted its place on the map of Western civlization thanks to the active and destructive movement of deviation from the norm, a movement that transfigures the ready made and unchangeable elements that Europeans exported to the New World. (16)[1]

The source for Brazilian cultural production should now be found in regional and folkloric themes, the scenery should be Brazilian in its native elements, not idealized, and it should no more reconstruct the imitative urban centers and their miming of the European metropolis. Macunaíma, not Othello, Romeo, or Hamlet, should be our hero—a half-breed, with traits typical of tropical climates, a precursor of the type that Retamar alludes to when he states that "... there is in the colonial world, all over the planet, a special case: a vast zone where hybridism is not an accident, but the essence, the central line: we, 'our America mestiza'!" (1988, 15).[2]

Lazy, lascivious, but highly intelligent, Macunaíma embodies the antihero dreamed of by the revolutionary Brazilian modernists. Nature replaces culture and progress is valid when it aims at the attainment of our original inheritance. Against the mediating conformist attitude, we begin searching for originality and authenticity based on the absolute denial of imported material. Oswald de Andrade said, in 1924: "The job of the futurist generation was cyclopic. To put right the empire-watch of national literature. This job done, there is another task. To be regional and pure in one's time. . . . The counterpart of native originality to render useless the academic adherence" (207).[3]

Oswald de Andrade's position is developed in his *Manifesto Antropófago (Anthropophagous Manifesto)*. For him, it is necessary to be aware of the irreversible situation, the presence of foreign blood in us, the unquestionable reality of the European mind that has grown among our intelligentsia and given rise to works of art now extant and established within the ranks of our artistic and intellectual tradition. Therefore, what has to be done is to devour the foreigner and then digest its parts, making the old nonnative element become one with the really national, the regional, the autochthonous, giving birth to a half-breed that will ostensibly show his marks of Brazilianity. Macunaíma! In 1928 Andrade stated:

> We had justice codifying vengeance. Science codifying magic. Anthropophagy. The permanent transformation of taboo into totem. (228).[4]

> Before the Portuguese discovered Brazil, Brazil had discovered happiness. . . . Against the Indian carrying tapers. The Indian son of Mary, God-son to Catherine of Medici and son-in-law of D. Antonio de Mariz . . . Against memory source of custom. Personal experience renewed. (231)[5]

This position, to be echoed in Retamar's *Caliban* of 1971, that we have to deal with the miscegenation brought about by colonization but react against the colonial intentions of exploitation and oppression, paves the way for a new Brazilian literature. Caliban may speak the language of the center, but he will do it for his own purposes, to affirm his unique being in opposition to the destructive, plundering European invader. This reversed attitude moves from initial hints at the Shakespearean canon, through quotations used to reinforce themes, to subversive appropriations, intertextual counterpoints, ambivalent "Shakespeares." Transformed, transfused, the "Bard" looks and sounds Brazilian. Taboo become totem.

With the military dictatorship of the sixties and seventies, Shakespeare, like other canonized workers, was carnivalistically appropriated as a suitable means of subversion. Subverting the canonical text would run parallel with subverting the system. Shakespeare flickered here and there in parodied texts, in quotations, suggesting, and somehow contesting. It is doubtful, however, whether the unlearned mass, the majority of the Brazilian people, were able to read between the lines. It was then that one play appeared, written by the exile Augusto Boal outside Brazil, of course, dealing with the subject of domination: *A Tempestade*. Halfway between translation and contestation, this parody of *The Tempest* was more an angry cry, derisively attacking the system, using abusive terms, travestying characters, ridiculing the Shakespearean myth, denouncing capitalist inequality and right-wing hegemony. In Boal's *Tempest,* dedicated to Retamar, anarchy and decentering are explicit. The first page indicates not only the setting but also the author's mind:

> This performance may take place on a stage of the Italian kind or within an arena; in a theater house or in a circus; in a garage or in the street.

What matters to me is that it be done with a lot of truth, a lot of sincerity, a lot of color, that it may even be a bit exaggerated, but let it be clear, very clear, that we are beautiful because we are ourselves, and no culture imposed on us is more beautiful than ours. It must needs be clear that we are Calibans.[6]

This is a play of revolt, of dessacralization of all taboos, including language. Fernando's virginity, for instance, comes close to behavior that resembles the mannerisms of Brazilian gay men. Miranda is no innocent girl. On the contrary, she is seen at the end as a very lascivious young woman. All representatives of the civilized European and North American center are clearly shown as mercenary, disloyal hypocrites. Prospero's power is reached by way of extreme violence. Even the masque bears the marks of Boal's intention: there are no Greek goddesses and nymphs, but North American creations such as Zé Carioca, Latin Lover. They dance grotesquely to the sound of voodoo and Indian music, imitating Hollywood stars. Among them you see Carmen Miranda, the Brazilian myth of the samba singer, who, besides having been born in Portugal, lived and prospered in the United States. In the end, there is no utopia. The conclusion one arrives at is that there is no way out. The powerful will always win. Though Caliban tries to overcome Prospero, he ends up, not converted, but, together with Estêvão and Trínculo, beaten up by Antônio who, in a deal with Prospero, leads them to work, the only thing there is left them. It is worth noticing how Boal works out the demonstration of his thesis. At he final moments of the play, after having been defeated in their attempt to gain control of the situation, Caliban, Trínculo, and Estêvão talk about their duty towards their superiors and offer their good wishes to the newlyweds. Caliban is the only one who remains loyal to his principles. Nevertheless he will still be a slave/laborer:

> *Trin.* We must love our masters above all things!
> *Cal.* We must learn good words and have good manners.
> *Est.* We must serve them in the best possible way . . .
> *King.* And these monsters, what are they?
> *Seb.* Are they for sale? I smell some business.
> *Pros.* I am taking some for a display in Europe. Come, Ariel. (*Ariel enters, dancing*). This is the most exotic of all!
> *Est.* May the noble couple be very happy and may their life be full of bliss.

INTRODUCTION: BRAZILIAN APPROPRIATIONS OF SHAKESPEARE

Trin. May the noble couple increase their possessions, may they be richer and richer and multiply their inherited assets for years to come, amen.
Cal. May the noble couple have lots of children, to fulfill Mr. Prospero's wishes . . .
Pros. At last you've learned good manners . . .
Cal. May their children be hanged with their umbilical chord, and may they rot in their mother's womb, and may the gangrene destroy every fibre of their bodies and may the devil himself . . .
Pros. What are you saying?
Cal. May they live long . . .
Pros. Good . . .
Cal. In hell!

Ironically Boal shows that, as the original Caliban said, the language learned from the colonizer is all that is left the "barbarian"—not for the rhetorical domineering use but to curse, and even that, unnoticed.

It was with Globo network TV that Shakespeare found his way to the common people. Paulo Afonso Grisolli directed two short serials based on his work: *Romeu e Julieta,* in 1980 and *Otelo de Oliveira,* in 1983. For the first time in Brazil, Shakespeare appeared as popular culture. This appearance coincided with the slow movement towards freedom and the construction of identity. It was Shakespeare, but its components were Brazilian. These adaptations were aimed at the uncultured populace, which was unaccustomed to theater. These two versions managed to highlight some of the themes and issues then seen as central to the Shakespearean text and, at the same time, some feeling of recognition was aroused in the audience through the conjunction with national peculiarities. The symbiosis made the plays easily "edible." They brought theater to the small screen, in some sort of composite film, theater, and TV mode. Not quite purely television form, Grisolli's work was perhaps the foundation of Shakespeare on TV. Unfortunately, his efforts came to be blurred by the advent of soap opera, excellent commodity entertainment, responsible to a large degree for the continuation of low-level performances and alienating dreams.

Grisolli's *Romeu e Julieta* was made in Ouro Preto, an oppulent souvenir of the mining wealth that made a few people rich (mainly Portuguese) at the expense of slaves and the rural poor. Ouro Preto was the appropriate setting for the film, as it mixes Veronese quaintness and the twentieth-century Brazilian sense of imbalance. Home of one of Brazil's best schools of mining engineering, the Escola de Minas, it gathers students from all parts of the country, who live at the famous *repúblicas,* old and grave seventeenth-century buildings lodging turbulent youth. The oxymoronic setting frames national contrasts and symbiosis of all sorts. Veiled by the central hegemonic text, Grisolli's version, instead of offering the everlasting tale of love, sharply criticizes pseudovalues as it displays the struggle for power in society, in the Catholic church, and among the students. The film was made in 1980, during the military dictatorship. Social tension had spread throughout the country, but was unable to culminate in action. Different socioeconomic groups lived in controlled disagreement. University students were believed to represent danger; they were viewed as latent subversive forces. Grisolli shows the conflict by means of the three opposed and simultaneously collaborative social strata: the Mining School, signified by the students, among whom are Romeu José da Rosa, Aristides, or Tidi (Julieta's brother, not her cousin), and Grisolli's Paris, Paulo Roberto, the *Caveira* (Portuguese for "skull"); the Church, signified by the rather ignorant and radical priest; and the rich, represented by Julieta's father, Dr. Cristóvam, who would not carry the image of the Virgin Mary in the procession beside Romeu's father, a working class man, a barber.

To make his point more telling, Grisolli has Romeu studying at the school of Pharmacology, a minor branch of the Escola de Minas, while Paulo Roberto attends the Mining School, the famous branch of the same institution. This seemingly naïve fact signals the conflict permeating his text: hegemonic societies are composed of smaller power units: Brazil contains Ouro Preto, which contains the Escola de Minas, which contains the Mining School and the School of Pharmacology; the Church contains the rich and the poor classes, which contain families. The dominating groups interrelate so that order may be maintained. On the other hand, the smaller groups support one another, so as to confront the oppressor. This is what happens when the police officer tries to punish the student (Romeu) who has appeared naked on the street during the religious procession: the officer has to face the group of young men living at *Ninho do Amor* (Love Nest) plus their opponents from *República Cemitério* (Graveyard Republic) who, confessing their joint fault, force the officer to give up, as the prison does not have room for all of them. The three social conflicting sections vary their interrelationship. From time to time, one supports the other, so as to oppose the third. Julieta's father, for instance, wants her to marry Paulo Roberto, a youth belonging to their social circle but still "dangerous," because a student; their compromise is necessary to the maintenance of wealth. The priest manages to control some people, but does not have much sway over the students. He deals more with the adult rich so as to oppose the rash young men living in the *repúblicas*.

Shakespeare's play thus becomes a critical 1980 Brazilian construct, crying out against the unequal treatment received by different social groups, simultaneously recreating the typical folklore elements of religiosity and the aggressive, disturbing, self-assertive behavior of the students at Escola de Minas, itself part of the town folklore. A drunkard, a common type in the interior of Brazil, opens and ends the story, functioning as the chorus, speaking Shakespeare's lines.

At the moment when voices were silenced, Grisolli's visual creation for TV manages indirectly to convey a message of revolt and accusation, through the appropriation of the English play. In this 1980 *Romeu e Julieta,* Brazil shows up, in its oppression and its hope, in its protests and its beauty. The original text becomes both the same and another, serving as a means of expression of man's anguish and desire. As Anthony Easthope (1991) has pointed out, a good artistic piece is always open to new readings. So is *Romeo and Juliet* in Walter Durst's adaptation, directed and produced by Afonso Grisolli, which appeared as part of a definite social milieu and was politically committed in a way different from the sixteenth-century original. In it, all the splendor and uniqueness of Ouro Preto intermingles with the beauty of Shakespeare's play. At some special moments, chiefly at the masqued ball, the sixteenth-century text is heard, and the conflation is excellent. It is Juliet and Romeo who say the words one hears; but these words are spoken from the yard of an ancient Brazilian building in the heart of Ouro Preto.

In 1983 Grisolli produced and directed for Globo TV another appropriation of Shakespeare: *Otelo de Oliveira.* As the title shows through the hero's surname, Oliveira, this is a recreation by Agnaldo Silva of the English *Othello.* The story is the same, but its setting and characters are Brazilian and it highlights Brazilian folklore and religious symbiosis. Otelo de Oliveira, a gypsy, has devoted his life to a Samba School, not to the wars against the infidels. He is the harmony director of the school.[7] Nobody knows much about him, except that he is one of the best at his job. A young girl,

Denise, or Dé, the daughter of Barbosinha, a *bicheiro*,[8] falls in love with Otelo when she goes to the Samba School with her father and sees him "commanding" the Carnival rehearsal. Unlike the original Emilia, Grisolli's is a servant who has been Dé's nurse from her birth. Married to Tiago (Iago), who is Barbosa's driver, she knows all the time the sort of man her husband is and suspects that he is up to some evil doing. The latter works under Otelo at the Samba School and hopes to become his *segundo* (second), but his hopes are thwarted when the leader chooses Cassio, an educated middle-class young man, loyal to Otelo, who will become Dé's guardian when her husband has to remain at the Samba School to protect it against rival dancers.

Rodrigo (Roderigo) is a rich young man who has also been working at the Samba School expecting to win Dé's love with Tiago's help. Heloína, Cássio's former lover, is a good-looking girl that participates in voodoo rituals to take vengeance on Cassio, who abandoned her. The main changes fall thus on characterization, making the people in the story more contemporary and common to the twentieth-century Brazilian TV spectator. The fact that Grisolli's Otelo is a gypsy makes him closer to the Shakespearean position, since, due to our racially mixed formation, in Brazil a gypsy is much more fraught with danger and mystery than a black man, who, though seen as inferior, is nevertheless always present in Brazilian environments, even if he is there only as a servant, a policeman, or a thief.

The action takes place about a month before Carnival, and the drums and *cuícas*[9] are heard in the background. The Samba School, with its preparation for the parade, shares the scenery with Otelo's home, a typical low-class Brazilian dwelling, situated on the periphery of Rio, though not a slum house (pointing towards the Brazilian social strata, where there are divisions even within one class) and Barbosinha's place, characteristic of rich, but not necessarily refined owners. Tiago's role is superbly performed by Milton Gonçalves, a black actor. Grisolli's villain, unlike the original Iago, does not display verbal mastery; his character highlights instead the hidden hatred of a socially marginalized man. Tiago's triumph lies in the destruction of someone who has managed to ascend a position he himself would like to hold but has been unable to. Like lots of men in the slums, he smolders with hatred. Having risen in the class structure by participating in the arrangements of the Samba School and in the life of the Barbosas because he is necessary, not

INTRODUCTION: BRAZILIAN APPROPRIATIONS OF SHAKESPEARE   23

because he is liked, he wants revenge. He gives vent to his hatred in a way quite different from his English model.

While Shakespeare's villain is a master of the words, Tiago silently prepares his trap for Otelo, seizing the opportunities that will serve his purpose. In the Brazilian appropriation for TV, the thoughts and feelings one perceives are directed by the camera that focuses on the black man's facial expression above any other aspect. The spectator follows his evil thoughts as they are manifest in the actor's face, along with his way of walking, his movements. The physical contrast between the two main characters is the kind of usurpation/transformation that deeply talks to and about a Brazilian audience, an audience that participates in a culture of the body, quite distant from the culture of the *ingenio* that characterizes Shakespeare's time, when "Othello's music" (Wilson Knight 1983) is contrasted with Iago's machiavellian and often vulgar linguistic *tour de force*.

Various controversial aspects of Brazilian life are displayed in *Otelo de Oliveira*. Though very *carioca*,[10] a picture of Rio de Janeiro and Carnival, it manages to suggest other national traits and undesired marks of third world social stratification and cultural manipulation of the unlearned poor. Ironically, the poor that are being manipulated on the screen are the "reproduction" of the people who live in slums, barely earning enough to eat, often stealing, but finding pleasure in watching this kind of program, somehow identifying with the rich and forgetting their own subhuman condition. These spectators, who own a TV set but may not have even a table in a three-room house where some ten people live, remain unaware of their controlled situation. They are unable to change, not realizing that they are themselves manipulated by their demi-god, TV. They watch and dream.

It is the task of a group trained in the arts of the circus and working under a young director, Gabriel Vilela, to bring to the streets and the stage a truly Brazilian contemporary Shakespeare: the Galpão (warehouse) troupe, performing *Romeu e Julieta*. This production, which started in 1993, blends the original text (in a brilliant translation by Onestaldo Penaforte) with the roots of one of the most traditional Brazilian states: Minas Gerais. Unlike Boal, Vilela uses the Shakespearean text with cuts that do not interfere with the central dramatic effect and add to it passages after the *mineiro*[11] novelist, Guimarães Rosa, and songs from *mineiro* folklore. This is a new text, but at the same time, not new. Shakespeare's *Romeo and Juliet* is there, but the lovers are no longer from Verona. They live in every Brazilian, because they relive the love affair of the young Renaissance couple, but in Minas Gerais, in the twentieth century, dressed in shabby clothes that characterize the *teatro mambembe,* the kind of performance by traveling actors that could be seen, some years ago, in the interior of Brazil, clothes recognizable on the streets of our small towns and villages. Vilela and his dramaturg, Antônio Carlos Brandão, reconstructed the Shakespearean play in a new form, retaining the original text (if one can safely talk of original texts when dealing with Shakespeare) and bringing into focus its universal aspects. They put new garments on old ideas and foreign but respected language. In 1978, Silviano Santiago said that

> Latin America has established its place on the map of western civilization thanks to an active and destructive movement of deviation from the norm, that transfigures the unchangeable and finished up elements that Europeans used to export to the New World. . . .
> The Latin American artist accepts prison as a form of behavior, transgression as a form of expression. (27)

Prison in the case of the popular performance by Galpão is the Shakespearean text itself, within which the protagonist "will live, and pray, and sing and tell old tales." It is in their singing and telling of old stories that transgression takes place, transporting to our regional/natural environment the emotions of the "star-crossed lovers." Deviation from the rigid norm of classical performances establishes a link with the Brazilian audience, contemporary relationships, and ever-present tribal antagonism. Thanks to songs taken from the folk repertoire, the tragedy is turned into a lyrical drama tinted with the comic nuances of the popular *mambembe* theater. These songs appear at the right moment and in the correct place, not distorting the meaning but complementing it. The action begins, like some circus performance, with a mixture of gangsters shooting, women screaming—all to introduce a fat, exuberant nurse who, getting into a big old car, shoots at the gangsters and brings about quiet. Out of the car windows two puppets representing Romeo and Juliet appear and present a pantomime while a song is heard. The lyrics of the song go somewhat like this:

> You like me, little sister.
> I like you too, little sister.
> I'll go to your dad, little sister,

INTRODUCTION: BRAZILIAN APPROPRIATIONS OF SHAKESPEARE 25

> For permission to marry you.
> If he says yes
> I'll see to legal arrangements
> If he says no
> I'll die in suffering.
>
> Applaud, applaud, applaud, little sister
> Tread, tread, tread, little sister.
> Move round, round, round, little sister.
> Embrace whoever you wish, little sister.

With this *introitu* directly relating the pains of love and parental interference in marriage, instead of the original prologue, one has a narrator who sometimes sums up the incidents that have been removed from the text. This narrator, who physically reminds one of Shakespeare himself, uses the storytelling tradition of Brazilian folklore and the style of Brazil's greatest contemporary prose writer, Guimarães Rosa, the regionalist/innovator, whose unique way of constructing texts reproduces artistically the way of speaking and the customs of the rural folk of Minas. Beginning with the customary "Once upon a time . . ." he summarizes the situation, places the action in Verona, and ends up by saying: "Look and see!" The scene moves on to the Prince and his law on those disturbing the peace in Verona and, after a short speech by the narrator, we have Romeo and Benvolio talking of the former's love for Rosaline. The Romeo we are introduced to is a sad looking youth, walking on wooden legs and playing a *sanfona* (a kind of accordion popular in the interior of Brazil). Before the party where Romeo and Juliet will meet, one hears a song whose lyrics foretell what will happen. They go like this:

> Ashes, only ashes in my heart.
> Ashes from our love.
> I swear I was lying when I swore
> To be forever faithful to this love
> That I have abandoned.
> Enough! So hard suffering is too much
> I am no Pierrot
> I am a very modern Harlequin.
> I don't believe in love.

The melody of this song, instead of sounding like a lament, however, has a joyful rhythm very much in tune with the feelings of a young group going to a party. Like the Pierrot of the song, Romeo and his love for Rosaline will soon be ashes and nothing else. Throughout the play, insertions of this kind, always using folklore music, point to the action at the same time as they create a link between incidents and emotions, exploiting the audience's familiarity with the songs and offering a melodious background for the development of the drama. Observations of the reaction of the audience, among which foreigners were present, showed that the melodies did have influence on their behavior and attention, especially the song that ends the performance and is recurrent from the moment just before Romeo and Juliet meet for the first time. A rhythmical song, it tells of a false stone ring that is broken and of weak love that is gone, and uses as a refrain the words "flower, my flower, come here." When the play is over, all the actors join in and sing this song accompanied by the *sanfona,* and an enthusiastically sympathetic audience sings with them.

Carnivalization, another element characteristic of contemporary literature and very much related to Brazilian ways of life, is introduced into the performance rather than into the text proper. Parody of Guimarães Rosa, a Shakespeare/actor intradiegetically directing the events, a mixture of linguistic resources such as the artificial French spoken by Mercutio when the Nurse takes Juliet's message to Romeo—a kind of semi-invented French, typical of circus theatrical performance, when the actors often speak nonstandard Portuguese. These and other devices are created and manipulated within the Shakespearean text, giving it new texture, enriching it with the transfiguration that Oswald calls for in his *Manifesto Antropófago.* Besides the old car, the scenery is arranged with leaves of plants that carry a charge of superstition in them. The graveyard is created out of these leaves and a small, fragile wooden cross, suggestive of death but, with the song in the background telling of broken rings and dead sentiments, paradoxically signaling the frailty of love.

Put together, circus and tragedy, life and death, mirth and dirge, the unquestionable fact of performance, all help us experience the play and feel that we are in our own world, at the same time that what we experience appears as the essence of reality, not simply that which "dreams are made on," but just normal moments in everyone's life. Removing the tragic burden from the Shakespearean tragedy, inconceivable in popular entertainment, and in need of something to help one cope with contemporary reality, through escape and fulfillment, Vilela's production is pregnant with a carnivalized sense of the world that makes of *Romeo and Juliet* a new old play, as everlastingly ambiguous as love, life, and death themselves.

Simultaneous with Vilela's *Romeu e Julieta,* a new version of *Hamlet* was staged in São Paulo, a contemporary Brazilian reading, *Ham-let,* directed by Zé Celso, and lasting four hours. Due to the director's use of the space in the theater, the spectators had to sit uncomfortably on benches, could leave before the end, and were somehow made to identify with and approve of Claudius and so, in a way, go against Hamlet. As Marcelo Coelho (1993, 4), writing for *Folha de São Paulo,* stated: "Subtle mockery of the audience, then: to reveal that we back Claudius, this easy-going, debauching, untrustworthy seducer king, instead of Hamlet, this wet-blanket . . . non-conformist . . ."

This *Hamlet* is a cry of revolt against the predicament of Brazilian culture. Zé Celso, who, in 1968, during the dictatorship, was seen as a reverenced myth of contestation, now, after the return of democracy, came to the fore once more, trying to rouse the people's anger at the rotten state of . . . Brazil? Once the weak and doubtful Hamlet is dead, what is left us? The foreign strength of Fortinbras, maintaining the same values as there were before and during the military dominion. Under the influence of *Ham-let,* it was reported in newspapers of São Paulo that numbers of young people began dressing in black, in an attempt to emulate the Prince, which attests to the significance of the performance. As usual, Zé Celso took hold of the canon to usurp its main ideas and subvert/convert them into a brilliant weapon against what he did not approve of and wanted very much to change, provoking debates and managing to alert his audience.

In 1997 another *Hamlet* appeared, this time in Curitiba, capital of the state of Paraná, in the south of Brazil. Written and directed by Felipe Hirsch, Shakespeare's play is used, as Hirsch says, for the construction of an essay, something coming from a page that he liked very much, an essay "like the wind that cleans the pages made dusty with time."[12] This essay is the new play *Estou Te Escrevendo De Um Lugar Distante* (I am writing you from a far away place). Aiming at a contemporary Brazilian audience, it can no longer be a tragedy. It goes deep into the human search for meaning in life and death but seems to find no solution, only the void. As the protagonist says in the end, addressing the audience: "We are all made of the same shit!" And, after all, shit is unable to create or cope with tragedy. Reality—unbearable reality is quite enough. To better simulate the reality of life, there is comedy, cruder than one finds in Shakespeare's text, but the sort of comedy that appeals to the common people who go to the theater in twentieth-century Brazil in need of escape, but hopelessly aware of their poor human condition. Most of the comedy in the play comes from Gertrude, a mixture of sensuality, pretence, and awareness of her status as a queen and a woman. A moment of excellent comedy occurs, for example, when, by Ophelia's tomb, Hamlet and Laertes start quarreling in words that go beyond the original, revealing attitudes that suggest not nobles, but uneducated, middle-class contenders. As the noise gets louder, the Queen suddenly shouts at the two young men, asking them if this is not a burial and, going back to her place, commands all those around: "Everybody crying, now!"

The actors in the performance at Teatro Novelas Curitibanas were travesties of the original. Gertrude was played by a man, Guilherme Weber, while the male characters were played by women. Only Ophelia, whose part is small, was not travestied. There is a young Hamlet, a child, who, at the beginning and the end, comes to the author/chorus, looks at him in silence, and is led off the stage by Yorick. Metatheater is quite explicit in *Estou Te Escrevendo De Um Lugar Distante,* and the audience is constantly reminded of the play's debt to *Hamlet.* Most of the best-known moments in Shakespeare's text are transported into Hirsch's work and transmuted in the questions on the human condition that it unrelentingly tries to answer to no end. Its composition, nevertheless, is a complex amalgamation of other texts that have preceded it, such as the *Hamlets* by Geovanni Testori, Heiner Müeller, Tom Stoppard, Antonio Abujamra, Karel Tchapeck, and even a *SkinheadHamlet,* found on the Internet. This carnivalized openness, this carnivalesque laughter resounding on the threshold, relativizing the supreme value of the literary and artistic canon, disrupts the status quo, disturbing those attending the performance, the "cadavers in the audience," as Hirsch's Prince sees them.

Without being a psychoanalytical reading of Shakespeare, *Estou Te Escrevendo De Um Lugar Distante* sees in Hamlet's vision of his father a projection of his feverish mind, that his friend Horatio is forced to represent, in a scene that may be taken either as the Prince's demented imagination or as a spiritualist scéance in which the dead King is incorporated in his son's best companion. The Ghost is seen only in a kind of retrospective view of his burial, when his corpse is carried, covered, along the stage, first, to have his death lamented by Gertrude, who then mounts the corpse. Claudius joins her and they have sex right there on top. The scene with Hamlet, though, takes place only with the help of Horatio, who performs the Ghost, against his will but forced into it by Hamlet. Hirsch's reading of *Hamlet* testifies to the richness of Shakespeare's text, its potential to always suggest new interpretations and the subversion of beliefs.

In 1994 the Globo television network produced a soap opera, *Fera Ferida* (Wounded Beast) that not only merged Shakespearean themes with current political issues, social types, and gossip with utopian class blend but also incorporated (as is usual in Brazilian soap operas) speeches such as the appropriation of *Hamlet:* "There is something rotten in Tubiacanga" (Tubiacanga being the imaginary town where the action of the soap opera took place).

Fera Ferida is an appropriation of the work of the Brazilian writer Lima Barreto or rather it hints at Barreto but distorts his work so much that there is little left that one could distinguish as being his. Barreto lived in the beginning of the century and was a confessed anarchist, disappointed with the military-political power of the newly established republic. Lima Barreto dealt with a lot of politics, ridiculed the army, and pointed to the brutally unfair treatment of women. He was not much concerned with romance and did not specifically go to Shakespeare for his arguments. Yet the soap opera presented on TV, professing to be an adaptation of Barreto, begins by transmuting the non-Shakespearean texts of the Brazilian writer and offering the spectator a mixture of *Romeo and Juliet* and *Hamlet.* A son who had promised his dying father to revenge his untimely and unjust death at the hands of Tubiacanga's mayor and of an ignorant exmajor, the "guardian of Tubiacanga's national safety," returns incognito to the town, where he meets the girlfriend of his childhood, who does not recognize him and is, of course, the mayor's daughter. Independent, intelligent, this girl is a twentieth-century Juliet. The themes of the son responsible for the revenge and the star-crossed lovers are put together. But these ideas and some lines from Shakespeare are all that is taken from the playwright. What one has here is the common formula of soap operas where social mobility is overtly seen as an open possibility, light topical political criticism is offered as consolation for Brazil's difficult predicament, and religious syncretism and a false scientific outlook blur appearances.

In July 1999, in Belo Horizonte, Minas Gerais, the Galpão Group offered, with a grant from the Ministry of Work, a workshop on comedy entitled *Oficinão do Galpão* for actors and directors. At the end of this workshop, centered on Shakespeare, a play was to be performed, chosen among the comedies studied during the *Oficinão*. The choice fell on *Twelfth Night*. Chico Pelúcio, from the Galpão Group, and coordinator of the workshop, directed it. This was an interesting adaptation. I call it an *adaptation,* since to me there is a difference between this term and *appropriation* (as is the case with Boal's *A Tempestade*). An adaptation is the use of the source text without modification of the main ideas or of the text as a whole, without cuts and/or additions that would interfere in these ideas and ideologically give the text another meaning and object entirely different from the original. *Adaptation* then implies the creation of mise-en-scène with changes in location, language transposition aiming at a better understanding of the word-play by the nonnative audience, and swift topical allusions for audience involvement. An appropriation, on the other hand, takes hold of the source text for one's ideological purpose (often sociopolitical), making it one's own and transforming it, practically, into another text, not only with minor changes, but thoroughly dressed in new clothes, made up so as to plunge the audience into another universe, full of implications regarding contemporary life and world.

In the case of this performance of *Twelfth Night,* Shakespeare's text—as far as one can talk of Shakespeare's text—was preserved in a translation by Sérgio Flaksman, and the action moved from Illyria to a little village by the São Francisco river, the second longest river in Brazil, located in the north of Minas Gerais and running through part of the northeast of the country. As the region on the margins of the São Francisco is still very poor, the population living mostly on fishing and regional handicrafts and immersed in its own very authentic culture, Chico Pelúcio and his troupe spent some time in one of its villages, trying to absorb the people's way of living, their customs, and their stories.

Some changes then took place in this production of Shakespeare's comedy. For one, as the play was to be performed at the Galpão Group's arena theater, the scenery was created with both requirements in mind: that theater and the margin of the river. For the transposition of the location, two platforms were raised on opposite sides of the round grandstand, and above them, on one side, was a huge ship, and on the other, a moveable section representing the upper part of a ship. This part was used at the very beginning, to give the feeling of despair as actors shouted and tried to control the ship's ropes, as they were furiously tossed backwards and forwards, and a lot of noise was heard, indicative of the storm and consequent shipwreck. Later on, this upper part of the ship gave way to two doors that were used by Orsino and Viola in act 2, scene 4, when she almost confesses her love for him, by telling of her feelings and her pseudosister's unrequited passion. This was an interesting conception, as Orsino and Viola seemed to be separate in space, being each at one door, but simultaneously, due to coordinated movements, giving the impression of getting nearer and nearer as she disclosed her heart to him. One had the feeling that the Duke himself was entrapped by her charms, but he suddenly moved a little way away and told her to go to Olivia's.

Another rich transformation occurred in Feste's characterization. There is a common type in the interior of Minas Gerais, of either a man or a woman—usually a woman—a mixture of a wise and mad person who gives advice to those around her and at the same time amuses them with her puns and wise-comical ideas. She is often shabbily and sometimes fantastically dressed, looks bizarre, but sounds philosophical. Shakespeare's jester is turned into such a woman but his name is kept. It was worth keeping this name, as *Feste,* pronounced through the Brazilian phonetics, sounds somewhat like the word *peste,* meaning "you damn thing," or, literally translated, "plague." When Sabastião (Sebastian) comes for the first time to Olivia's house, he addresses Feste as "Peste," to which she reacts immediately, giving rise to laughter in the audience. The Brazilian Feste dances and directs the comic group in the play with her unique behavior, her movements, and her songs, which Pelúcio had brought from the São Francisco region and inserted into the text. This insertion, as happened with Vilela's *Romeu e Julieta,* instead of distorting the original, gave a new and richer flavor to it at the same time as the songs brought the audience closer to the play, making them coparticipants in it. Shakespeare's song "The rain it raineth every day" was maintained, and at the end of the play, while the rain falls on the huge ship on one side (as occurred at the beginning), Feste moves away singing and a boy, who had appeared at the start, playing with a toy ship, leaves the toy and crosses the central stage, creating a feeling of the endlessness of the predicament witnessed by the audience. It was both beautiful and touching.

In this production, the love affair gave way to comicality, not only because the latter appeals more to a twentieth-century nonromantic audience, but also, perhaps, because the comic actors, playing Toby, Aguecheek, Fabian (Fabiana, a woman, in Pelúcio's production), Feste, and Malvolio were much better than the ones playing the romantic characters. Their performance was a tour de force, and little topical change was necessary to enthrall the audience and keep the comical tone of the play always high. The presentation lasted about one hour and a half, with no interval, and there was no sign in the audience of fatigue and/or lack of interest. Regional music was aptly used, and there were moments when it was linked to the characters' verbal ability, which extended the lively comicality to real life situations. Such was the case, for instance, when, before Olivia's house, at the beginning of act 2, scene 3, Toby, André (Andrew), Fabiana, and Feste are singing and dancing and then Maria comes to quiet them. Feste stops singing, bends over Maria, seems to be showing something on her shirt, exclaiming: "Ó . . . Ó . . ." (Look . . . Look . . .). As Maria, unable to see anything on her skirt, asks what it is, Feste continues, singing as he answers: "Ó . . . lha a pulga!" (Loo . . . k, the flea!), and a song thus starting is heard, happily sung by the whole group, to be interrupted by Malvolio's entrance. As can be seen from this example, regionalism is introduced in Shakespeare's text to make it sound more Brazilian without distorting its central tenet.

Twelfth Night by Oficinão do Galpão is another good example of the extensive flow of Brazilian readings of Shakespeare that seem to add to the playwright's amplitude, coming not only from his great strength but also from new possibilities appearing in "accents yet unknown."

The productions above discussed are among a few of those made in Brazil since the nineteenth century. This introduction cannot hope to analyze or even mention all those that have been performed, either good or bad. It seems, however, that the most promising productions have been directed by young people whose ability to assimilate and/or subvert, while at the same time respecting, Shakespeare, proves that, although there is no *essential* Shakespeare, his work provides everlasting inspiration to creative imaginations.

Faced with this puzzling simultaneousness in the art of performance, having read from Fernando Retamar to Oswald de Andrade and Sérgio Bellei, a perplexed critic might ask: "Which Brazil is here? What Shakespeare is appropriated? What is the point of appropriating his work?" The articles in this volume will, I expect, answer some or part of these questions.

In "Theater for the Oppressed: Augusto Boal's *A Tempestade*," Marlene Soares dos Santos deals with postcolonialism and Boal's Brazilian appropriation of Shakespeare's *The Tempest*. She gives us an overview of the interpretations/appropriations of *The Tempest*, from its appearances in Britain and the United States to its use by Latin American writers, both in plays and in essays. Contextualizing the work of the Brazilian playwright and theater theorist, showing in detail its insertion in the twenty-year dictatorship that attempted to destroy our arts, Santos talks about the evolution of Brazilian theater and especially the creation and power of the Arena Theater, Boal's company that has so much influenced our stage. She goes over Brazil's most prominent dramatic works of the first half of this century and the left-oriented groups that paralleled the Arena, to focus her attention on Boal's play, highlighting its subversive and thought-provoking qualities, meant, as is common with Boal, to make the audience realize their sociopolitical plight and try to find means to change it. In this chapter, the Brazilian appropriation is seen as a postcolonial rereading that deeply shows European and North American colonialist exploitation not only of Brazil, but of Latin America in general. This piece by Marlene Soares dos Santos was previously published in the *Anais do XXVII SENAPULLI* (Águas de Lindóia: ABRAPUI, 1995).

In "Shakespeare's Sonnets: A Case of Nontranslation," Solange Ribeiro de Oliveira discusses the question of omission in Péricles Eugênio da Silva Ramos's translation of thirty-three sonnets by the Bard. The absence of Sonnets 130 and 132 strikes Oliveira as being typical of an era, now about to end for the Brazilian intelligentsia, when, unaware of our own Brazilianity, and enmeshed in European values, we read and reread the Eurocentric canon from the standpoint that originated that canon. Her discussion identifies the process of change not only hinted at but also developed by Shakespeare. She describes conventional standards for the sonnet and shows how Shakespeare was innovative on both formal and thematic levels. In such innovation, according to her, the Bard precedes postcolonial readings of the establishment. She sees the color of the Dark Lady as well as her ascendancy within the sequence, and the use of imagery taken from everyday life (as is found in Sonnet 143) as proving his role as an anticonservative writer. Silva Ramos's omission is consistently analyzed as characteristic of "racial associations between color and contrasting moral attitudes." Her peripheral reading stimulates thought on the use of translation as a sociopolitical weapon.

Purveying world and Brazilian performances of *Hamlet* in Brazil of the eighties, Anna Stegh Camati focuses her attention on *Hamletrash,* a parodic recreation of Shakespeare's play, written by Cesar de Almeida, and performed by two actors: Ceasar/Hamlet and Pagu/Ophelia. Based on theories of parody and appropriation, Camati analyzes Almeida's play in its use of the classical text in a Brazilian context, aiming not only at the reconstruction of *Hamlet,* but also at the presentation of sociopolitcal situations in contemporary Brazil, and the discussion of the predicament of the contemporary artist by the intellectually ill-prepared media, an artist threatened by social, cultural, and political inertia and devaluation. In her study, she considers the value of theatrical satire and parody to deconstruct canonical works, simultaneously creating a powerful tool for the criticism of social reality. In her detailed presentation and discussion of Almeida's text, the author offers an overview of Brazilian playwrights of the nineties who have experimented with form, like the author of *Hamletrash.* Permeating the play, where the canon maintains its place, are elements from the media, especially from Globo TV, which Almeida calls "trash," and which are meant to attract the spectators' attention, once it is understood that the only way to confront the contemporary "aesthetics of consumption" as it is disseminated by television is the use of its own tools, that is, "cultural trash."

Silvia Mussi da Silva Claro offers an intertextual reading of Machado de Assis, one of Brazil's greatest writers, in the light of *Hamlet.* Though Machado is better known for his novels, the chapter shows how much Shakespeare and, in this case, *Hamlet,* have influenced his *crônicas* (here translated as "chronicles"), a Brazilian literary genre, consisting of short essays on topical subjects, usually published in newspapers. Machado wrote these little essays in the nineteenth century and his contact with Shakespeare occurred through performances by Brazilian actors, especially João Caetano, and the touring foreign actors such as Rossi and Salvini. He also read the plays in textual editions found in Rio de Janeiro and in his own library. Claro's analysis of the way Machado quotes and parodies Shakespeare's words is an engaging reading of the dialogical process that so deeply constitutes the Brazilian novelist's style. His Shandian techniques come to the fore as his chronicles are discussed through the voices found in *Hamlet*. The way Machado appropriates/adapts the Prince of Denmark's words enlightens not only our understanding of the Brazilian writer but also of the Bard's own text as it is apprehended and elaborated by the former.

In her chapter, Maria Clara Versiani Galéry concentrates on the new possiblities—suggested by recent excavations of the Rose, Henslowe's theater—concerning the use of the Elizabethan stage. To her, the remnants of that theater appear as evidence of staging that can be confirmed by the study of Shakespeare's First Quarto of *Titus Andronicus* (1594). After a rapid view of different scholarly opinions concerning the use of the stage, including that of the Globe, by playwrights of that time, especially Shakespeare, the author discusses the innovative and experimental ways in which Shakespeare explored the physical possibilities of that space. The platform as well as the upper stage and trap door are considered as they appear to have been used in *Titus Andronicus* based on the evidence of stage directions found in the 1594 Quarto. Galéry talks of the centrality of the trap door to the construction of ideas in the play, resulting in the representation of the development of violence and treachery in the text. This provoking analysis may open a new door to studies of performance in Shakespeare's time.

In his reading of *Macbeth*, Tom Burns discusses the importance of the concept of masculinity in the play, through the dichotomy *homo versus Vir*, or man as potentially decent human being versus man as rogue male, as the dichotomy appears in the imagery and language in Shakespeare's text. Beginning with the ideas about disturbed nature as a reflex of social and individual deterioration, he focuses his attention on the playwright's concept of the imbalance created by two opposing forces in human beings, as they are portrayed in gender contrast. While woman is seen as mild, the body producing life-giving milk, the body denied by Lady Macbeth in her quasi-masculine behavior, man is doubly represented: he is either *homo*, that is, the man of potentially positive human traits, or *vir*, the "manly" man who carries in him the constant potential for violence. Burns discusses how *vir* gradually takes over in the protagonist's character, leaving behind his "milk-livered" aspects that were concomitant with his soldier's behavior. In this chapter, other male characters are discussed to highlight these traits: Malcolm, Macduff, and Edward of England, whose saintly health is contrasted with Macbeth's evil illness. Disease is seen not only as inherent in man's state, but pervading the text, spreading over society and nature, finally to become contemporary with ourselves. Tom Burns's chapter was previously published in *Anais de VII Semana de Estudos Germânicos e Encontro com Shakespeare* (Belo Horizonte: FALE-Dpto. LETRAS GERMÂNICAS, 1990).

In *"The Taming of the Shrew:* Shakespeare's Theater of Repetition," Maria Lúcia Milléo Martins considers the openness of Shakespeare's play, an openness confirmed by the inexhaustible rereadings of the play. She summarizes the endless discussion of whether Shakespeare was a chauvinist portraying the male values of his time or an early proponent of feminism, offering a possible critique of these values. Basing her study on Deleuze's view of the theater of repetition, she shows how the playwright may be seen as an untimely-born postmodernist. To clarify her assumptions, she compares three rereadings: John Fletcher's 1613 *The Woman's Prize or the Tamer Tamed* and two film versions—Zefirelli's and Marowitz's. Milléo Martins sees Shakespeare's time as a moment of crisis that prepares for changes in gender roles, and so she comes to the conclusion that this very imbalance is recreated in *The Shrew* as Shakespeare opens up possibilities that prove his text to be marked by ambivalence, which in its turn allows myriad interpretations born out of its inconclusive assumptions concerning male versus female power. In her discussion, language is considered as a weapon used not only by the protagonists but also and perhaps most prominently by Shakespeare himself. Ambivalent language is thus considered in its function of value mirror and status reverser, recreating within the text the inconsistency found in reality.

Adelaine La Guardia Nogueira reads Salman Rushdie's "Yorick" as a joyful possibility of "destroying dualities as fixed entities." She analyzes Rushdie's position as a policultural writer and, in this short story, his Oedipal attempt at murdering his father(s), that is, his literary predecessor(s)—Shakespeare and the canon in general—both in the East and the West. After a rapid overview of the work of the Bombay-born British writer and his output within postcolonial literature, Nogueira discusses "Yorick" in its relation to Shakespeare's *Hamlet* and unravels the threads of both works in what each of them has of Mikhail Bakhtin's concept of the "carnivalistic sense of the world." Rushdie is seen in his decentralizing attitude towards literary sources, his concern with the writing process, and his techniques of text construction/reconstruction out of annihilation. Through comparative analysis, Nogueira shows how intertexts are juxtaposed, creating the ironic stance characteristic of the joyful relativity found in dialogical constructs.

José Roberto O'Shea's " *'Uhuru!'*: Césaire's and Shakespeare's Uncontainable Calibans" deals with a possible reading of both texts in what they offer of unpredictability concerning the two main characters, Caliban and Prospero. He discusses the ways in which Aristotle's concept of the natural slave is erroneously used by traditional criticism, which sees in *The Tempest* a message of forgiveness and reconciliation, and in Caliban a hopelessly uncivilized "thing of darkness." After a review of peripheral rereadings of the Caliban metaphor, especially in Latin America, from Ernest Renan's 1878 *Caliban: suite de "La Tempête,"* the author uses the ideas of *pensée sauvage* and interdependence as cornerstones in his discussion of both Shakespeare's and Césaire's plays. The latter's representation and minimization of other characters, such as Miranda and Ferdinand, are seen in comparison to the reinforcement of the dialogical construct that comes out of the Prospero-Caliban opposition/interdependence and, instead of the manichean traditional reading, one has an interesting approach to the possibilities open to the reader from the contemporary postcolonial point of view. José Roberto O'Shea's article, revised and enlarged, was previously published with the title " 'Uhuru!' Aimé Césaire's Contained Caliban," in *Anais do XXVII SENAPULLI* (Águas de Lindóia: ABRAPUI, 1995).

In his article "Intertextuality in Shakespeare's *The Tempest* and Césaire's *Une Tempête,*" William Valentine Redmond discusses the way the two plays may be mutually used for better understanding of either as representative of sociopolitical moments. In his analysis, topicality in either work points directly towards the exploitation of colonized people by their colonizers by means of violent distortion and subsequent annihilation of the former's self-respect and sense of belonging. Topicality and use of space are here seen, in the light of adaptation to the moment and geographical milieu of their creation, as they move from one play to the other. Redmond considers Césaire's insertion of *The Tempest* in the context of black consciousness and sees the improbability of final reconciliation from a postcolonial stance, discussing the possibility of a reading of *The Tempest,* after *Une Tempête,* in its relation to the course of history. William Valentine Redmond's article was previously published in *Painel de Humanas ICHL/UFJF* 3 (Juiz de Fora: Oct. 1991): 109–23.

Metatheater is the focus of Bernardina da Silveira Pinheiro's "Stoppard's and Shakespeare's Views on Metatheater," a comparative study of Shakespeare's *Hamlet* and Stoppard's *Rosencrantz and Guildenstern Are Dead*. From the view of *Hamlet* as the greatest example of intuitive metatheater, the author sees Stoppard's play as a virtuoso display of techniques pertaining to this sort of drama. While Hamlet is here seen as the complete embodiment of theater on theater and his companions Rosencrantz and Guildenstern as representative of the rotten aristocratic society of Shakespeare's time and of dubious mankind in its greed and lack of loyalty, Stoppard's protagonists are discussed as prototypes of contemporary nonentities, automatons more than human beings, nonthinking people who live only to be directed. Pinheiro analyzes both texts and shows how the source gives way to the appropriation, in the latter's use of criticism, parody and play-within-the-play as well as in Stoppard's critical stance concerning not only mankind, but theater, actors, and playwrights in general, including Shakespeare and himself. Pinheiro's discussion highlights the playwrights' concern with values that have changed, from Elizabethan times to our own. This chapter by Bernardina da Silveira Pinheiro was previously published in *Anais do XVI SENAPULLI* (Belo Horizonte: PUC-MG/ABRAPUI, 1984).

In "Godard: A Contemporary King Lear," Thaís Flores Nogueira Diniz sees the French film as a transcultural creation that offers a change of genre. From the Renaissance feeling of despair and skepticism, according to the author, the film moves on to reflect twentieth-century chaos and meaninglessness, typical of our time's existential revolt. This mindset seems to show up in Godard's disconnected work. All sorts of rupture in the order of things, in sequential narratives intermingle with superimposed images, characters, voices, forms of art, making Shakespeare look entirely new or, perhaps, decentering the Bard to such a point as to remake the ideas of paternity and reverence in art. Diniz's essay discusses the possible changes that can be found in such rupture, as she shows how Godard works somehow on lines similar to Shakespeare's, but through his own and different medium, the cinema. Visual puns are analyzed together with subtitles—words—as they appear in the French director's reading of *King Lear*. Godard's work is technically considered, not only on the thematic level but also on a filmic register.

The end of a playtext is performance. In the same way, a book on

Shakespeare should end with a textual study aiming at performance. This is what Margarida Gandara Rauen does in her "Multiple Texts and Performance in the Final Scene of *Henry V.*" Her discussion of the 1600 Quarto and the 1623 Folio offers a wide range of possibilities for the production of the play from the awareness of the differences in such texts and especially how either deals with the questions of power, gender, and irony. Comparatively analyzing passages from Q and F, Rauen shows how strongly influenced the director's decisions may be concerning characterization, political and gender representations, decisions that will include even the choice of the text to be used since, from her point of view, on such a choice the whole process of performance will depend. The reading of this essay, mainly in countries where textual study is still rather new, will help not only directors, but also editors, translators, actors, and teachers of Shakespeare to realize how multiple are the playwright's works and how open to new readings/productions.

It seems to me that Brazilians really are on the way to artistic self-respect. We already have a national creative art. We no longer need to mediate. Grisolli's, Zé Celso's, Vilela's, Hirsch's, and others' productions are here, holding their positions along with the work of Machado de Assis, Jorge Amado, Carlos Drummond de Andrade, Nelson Rodrigues. Other creations will come where the digested production from the Old World, like all European traits that are components of the Brazilian blood, will be transformed and transmuted, will become a unique form of national expression. Shakespeare's universality will from now on have its place within the *mestiço*'s blood. His qualities will remain in new renderings of his work, but these renderings will hopefully introduce and establish a Brazilian art without submissively copying canonized performances of his text. Transmuted, a Brazilian Shakespeare. *Macunaíma!*

NOTES

Throughout this volume, all quotes from Shakespeare's work in English are taken from *William Shakespeare: The Complete Works,* ed. Stanley Wells and Gary Taylor (Oxford: Clarendon Press, 1986).

Part of this essay was published in *Anais do XXVII SENAPULLI* (Águas de Lindóia: ABRAPUI, 1995). The present work was revised and enlarged for publication in this volume.

1. This is my translation into English.

2. Ibid.
3. Ibid.
4. Ibid.
5. Ibid.
6. The translation of Boal's *A Tempestade* was made by Michael Warren and myself.
7. The harmony director is the person responsible for the quality of music and rhythm at a Samba School.
8. Numbers man.
9. *A cuíca* is a musical instrument with a distinctive creaking sound.
10. *Carioca* refers to someone or something from Rio de Janeiro.
11. *Mineiro* refers to someone or something from the state of Minas Gerais.
12. Hirsch's words in the presentation of the play *Estou Te Escrevendo De Um Lugar Distante*.

Bibliography

Andrade, Oswald de. "Manifesto Antropófago." In *Vanguarda Européia e Modernismo Brasileiro,* ed. Gilberto Mendonça Teles 226–32. 2nd ed. Petrópolis: Vozes, 1973.

———. "Manifesto Pau-Brasil." In *Vanguard Européia e Modernismo Brasileiro,* ed. Gilberto Mendonça Teles 203–8. 2nd ed. Petrópolis: Vozes, 1973.

Bakhtin, Mikhail. *Problems of Dostoevsky's Poetics.* Trans. Caryl Emerson. Minneapolis: University of Minnesota Press, 1984.

———. *Rabelais and His World.* Trans. Hélène Iswolsky. Bloomington: University of Indiana Press, 1984.

Bellei, Sérgio L. P. "The Culture of Mediation." In *A Literatura dos Descobrimentos—Anais do XXIV SENAPULLI* 9–18, João Pessoa: ABRAPUI/CCHLA-UFPB, 1993.

Bhabha, Homi K. *The Location of Culture.* London: Routledge, 1994.

———, ed., *Nation and Narration.* London: 1995.

Boal, Augusto. *Teatro do Oprimido e Outras Poéticas Políticas.* Rio de Janeiro: Civilizacão Brasileira, 1975.

———. *A Tempestade e As Mulheres de Atenas.* Lisbon: Plátano, 1979.

Boose, Lynda E., and Richard Burton, introduction to *Shakespeare: the Movie,* ed. Lynda E. Boose and Richard Burton. London: Routledge, 1998, 1–7.

Bulman, J. C., and H. R. Coursen, eds. *Shakespeare on Television.* Hanover: University Press of New England, 1988.

Coelho, Marcelo. "Zé Celso Pede Vingança Contra Usurpadores." *Folha de São Paulo,* October 29, 1993, 4, 13.

Dias, Gonçalves. *Leonor de Mendonça.* Belo Horizonte: Vega, 1976.

Drakakis, John, ed. *Alternative Shakespeares.* London: Routledge, 1985.

Fanon, Frantz. *Black Skin, White Masks.* Trans. Charles Lam Markmann. New York: Grove Press, 1967.

Gomes, Celuta. *William Shakespeare no Brasil.* Rio de Janeiro: Biblioteca Nacional, 1961.
Gomes, Eugênio. *Shakespeare no Brasil.* Rio de Janeiro: Imprensa Nacional, 1961.
Hodgdon, Barbara. "The Critic, the Poor Player, Prince Hamlet, and the Lady in the Dark." In *Shakespeare Reread: The Texts in New Contexts,* ed. Russ McDonald. Ithaca: Cornell University Press, 1994, 259–293.
Knight, G. Wilson. *The Wheel of Fire.* London: Methuen, 1983.
Loomba, Ania. *Gender, Race, Renaissance Drama.* New Delhi: Oxford University Press, 1993.
Lotman, Iuri, and B. A. Uspensky. "On the Semiotic Mechanism of Culture." In *Critical Theory Since 1965,* ed. Adams Hazard and Searle Leroy. Tallahassee: Florida State University Press, 1986, 410–13.
Matta, Roberto da. *Carnavais, Malandros e Heróis.* Rio de Janeiro: Zahar, 1983.
———. *A Casa e a Rua.* São Paulo: Brasiliense, 1985.
Retamar, Roberto Fernández. *Caliban e Outros Ensaios.* Trans. Maria Elena Matte Hiriart and Emir Sader. São Paulo: Busca Vida, 1988.
Rodó, José Enrique. *Ariel: Breviário da Juventude (1900).* Trans. Hermes da Fonseca Filho. Rio de Janeiro, Companhia de Livros e Papéis, 1926.
Rothwell, Kenneth S. *Shakespeare on Screen.* Cambridge: Cambridge University Press, 1999.
Singh, Jyotsna. "The Postcolonial/Postmodern Shakespeare." In *Shakespeare: World Views,* ed. Heather Kerr, Robin Eaden, and Madge Mitton. Newark: University of Delaware Press, 1996, 29–43.
Santiago, Silviano. "O Entre-Lugar do Discurso Latino-Americano." In *Uma Literatura nos Trópicos,* 11–28. São Paulo: Perspectiva, 1978.
———. *Vale Quanto Pesa.* Rio de Janeiro: Paz e Terra, 1982.
Vaughan, Alden T., and Virginia Mason Vaughan. *Shakespeare's Caliban.* Cambridge: Cambridge University Press, 1993.

Theater for the Oppressed: Augusto Boal's *A Tempestade*

MARLENE SOARES DOS SANTOS

So, from old Shakespeare's honour'd dust, this day
Springs up and buds a new reviving Play
—Davenant and Dryden, *The Tempest*

É preciso que fique claro que nós somos Caliban
[It must be made clear that we are Caliban]
—Augusto Boal, *A Tempestade*

WHEN WILLIAM DAVENANT AND JOHN DRYDEN WROTE THE LINES that make up the first epigraph of this essay, they were referring to their adaptation of *The Tempest,* which they wrote in 1674. They could not foresee the number of "new reviving plays" and poems that would spring up "from old Shakespear's honour'd dust" scattered on English and American soils. An early offshoot, to use Ruby Cohn's term (1976), belongs to John Fletcher, Shakespeare's former collaborator, who borrowed the storm, the desert island, and the girl who had never seen a man for his *The Sea-Voyage* (1622). Late in the following century (1797) F. G. Waldron rewrote *The Tempest* and gave it the title of *The Virgin Queen.* In the nineteenth century, Robert Browning's dramatic monologue *Caliban upon Setebos* (1864) added to the history of the play. The twentieth century saw Percy MacKaye's version, *Caliban by the Yellow Sands,* staged in America in 1916, as well as W. H. Auden's poem, *The Sea and the Mirror,* published in England in 1944. It is worth observing that these English and American "adaptations," "versions," or "offshoots" show a preference for Caliban rather than Prospero, as some of the titles indicate.

The second half of the twentieth century witnessed a new direction in the destiny of the play. With the process of decolonization gaining strength in the fifties, *The Tempest* began to be read by writers of Britain's colonies, sometimes in English—as in the case of Edward Braithwaite's poem *Islands* (1969) and George Lamming's novel *Water with Berries* (1971)—and sometimes not—as in the case of Aimé Césaire's play *Une Tempête* (1969) and Roberto Fernández Retamar's essay *Caliban: Apuntes sobre la Cultura en nuestra America* (1971). Thus, with the exception of Ernest Rénan's *Caliban* (1877) and its sequel, *L'eau de Jouvence* (1879), we can say that the possibility of reading Shakespeare's play remained a privilege of British and, to a lesser extent, American authors for three and a half centuries.

It must be added that modern readings are no longer called "interpretations" but "appropriations," which denotes their ideological and political orientation. It is not my intention to discuss definitions; I only want to state my position, which is the same as Ania Loomba's (1993, 142) when she says that "a demarcation between the two terms is in one sense false, for they spill into one another," and, she goes on, it marks the distinction of a reading/criticism "that explicitly acknowledges its partisanship and another that defends itself claiming that it is *objective,* and not 'devoted to special purposes'—which is how the *Oxford Illustrated Dictionary* defines *'appropriation.'* " And this explicit partisanship is present in the idea and practice of Augusto Boal's theater.

His appropriation of *The Tempest* can be included in the corpus of Latin American transgressive rewritings of Shakespeare's master text. Boal's play, oriented by Retamar's influential essay and supported by the playwright's own dramatic theories, includes Portuguese in the choir of many voices—Spanish, French, and English—calling for resistance to and liberation from colonialism in Central and South Americas. Of course there are differences in these claims and we should bear in mind Edward Said's words: "each new American reinscription of *The Tempest* is a local version of the old grand story, invigorated and inflected by the pressure of an unfolding political and cultural history" (1994, 213). To examine our "local version of the old grand story," I should like first to look into the Brazilian sociopolitical context of the sixties and the seventies into which the theatrical scene which made possible the production of Boal's play is inserted.

In 1964 what some people called "revolution" and others called a "coup d'état," took place in Brazil. It really took place on April 1, but the High Command of the Armed Forces, fearing the possible humorous connotations of April Fool's Day, decided to designate

March 31 the official date. It marked the beginning of a twenty-year period of military dictatorship, the terrible consequences of which can still be felt today.

The military coup interrupted the development of Brazilians' self-esteem, which had begun in the previous decade. We were losing that uncomfortable feeling of not deserving the beautiful and rich country God had blessed us with. This feeling of inferiority, developed through years of European and then North American economic and cultural domination, was gradually disappearing owing to the country's growing prosperity. The building of the new capital, Brasília, called the world's attention to the high level of Brazilian architecture; cars started being made in Brazil; our soccer team won the world championship twice in succession (1958 and 1962); our popular music, *bossa nova,* became internationally famous; our cinema, the so-called *Cinema Novo* [New Cinema]—was gaining recognition and prizes in European festivals, and our theater was beginning its most remarkable period so far. But Brazil, caught in the middle of the Cold War between the United States and Soviet Union, affected by the Cuban revolution, and shaken by its internal political turmoils, provided the Armed Forces with the opportunity and the excuse they were waiting for to occupy their own country.

At first they said their aim was only to reestablish order; that being done, they would return to the barracks. Yet holding power proved to be too attractive for them to let it go, and they stayed on. Doing so, they lost the support of institutions like the Catholic Church, conservative newspapers like *O Estado de São Paulo,* and a great many people who felt betrayed by them. As the opposition grew, the methods to crush it increased in number and cruelty: censorship, arrests, tortures, exiles, total abolition of civil and human rights. At the same time, other South American nations were going through the similar experience of having democratic governments overthrown and replaced by military dictatorships. The most well-known case is Chile, where President Salvador Allende was killed and General Augusto Pinochet ascended to power.

Resistance in Brazil was organized everywhere: in the schools, universities, unions, newspapers, all kinds of associations. The Catholic Church redeemed itself by becoming one of the strongholds of this resistance because of its prestige and international power. Artists were among the first to join the ranks of opposition, and the two cultural areas that were thoroughly engaged in the fight were those of popular music and theater.

The history of the modern Brazilian theater can be divided into two phases: before and after Teatro Brasileiro de Comédia (The Brazilian Theater of Comedy), known as TBC. Until 1948, when TBC started its activities, theater in Brazil (when I say *Brazil* I really mean its two biggest cities, Rio de Janeiro and São Paulo) was synonymous with amusement. Playwrights were supposed to give the public what they supposedly wanted: a pleasant afternoon or evening, no more. Of course there are honorable exceptions: in 1932, Jarocy Camargo wrote *Deus lhe Pague* (*May God Reward You*), a melodrama inspired by his preoccupation with class difference. Invited to think, the audience reacted well and the play was a great success. In 1933 Oswald de Andrade, one of the founders of our modernism, translated his *Manifesto Antropófago* (*Anthropophagous Manifesto*) into theatrical practice and wrote *O Rei da Vela* (*The King of the Candle*), affirming his nationalist and anti-imperialist position. Never staged during the author's lifetime—considered too crude by contemporary aesthetic standards—the play had its actuality proved in an epoch-making production in 1967. Another epoch-making event, this time in 1943, was Nelson Rodrigues's *Vestido de Noiva* (*Wedding Dress*) which put Brazilian urban society in the spotlight. These three playwrights in isolation tried to point out a new road to our theatrical scene.

This new road was partially taken by the creation of TBC by a rich Italian industrialist, Franco Zampari, who wanted to prove that in São Paulo it was possible to create a theater and a company as good as the American and European ones. The moment could not have been more propitious since during and immediately after World War II, many actors and stage directors tried a new life in Brazil, such as the French Louis Jouvet, the Polish Zbigniev Ziembinsky, and the Italians Adolfo Celi, Luciano Salci, and Ruggero Jaccobbi. Except for Jouvet, all of them were involved with the construction of the TBC and its tremendous success for over ten years. The importance of this achievement cannot be praised enough: the TBC introduced the notion of art in our theater, the figure of the stage director, the painstaking care with scenery and lightning, the careful choice of a repertoire, which included the great classics of the American and European theaters and gave our great actors and actresses the opportunity to show their talent in productions marked by a high level of professionalism, thus creating a faithful public among the high bourgeoisie of São Paulo and Rio de Janeiro.

I said that the road pointed out by Joracy Camargo, Oswald de Andrade, and Nelson Rodrigues had only been *partially* taken by the TBC. Regardless of its enormous importance, they were a company and a theater *in* Brazil, not a company and a theater *of* Brazil. Owing to their European roots, the foreign directors chose to work with what they knew best—which was, obviously, European dramaturgy—and there was no room for Brazilian playwrights. The actors were encouraged to cultivate a European acting style, and even their diction betrayed their rehearsals under the Italians since they spoke Portuguese with an Italian intonation. It must be said that, towards the end of its existence, the TBC did try to attract national authors and adjust its characteristic acting style to the demands of Brazilian plays. But it was too late: this part of the road had already been occupied by new groups and companies, left-oriented, who, through different methods, were working towards the idea of a national and popular theater. Among them, the most outstanding was Augusto Boal's Teatro de Arena (The Arena Theater).

In the search for a truly Brazilian theater, the Arena created a laboratory for actors and a workshop for playwrights. The results came sooner than expected for in 1958, the play *Eles Não Usam Black Tie* (*They Don't Wear Black Ties*) by a young author, Gianfrancesco Guarneri, was the group's first success. Yan Mychalsky (1985, 14) states the relevance of that production when he says:

> Thus was born a new kind of drama that would impose itself on our theaters during the next years: in the first place, it was a ferociously nationalistic drama which toiled to reflect an essentially Brazilian way of living, speaking and behaving at the same time that it rejected the imported models of European and North-American playwriting. In the second place, it was a drama that looked into the problems of the less privileged classes of our society—the workers and the peasants—aiming to become the voice of their demands.[1]

It is obvious that with such a proposal, the Arena was soon labeled *teatro politico* (political theater). Here we find the same case of the use of the word *appropriation* already mentioned: the so-called political theater is clear about its conception of art and its objectives. As Bernard Dort (1977, 365–81) says, "every theater is ontologically political." He sees the label as a tautology; as a solution, he suggests the qualifying "deliberately political," which is more accurate. What makes the label "political theater" even more imprecise when we talk about our theater at the time of the dictatorship is that all of it—regardless of its proposals—became deliberately political and all its members subversive. The newspapers of October 23, 1967, exemplify this, publishing General Façanha's well-known diatribe against the artists: "The theatrical class consists in its entirety of fake intellectuals, dirty people, madmen and vagabonds who know about everything except theater." Thus the theater became a special target of the regime, which feared it more than any other cultural manifestation. And the campaign against the theater began mainly through censorship: there is no agreement concerning the number of dramatic texts forbidden by the military regime; the account goes from four hundred to one thousand. Our censors, in their zeal, did not spare even foreign companies. They forbade the two performances of Giorgio Albertazzi's *Pilato Sempre* (*Always Pilate*) on a tour sponsored by the Italian government, which caused a diplomatic incident. Another was caused by the arrest of all the members of the American Living Theater—Julian Beck, Judith Malina, and fifteen other actors—under the excuse that they were carrying marijuana. The group was expelled from Brazil by a governmental decree. Such was the climate in which the Brazilian theater had to survive and in which Boal developed his theories and tried to put them into practice.

The relationship between Boal and the Arena Theater started in 1956. In 1953 he had gone to the United States to study chemistry and finished by studying drama for two years. He frequented the Actor's Studio under the direction of Elia Kazan and became familiar with the Stanislavsky's method of interpretation. Still in the States, Boal directed his first play. The meeting between Boal and the Arena Theater took place at the right moment for both: Boal was looking for a company and for a space where he could display everything he had learned abroad, and the Arena was looking for a director who could lead its hesitant steps towards a fixed goal. Boal brought to the Arena his recently acquired professional techniques and imprinted on it his clearly defined leftist political position.

Going against Boal's own division of his history with the Arena into four phases, for the purposes of this essay I shall divide it into two: before the military coup (from 1956 to 1964) and after it (1964–71). In its first phase, the Arena established itself as the antithesis of the traditional TBC. For eight years Boal and the Arena could try, develop, and actually realize their idea of a national theater, with a popular voice, that aimed at making its audience politically aware and encouraged it to believe in its power to change the status quo. Boal's play *Revolução na America do Sul* (*Revolution in South America*) (1960) is illustrative of this phase.

In its second phase after the coup, the Arena had to find a way to evade censorship. One solution was to present the literary-musical collage, inaugurated with an extraordinary show called *Opinião* (*Opinion*). The author told a story accompanied by music, which resulted in the development of the musical play *Arena Conta Zumbi* (*Arena Narrates Zumbi*), by Boal and Guarnieri in partnership with a then very young composer, Edu Lobo. It centers around Zumbi, the leader of a large group of runaway slaves who dies fighting for the freedom of his people. The relationship between Boal and the Arena was over in 1971, when he was arrested, tortured, and obliged to leave the country.

Boal's theatrical theories and techniques can be found in three books: *Teatro do Oprimido* (*Theater of the Oppresssed*), *200 Exercícios para o Ator e para o Não-Ator com Ganas de Dizer Algo Através do Teatro* (*200 Exercises for the Actor and Non-Actor Willing to Say Something through the Theater*), and *Técnicas Latino-Americanas de Teatro Popular* (*Latin American Techniques for the Popular Theater*). In the first book, among other issues, he explains the methodology of his poetics of the oppressed.

For Boal, every theater is necessarily political, because man's activities are all political; he believes the theater is a weapon and people should use it. He also believes that the theater is not revolutionary itself, but can surely become an excellent rehearsal for revolution.

In some plays—those that require that the audience should make an immediate connection with Brazil's political reality—Boal employs a Manichean technique. Dividing the world between good and evil, he simplifies the structure of the play and the delineation of the characters to provoke a quick response from the spectators. Boal justifies it by saying that it belongs to the best tradition of popular theater, such as the religious theater of the Middle Ages. He has been attacked for this, but Silvana Garcia (1990, 119) defends his use of Manicheanism as absolutely indispensable to the kind of play Boal wants to produce:

> The repeated attacks against Manicheanism always originate from right wing views which insist to create—at any price—the possibility of a

third position of neutrality, impartiality, objectivity or of any other mystifying concept. In reality, we know there exist good and evil, strength and weakness, left and right, exploiters and exploited.

It must be observed that Boal's preoccupation with the oppressed goes beyond our frontiers and includes all of Latin America. This concern is manifested not only in his theoretical writings but also in his practice as playwright, director, and producer. This deep sense of identification with our Latin American neighbors has been constant in his career: it can be found in one of his first plays, *Revolução na América do Sul* (1960), and in one of his latest, *A Tempestade* (1979).

The reading I propose for Boal's *A Tempestade* should take into account both its sociopolitical context and Boal's theatrical ideas and practices. It should also follow Silviano Santiago's suggestion of how to read a dependent literature like ours; according to him there is

> ... the need to create a new reading strategy: to *minimize* every literary debt (in spite of its presence and force) to foreign literature, at the same time trying to *maximize* (in spite of its minimum size) our original contribution which, despite everything, is the guarantee we have to make our own mark on culture. (1982, 194)

The dedication of the play hints at its guidelines: "this play is dedicated to the Cuban poet Roberto Fernández Retamar, who gave me the idea and the motivation." Those of us familiar with Retamar's well-known essay "Caliban" know he developed the identification of Caliban with Latin American nations and cultures, oppressed by European colonialism and North American neocolonialism, as it has been correctly described:

> Cuba straddles the Caribbean and Latin America geographically and culturally, and Fernández Retamar's arguments are marked by this double affinity. His focus is hemispheric, and his Caliban, originally the victim of European conquistadores, now labors more directly under North-American imperialism. (Nixon, 1987)

We cannot speak, in the case of Retamar and Boal, of an influence of the former on the latter; it is a clear case of confluence. Since Boal's approach to the problem of colonialism and oppression has always been hemispheric, it is not surprising that his Caliban, who defines himself as black, Indian, and yellow, is not portrayed as specifically Brazilian but as Latin American. Boal shows, in his initial stage directions, that he and Retamar share the same opinions about oppressed cultures: "but it must be made clear, very clear, that we are beautiful because we are ourselves, and no imposed culture is more beautiful than ours," and he finishes by affirming this position in the words that make up the second epigraph of this work: "it must be made clear that we are Caliban."

A very important point raised by Boal's and Retamar's readings of *The Tempest* is their revolt against the visible presence of North American neocolonialism, which Retamar dates back to 1898, the year of North American invasion of Cuba. This revolt increased considerably during the sixties and the seventies, when many Latin American countries had dictatorial governments openly protected by American foreign policy, which even arrogated itself the right of intervention as it did in Chile. The duplication of oppressors poses a very interesting problem concerning the identity of the United States: colonized or colonizer? I shall only touch on the problem since it takes us back to Edward Said's idea of the different local versions of *The Tempest*.

America was once Britain's colony, and even after its independence it felt the consequences of Britain's colonialism. At one time, American intellectuals claimed an identification of their native Indians with Caliban and saw *The Tempest* as an allegory of colonial America.[2] What seems ironically amusing today is the typical colonialist opinion that the British held on to about Americans until the open involvement of the United States in the affairs of Europe, during World War II. As Terence Hawkes comments, a kind of ideological adjustment was needed: "So far as Britain was concerned, the path of adjustment was clear. Americans were not savages. They were not Indians. They spoke our language" (Drakakis 1985, 36). The authors of *The Empire Writes Back* (1989) include American literature in the list of postcolonial literatures but recognize America's new position: "The literature of the U.S.A. should also be placed in this category. Perhaps because of its current position of power and the neo-colonizing role it has played its post-colonial nature has not been generally recognized."

A Tempestade exposes the expansion of colonialism and draws attention to the plight of Latin Americans due to the enormity of their task: to fight against the old and the new colonizers, Europeans and North Americans. Boal's play centers on the denunciation of the two types of colonialism and their mechanisms of oppression. He, once more, uses his Manichean approach, structuring Shakespeare's story as a fight between good and evil, that is, between the oppressors/exploiters/capitalists and the oppressed/exploited/workers, in two acts (act 1 has three scenes, and act 2, four). The protagonist of the play is Caliban. He is the politically conscious worker who is willing to fight for a revolution that will abolish tyrany. A slave in his own country, Caliban voices the accusatory discourse of the oppressed, constantly calling for revenge and freedom. He leads two rebellions against Prospero and loses both of them.

The end of the play betrays Boal's disillusionment with the possibility of a rebellion by the oppressed. Moved by the hope of profit, Prospero forgives his old European enemies and even proposes a commercial partnership for the exploitation of the island. The noblemen are united again as landowners, entrepreneurs, and exploiters. Prospero leaves Antônio and Sebastião on the island; they immediately assume their masters' roles of whipping Caliban, Trinculo, and Estêvão and obliging them to work. Prospero also takes some islanders to exhibit in Europe as exotic curiosities, in order to make even more money. Boal's "brave new world" is one of pure capitalistic exploitation.

Music functions as an essential theatrical device in *A Tempestade:* it is both didactic and choric, it clarifies parts of the action, it explains the behavior of the characters, and it comments upon the dialogue. The play includes fourteen songs on the whole, and their use takes us back to Boal's experiments in his musical plays.

The key to Boal's play is its deliberate lack of sophistication: it tells a simple story, through a simple structure, using a simple language that inserts the play into the long tradition of popular didactic theater. By treating Shakespeare's master text sacrilegiously, Boal radically transgresses it for the benefit of his audience in its contemporary political moment. He asserts his belief in the theater as a means of a sociopolitical transformation although the end of the play seems to contradict it.

Boal's *A Tempestade* was presented in Rio de Janeiro on December 17, 1981. The public's reception was warmer than the critics' as the play was shown until February 14, 1982. The critic Flávio Marinho was particularly hard on the play as shown by the title of his review, "Boal's version of *The Tempest,* a poor storm." His main target is the author's Manichean strategy, which deliberately reduces the complexity of the play. He considers it unacceptable in 1981, when Brazil was beginning to experience a gradual political liberalization that would culminate in 1984 with the restoration of a civilian and democratic form of government. He finishes by saying that "what could have been a powerful hurricane of liberal ideas is actually a poor storm. Moreover, it is dated—neither old, nor outdated—only dated." Besides magnifying the play's shortcomings, Marinho fails to read it according to Boal's idea of theater. He also exaggerates when he sees the sociopolitical context of the end of 1981 as characterized by freedom and democracy.

On the other hand, Yan Michalsky, another theater critic, although not raving about the play, to my mind, understood how it should be read as well as Boal's proposal. His review, entitled "*The Tempest:* better to forget Shakespeare," says: "It is practically the same story. But two different islands. Two different worlds. Two different aims. Let us forget Shakespeare when we go and see Boal's *A Tempestade.* It is only thus that we shall be able to do justice to each of the two authors."

The main difficulty with Boal's plays, and *A Tempestade* is no exception, is that they do not read well, for he writes them for the theater. If the proof of the pudding is in the tasting, the proof of the play is in the staging. *A Tempestade* requires excellent performers, who should at least be competent singers, and excellent music in order to be fully realized on stage. The production of *A Tempestade* in 1981 was under the charge of a semi-professional company, Gente de Casa, who ignored Boal's main ideas and techniques; and the music was composed by someone called Manduka, who remains unknown to this day.

I believe that to be fair to Boal's *A Tempestade,* besides watching a good or at least a competent production of the play, one should also have in mind the difficult situation of the Latin American writer described by Silviano Santiago as living "between the love and respect for what has already been written and the necessity to produce a new text which should *confront* the old and very often *deny* it" (1978, 25).

And to complement Santiago, I should like to quote Antonio Cândido's (1975) words: "Compared to other literatures, our own is poor and weak. Yet it is this very literature that expresses us." In the light of this statement, it can be said that compared to Shakespeare's *The Tempest,* Boal's *A Tempestade* is poor and weak, but there is no doubt that it expresses us in a very difficult moment of our history.

Notes

1. My translation into English. Heretofore, all translations of quotes from Portuguese into English will be mine.
2. See Alden T. Vaughan, "Shakespeare's Indian: The Americanization of Caliban," *Shakespeare Quarterly* 39 (1988): 137–53.

Bibliography

Ashcroft, Bill, Gareth Griffiths, and Helen Tiffin. *The Empire Writes Back: Theory and Practice in Postcolonial Literatures.* London: Routledge, 1989.

Boal, Augusto. *200 Exercícios e Jogos para o Ator e o Não-Ator com Ganas de Dizer Algo Através do Teatro.* Rio de Janeiro: Civilização Brasileria, 1977.

———. *Teatro do Oprimido e Outras Poéticas Políticas.* Rio de Janeiro: Civilização Brasileria, 1977.

———. *Técnicas Latino-Americanas de Teatro Popular.* São Paulo: Hucitec, 1978.

———. *A Tempestade e As Mulheres de Atenas.* Lisbon: Plátano, 1979.

Cândido, Antonio. *Formação da Literatura Brasileira: momentos decisivos.* 2 vols. Belo Horizonte/São Paulo: Itatiaia/EDUSP, 1975.

Cohn, Ruby. *Modern Shakespeare Offshoots.* Princeton: Princeton University Press, 1976.

Davenant, William, and John Dryden. "The Tempest, or The Enchanted Island." In *Five Restoration Adaptations of Shakespeare,* ed. Christopher Spencer. Urbana: University of Illinois Press, 1965.

Dort, Bernard. *O Teatro e a sua Realidade.* Trans. Fernando Peixoto. São Paulo: Perspectiva, 1977.

Garcia, Silvana. *Teatro da Militância: A Intenção do Popular no Engajamento Político.* São Paulo: Perspectiva, 1990.

Hawkes, Terence. "Swisser-Swatter: Making a Man of English Letters." In *Alternative Shakespeares,* ed. John Drakakis, 26–46. London: Methuen, 1985.

Loomba, Ania. *Gender, Race, Renaissance Drama.* New Delhi: Oxford University Press, 1993.

Marinho, Flávio. "*A Tempestade* na Versão de Boal, uma Borrasca," *O Globo.* December 16, 1981. Rio de Janeiro.

Michalsky, Yan. "*A Tempestade:* É Melhor Esquecer Shakespeare." *Jornal do Brasil.* December 18, 1981. Rio de Janeiro.

———. *O Teatro sob Pressão: Uma Fonte de Resistência.* Rio de Janeiro: Zahar, 1985.

Nixon, Rob. "Caribbean and African Appropriations of *The Tempest.*" *Critical Inquiry* 13 (1987): 557–78.

Retamar, Roberto Fernández. *Caliban e Outros Ensaios.* Trans. Maria Elena Hiriart e Emir Sadir. São Paulo, Busca Vida, 1988.

Said, Edward. *Culture and Imperialism.* New York: Vintage Books, 1994.

Santiago, Silviano. *Uma Literatura nos Trópicos: Ensaios sobre Dependência Cultural.* São Paulo: Perspectiva, 1978.

———. *Vale Quanto Pesa: Ensaios sobre Questões Político-Culturais.* Rio de Janeiro: Paz e Terra, 1982.

Vaughan, Alden T. "Shakespeare's Indian: The Americanization of Caliban." *Shakespeare Quarterly* 39 (1988): 137–53.

Shakespeare's Sonnets: A Case of Nontranslation

SOLANGE RIBEIRO DE OLIVEIRA

THE COMPLETE SEQUENCE OF SHAKESPEARE'S SONNETS HAS BEEN translated into Porguguese more than once. One example is Maria do Ceu Saraiva Jorge's 1962 translation in Portugal.[1] In Brazil, the complete series has been translated at least twice: by Jerônimo de Aquino[2] and by Oscar Mendes.[3]

The 1980s however, a decade rich in Brazilian translations of other challenging texts such as excerpts from T. S. Eliot by Ivan Junqueira (1981), from Ezra Pound by the Campos brothers Haroldo and Augusto, by Décio Pignatari, (1982) from Joyce's *Ulysses* by Antônio Houaiss (1982) saw no new complete version of the sonnets. The translation of thirty-three sonnets by Eugênio da Silva Ramos[4] remains the most celebrated as well as the most widely known Brazilian representative of the sequence. This was the version used for the bilingual recording of the reading of twenty-two sonnets by the English and Brazilian actresses Barbara Jefford and Maria Fernanda, issued by Editora Americana as part of the Brazilian celebration of the fourth centennial of Shakespeare's birth in 1964.

This recording seems remarkable more for the omission of certain crucial sonnets than for the solutions found for the translations of those that have been included. The absence of Sonnets 130 and 132—both essential for the interpretation of the series as a whole—proves particularly conspicuous for the purpose of my argument.

Sonnet 130 has been considered crucial both as thematic synthesis and as metalinguistic comment. On praising the beloved, the lyric persona rejects as inadequate a series of conventional similes. The mistress' eyes "are nothing like the sun." Her lips do not resemble coral, nor do her cheeks, roses, her breath, perfumes; nor does her gait resemble that of a goddess. His mistress, the poet sums up, "treads on the ground"; however, she proves more seductive than others praised by deceptive comparisons: "And yet, by heaven, I think my love as rare / As any she belied with false compare."

Thus denouncing the Petrarchan convention, the sonnet hints at the need to look for new poetic forms, simultaneously proclaiming the exhaustion of the sonnet and the urgency to renovate themes and attitudes associated with it. The proposed renovation is in fact already under way, with the appearance, in the sonnets, of the beloved with a dark complexion, the very opposite of the traditionally fair beauty sung by Elizabethan lyric poetry.

The absence of Sonnet 132 in Pericles Eugênio da Silva Ramos's collection—one of the most relevant from the viewpoint of the Third World reader—has also been noted. It is in this sonnet that the lyric persona most favorably presents the dark lady, whose creation we have associated with the formal and ideological renovation argued for in Sonnet 130. The exclusion of Sonnet 132 from Silva Ramos's series, can, in principle, be considered aleatory, and attributed to a number of causes, impossible to set down even if we had the translator's own word on the subject. Among the possible factors that may have contributed to the leaving aside of this text, however, it is not unreasonable to consider paramount a certain ideological stand, typical of an age which we hope to be about to end: a time in which the European perspective made us forget our own standpoint as Brazilians, the inheritors of colonized cultures.

Nowadays, after reader response criticism has been assimilated into the mainstream of critical tradition, Sonnet 132 strikes the eye of the reader—who insists on her/his own reading as a member of the peripheral societies of texts canonized by the ethnocentric hegemonic cultures. Among such texts, Sonnet 132, more than any other of the Shakespearean sequence, seems to ask for something Sergio Bellei calls an "interesting reading":[5] the sort of reading that displaces the critical viewpoint so as to fit that of a reader placed outside the culture where the text was generated—in brief, a reading at least partially freed from the temporal and social context of the so-called original. It is with this sort of reading that I would like to grapple here. I will try, on the one hand, to read the Shakespearean text from the viewpoint of a postcolonial culture, and on the other, to link my reading with Silva Ramos's exclusion of Sonnet 132. I will thus be reaching for the reading of an absence, a kind of zero sign that can be argued to be most meaningful. I do not intend, however, wholly to ignore the initial context. I would like only to widen it so as to move it towards the contemporary Brazilian reader. There is no harm then in recalling some information on the sonnets so as more effectively to shed some light on the lack of Sonnet 132 in Silva Ramos's translation.

The complete series—stylistically and thematically connected with some plays, especially *Romeo and Juliet, Love's Labour's Lost,* and *Two Gentlemen of Verona*—was published by Thomas Thorpe's initiative in 1609. Just as with the plays, Shakespeare did not seem interested in manuscript copies for friends and admirers. In writing the sonnets, Shakespeare was following a waning fashion, which had reached its height between 1590 and 1600. Before him several other poets had tried their hands at writing sonnet sequences, Spenser and Sir Philip Sidney being only two of the most famous. The most famous dominant themes, the relation of beauty to death, the work of art as the only undying value, the unattainable love of the coy mistress—a reminiscence of medieval love ethics—had been dealt with many times before. By resuming these themes, Shakespeare shows his disregard for a pretended originality which would place the author at the origin of the work. He seems to anticipate the modern notion of the text as a mosaic, a palimpsest where visible references to previous texts cross one another.

In Sonnets 1 to 126, the lyrical speaker has been traditionally held to address a seductive young man whose beauty his art is meant to make immortal. (The alleged homosexual undercurrent may also have belonged to the contemporary literary convention.) The last two sonnets also clearly echo traditional themes, adding variations on another conventional subject, the relation between eroticism and bathing. In Sonnets 127 to 152, the famous dark lady appears—the mysterious, cruel beloved, who in Sonnet 144 allies herself to the handsome youth of the previous sonnets, thus consummating a double treason. At a single stroke, she robs the lyrical speaker of both mistress and friend. The central knot is tied here, bringing together two themes and adding to the sequence a certain element of action and character which denounces the playwright in the lyrical speaker. (As a matter of fact, Sonnet 144 resumes Sonnet 42: in the latter, the double treason is rationalized, using an imaginative logic in the best euphemistic tradition, to force the conclusion that the two traitors only fall in love to find in each other the image of their single lover, the poet who, for this reason, would not have been betrayed).

By creating the dark lady, as well as some unconventional images (among them, in Sonnet 143, that of the mother who neglects her baby in order to run after a fleeing bird), Shakespeare introduces the differentiating element in his sequence, which in so many other respects resembles previous works. A female version of Othello, another fascinating being, the dark lady proves interesting chiefly because of her dark complexion, which contrasts with that of the handsome youth, explicitly described as blond or light-skinned ("fair") in Sonnet 18.

For the Elizabethans, the adjective *dark,* even *black,* could indicate a number of shades of colors of complexion or hair, from the brunette of southern Europe to the darker hue of Arabs invading Europe and blacks proper. Othello is not necessarily black and is clearly called "the Moor." The dark lady may then be simply a brunette. What matters is not the shade of color of her complexion but another, more meaningful, fact: for Europeans in the Renaissance, dark skin meant the exotic, the creature from the recently discovered America, or from the East, which the navigators had made accessible. Setting the European imagination on fire, these creatures rendered the exotic object strangely and erotically seductive. As such, they serve the purposes of the conquerors. They become their prey, offering their fantasies the promise of unknown pleasure. Remember that Othello wins Desdemona, as he tells the Duke of Verona, not only because of his exotic, enticing person; he multiplies his attraction by means of narratives about other exotic beings from the strange countries he had visited. Through narrative, through the seduction of language, the Third World, in the Moor's speech, yields to Europe. By so doing, however, he likewise conquers the conqueror.

In the process, a transgression is committed by both the exotic object and the seduced one, hence the need for the punishment of both. The European gaze is caught by the colonized object. However, with the implacable logic of the winner, it also punishes those who let themselves go too far in allowing themselves to be fascinated. Fascination by the exotic object does not exclude the idea of its danger or evil, which the conqueror projects onto his victim. Ambivalence towards the object of desire is inseparable from its attraction. Associated with evil, the exotic object justifies its own oppression. As transgressors, Desdemona and Othello must be punished. Iago's slander is merely a means to this end. As in Greek tragedy, the ideological balance must be restored by the death of the hero. This happens exemplarily in Shakespeare's play. Seduced Europe is symbolically punished when Othello kills Desdemona and then kills himself, closing the inevitable cycle with the destruction of the seducer and with his own.

In the dark lady of the sonnets, Othello's figure reappears. Like him, she is associated with seduction, presenting herself, besides, as the synthesis of all evil. In Sonnet 142, for example, she is identified with a "bad angel, devil, fiend" in contrast with the saintly handsome youth, the "good angel." From a European ethnocentric standpoint, the dark color is associated with evil, and the exotic creature, the object of erotic greed, is presented as ethically guilty and therefore dangerous, destructive, forbidden.

Silva Ramos seems ready to translate the sonnets where the representation of the dark lady follows this line. In Sonnet 150, he completely conveys the ambivalence of the lyrical speaker towards his dark beloved:

> Quem te ensinou a me fazer amar-te tanto
> Quanto mais ouço e vejo justas causas de ódio?
> [Who taught thee how to make me love thee more
> The more I hear and see just cause of hate?]

Translating Sonnet 144, Pericles mentions "a mulher de cor bem má [a woman colour'd ill] negra como o inferno, escura como a noite." Here as elsewhere Shakespeare and his faithful translator play with the opposites *black* and *fair,* which may either bear the literal meaning of brunette and blonde or the metaphoric ones of impure, heinous, in contrast with pure, imaculate. Silva Ramos's translation keeps all the force of the racist association between colors and contrasting moral attributes. In fact, as a translator, the Brazilian poet could hardly avoid doing so. What is meaningful, however, is that he translated the most virulently racist sonnets and ignored Sonnet 132, where the ethnocentric perspective, toned down, may evoke pertinent reflections for the reader from peripheric cultures, who may be interested in denouncing the connivance between literature and ideology.

In Sonnet 132, the lyrical speaker returns to the racist association, but only in order to reverse it. He praises the beloved's dark eyes, whose mourning, he declares, announces her pity for her suffering lover and better suits her face than the sun does the morning sky: "And truly not the morning sun of heaven / Better becomes the grey cheeks of the east / As those two mourning eyes become thy face." The lyrical voice proclaims then that beauty itself seems black, as black (impure, heinous, foul) are all those that have not got the color of the beloved: "Then will I swear beauty herself is black / And all they foul that thy complexion lack."

At this point, the dark lady is, up to a point, partially retrieved and becomes the pattern of beauty itself: she becomes "fair," and, therefore, not only white but also, because of the association between the color and moral attributes, lovable and virtuous as well. The exotic, black object is absolved from its associations with cruelty or evil. The inversion—the dislocation of negative attributes to blonde beauties—may also be considered racist but—at least in this context—it seems a move toward the redemption of this exotic object.

Shakespeare here seems to give us a foretaste of another dark lady, the Abyssinian maid in Coleridge's "Kubla Khan." To my mind, the Abyssinian maid seems to be no other than the romantic muse. Unlike her classical ancestress, she does not play the Greek lyre, but a comparatively modern instrument, the dulcimer. Nor are her features those of the Greek muse, an Aryan: like Othello, she was born in Africa. According to the poem, the mysterious dark maid who appears in the second part of "Kubla Khan," gives the poet the power of creation: could he remember her song, he would be able to build up in air—that is, with the power of imagination—the fantastic castle described in the first part of the poem. The castle thus emerges as an image for poetic creation. And the mysterious black maid is reprieved as the romantic muse. (According to this reading, the Abyssinian maid represents a link between the two parts of the poem, which would thus make up a whole, and not an unfinished piece as Coleridge would have us believe.)

With his praise of the black muse, Coleridge seems to continue the reprieve of Shakespeare's dark lady. He draws close to the theme of alterity, which hegemonic cultures have failed to tackle satisfactorily, preferring to see the other as the seductive object, whose danger justifies oppression—which brings us back to Silva Ramos's translation and his skipping the sonnet where black beauty is disconnected from its traditional association with evil. The translator unconsciously assumes the European perspective more than the implied author of the sonnets: the latter partially cancels his condemnation of the exotic object. The so-called Third World seems to introject the radical outlook of the hegemonic cultures, without realizing the self-condemnation built into the introjection.

This is what Silva Ramos apparently does when he ignores precisely the sonnet in which the exotic object—the Dark Lady—is recovered as worthy of love and becomes fair, which is as much "blonde" as "without blemish, respectable," and therefore acceptable as an object of desire. This is perhaps the change announced by the lyrical speaker in Sonnet 130; by rejecting the worn out Petrarchan similes, he points to the need for a renovation that may be ideological as well as formal.

The exclusion of Sonnet 132 from Silva Ramos's translation may have been the outcome of pure chance. It may also reveal a significant oversight, which a reading more attuned with the question of alterity could have prevented.

Notes

1. Maria do Céu Saraiva Jorge, *Os Sonetos de Shakespeare* (Lisbon: author's edition, 1962).
2. Jerônimo de Aquino, *Obras Completas de Shakespeare*, vol. 22 (São Paulo: Edições Melhoramentos, 1956).
3. Oscar Mendes, *William Shakespeare—Obra Completa*, vol. 3 (Rio de Janeiro: Companhia José Aguilar Editora, 1969). A list of other Portuguese and Brazilian translations of isolated sonnets can be found in Ivo Barroso, *William Shakespeare: 30 Sonetos* (Rio de Janeiro: Nova Fronteira, 1991).
4. Péricles Eugênio da Silva Ramos, *Sonetos de Shakespeare* (São Paulo: Edição Saraiva, 1953). Also (Rio de Janeiro: Edições de Ouro, 1966).
5. A term used by Dr. Sérgio Bellei from the Federal University of Santa Catarina, in a lecture delivered at the Second National Conference of ABEA (Brazilian Association of American Studies) held in Rio de Janeiro in 1986.

Hamletrash: A Brazilian *Hamlet* Made of Scraps

ANNA STEGH CAMATI

"A LITERARY WORK 'IS NOT A MONUMENT THAT MONOLOGICALLY reveals its timeless essence': much of its permanence lies in its ability to influence and be influenced." Marsden's affirmation (1991, 9) alludes to the common knowledge that man has an intrinsic need to construct myths and to manipulate them once they are established, which explains the basic drive of many writers to borrow works of art from the past in order to update and relocate them.

In *Nísia Floresta, o Carapuceiro e Outros Ensaios de Tradução Cultural,* Pallares-Burke (1997) investigates the Brazilian way of recycling ideas. She argues that the anthropophagous impulse in the Third World is very similar to the analogous occurrence going on in more developed countries, since there artists also tend to indulge in a process she denominates "cultural digestion," a term she coined. Certain notions concerning the circulation of ideas among different cultures are thrown into relief in a series of provocative essays, furnishing elements for the comprehension of a cultural phenomenon known under the generic label of "globalization."

Jyotsna Singh (Kerr 1996, 31), who contextualizes Shakespeare within the colonial/postcolonial history of British cultural hegemony in India, states that

> as we approach Shakespeare's works in the twentieth century, and in an increasingly interconnected, postmodern global culture, we have become keenly aware that not only do they illuminate the culture of Elizabethan and Jacobean England, but through their subsequent reception and reproduction they have continued to shape a variety of cultural paradigms and institutions—both in the West and in the "third world."

In productions and adaptations outside England, it is amazing to verify the infinite malleability of Shakespeare. As Michael Billington (Kerr 1996, 19) has pointed out,

Strip the plays of their original language and you are left with a series of all-embracing mythological narratives: a reminder of the way Shakespeare's plays work not just through their poetry but through a complex tissue of visual signs and symbols. The most obvious example is *HAMLET*.

Most contemporary *Hamlet* adaptations emphasize the corruption of the modern state and/or the existential problems of modern man. According to Billington, "In the Soviet Union and in Eastern Europe the play has become a potent, politically subversive weapon aimed at corrupt and decadent tyrannies: one in which Elsinore, rather than Hamlet, is the hero" (Kerr 1996, 19).[1]

Shakespeare's political spectrum is wide, accommodating the conservatives, the moderates, and the radicals.[2] The latter contend that it is salutary to appropriate cultural elements and insert them into a new context. Charles Marovitz (1991, 16) believes "there are no limits to the transformations that can be made to the Collected Works." He shows that "restructuring, juxtaposing, interlarding, collating one work with another; modern vernacular mixed with classical idiom; rock music copulating with Elizabethan madrigals" are just a few of the techniques that have been used by contemporary playwrights to "reinvent" Shakespeare. Among the radical reinterpretations that have won critical acclaim, Tom Stoppard's *Rosencrantz and Guildenstern Are Dead* and *Dogg's Hamlet,* Peter Weiss's *Haunted House Hamlet,* Heiner Müller's *The Hamlet Machine,* Joseph Papp's *William Shakespeare's "Naked" Hamlet,* Paul Baker's *Hamlet ESP,* and Marovitz's *The Marovitz Hamlet* are worth mentioning.

In Brazil a series of audacious, innovative plays that draw on Shakespeare's *Hamlet* started to appear in the eighties, among them *Denise Stocklos Unearths Hamlet in Irati* (1988) by Denise Stocklos, a production listed in Susan Bennett's *Theatre Audiences: A Theory of Production and Reception* (1994, 121), *Elsinore* (1990) by William Pereira,[3] a theatrical pastiche of images and dialogues from Hamlet blended with heterogeneous elements such as Beethoven's *Ninth Symphony,* Kafka's *The Trial,* and the music of Jim Morrison's Doors; *M.O.R.T.E.* (1990) by Gerald Thomas,[4] a postmodernist collage that focuses on the problem of the creative artist paralyzed with the lamentable state of contemporary art; *A Certain Hamlet* (1991) by Antontio Abujamra,[5] in which the protagonist is profane, perverse, and incestuous; *Ham-let* (1993) by José Celso

Martinez Corrêa,[6] a "work in progress" dissolving into new compounds in each successive presentation; and more recently *Hamletrash* (1996) by Cesar Almeida,[7] an experimental spectacle combining Shakespearean conventions and postmodern strategies; and *I'm Writing You from an Undiscovered Country* (1997) by Felipe Hirsch,[8] an intertextual dialogue of numerous voices incorporating Geovanni Testori, Heiner Müller, Karel Tchapek, Antonio Abujamra, and Tom Stoppard as well as Shakespeare, in order to contradict traditional readings and challenge audience expectations.

Hamletrash was written, produced, directed, and enacted by Cesar Almeida, a contemporary playwright living in Curitiba, Paraná. It had its première on July 10, 1996, at the Teatro da Caixa in Curitiba, remaining on show until September 1, and returning on September 19 for another short run.

Almeida makes use of theatrical collage, a swift, fragmentary method. He combines speed, which permits him to deliver, as he says in the unpublished version of this play, "a maximum amount of information in a minimum amount of time," with discontinuity and juxtaposition that allow him to escape from the stranglehold of the mythical narrative of the text providing "new and unexpected vantage points on the original" (Marovitz 1991, 32–35).

In *Hamletrash,* he roughly follows the plot pattern of *Hamlet,* his main source. However, he condenses, distorts, and trivializes the model, abridging the text drastically in favor of scenic images. His theater is highly visual and physical. The collaged lines from several scenes are accompanied by frenetic theatricality: exaggerated gestures, hysterical laughter, ostensive sexuality, and elaborate lighting.

A thorough reorganization of the source-text that includes reshuffling and cutting of scenes and dislocation of words and speeches, wrenching them out of their original context, enable the same material to mean radically different things. The playwright deconstructs the Shakespearean model, using the fragments as a pre-text[9] into which he weaves excerpts from Heiner Müller's *The Hamlet Machine,* quotations and allusions from several sources, modern colloquialisms, interpolations of his own, and bits and pieces from popular culture propagated by the mass media. However, he does not merely appropriate situations, characters, and speeches from the preformed literary material he borrows, but he wittily subverts the scattered fragments by creating a new text and context.

By using *Hamlet* as a paradigm or frame of reference, the playwright invites the audience to anticipate the main thematic issues in *Hamletrash,* such as ethical and moral uncertainties, melancholy, indecision, power, and vengeance. However, as Marovitz reports on his own *Hamlet* collage, even those people who had no familiarity with the original text could understand the critical questions raised because

> there is a kind of cultural smear of Hamlet in our collective unconscious and we grow up knowing Hamlet even if we have never read it, never seen the film or attended any stage performance. The "myth" of the play is older than the play itself, and the play's survival in the modern imagination draws on that myth. When one assembles a collage version of the play—or an anti-narrative gambol through its themes and issues—one reactivates the "myth" in such a way that people are reminded of it again. (1991, 19)

Thus, the Shakespearean model will serve as a basic structure for the playwright opportunistically to exteriorize the anxieties, dreams, desires, and doubts of the creative artist in Brazil today, to expose the prevailing sociopolitical situation of his country and to question the validity of the work of art within the contemporary Brazilian cultural context.

In a newspaper article published in *O Estado do Paraná,* entitled "Hamlet Nascido da Sucata Trash" (Hamlet Born from Scraps of Trash), Almeida asserts that he had aimed at presenting

> a stylized completely Brazilian version of *Hamlet.* Deconstructing a "classic" text does not destroy or invalidate it, because the mythological narrative remains intact and can be reactivated by the insertion of contemporary issues, local colour and naturalized characters, granting a greater complicity between stage and audience. (1996, 22)

Among the several forms of textual appropriation, Almeida has elected parodic theatricality[10] as an intertextual tool to shape his new synthesis. As Linda Hutcheon has put it, the parodist succeeds in establishing a close connection with the world by means of the interaction of parody and satire:

> Parody historicizes by placing art within the history of art; its inclusion of the entire enunciative act and its paradoxical authorized transgression of norms allow for certain ideological considerations. Its interaction

with satire overtly makes room for added social dimensions (1996, 109–10).

Through the integration of parody (refunctioning of "classic" texts) and satire (exposure of the sociopolitical and cultural reality in Brazil), the playwright expresses, in an emphatic way, his conviction that the theater cannot remain alienated from the social reality. He transforms the Shakespearean tragedy into a serious comedy.[11] His poetics of laughter provides him with the necessary critical-ironical distance to reach the spectators' sensibility, not via emotional identification, but through more speculative and rationalistic processes.

In *Hamletrash,* two overtly metafictional characters[12] play the players and act out several roles. The actor-protagonist Cesar Almeida/Hamlet roleplays the narrator and all the other dramatis personae except Ophelia. The actress-character Pagu/Ophelia also assumes the masks of a girl aspiring to become an actress and of the presenter of a popular television program.

As in Shakespeare's theater, stage properties are reduced to a minimum. Several sticks protruding from the ceiling suggest vengeance, the main motive evoked in the play. A structure of three superimposed man-high boxes are strategically placed at the mid-end of the stage. The front side of each of these boxes is opened during the play to bare its contents before the eyes of the audience. This structure is creatively used to simulate a series of different spaces and situations.

In scene 5, we see the protagonist Hamlet/Cesar Almeida in leather-jacket and dark sunglasses imprisoned within the box-structure. The open upper box reveals his tormented head procrastinating over his existential situation. The contorted and agonizing gestures of the actor feature a robot or a machine. This visual image of painful arrest metaphorically alludes to the actual situation of the creative artist confined within a space reduced to a minimum, as the result of the growing influence of the mass media that debase the aesthetic standards of people by submitting them to uncountable subliminal messages favoring formulaic art produced for commercial purposes.

In scene 7, the actress-character impersonates the "dead" Ophelia. The open lower box reveals a startling image: Ophelia's head is upside down and her eyes are staring at the spectators. Her discourse is aggressive, at times even obscene, intending to communicate complex feelings of repressed sexual desires and to elicit outrage against the perpetuation of traditional gender roles. This visual image projects the idea of the necessity of inverting the cultural stereotype of the submissive, naïve, and sexually passive woman. Ophelia's outburst of anger is complementary to her speech in scene 4, where she makes an ostensive critique of the dramatic situation of women in art and life. Here Almeida transcontextualizes almost verbatim from scene 2 *(Das Europa der Frau)* of Heiner Müller's *The Hamlet Machine*. The transcribed excerpts are themselves a collage of bits and pieces from other writers, constituting a stratification of female experience based on political history (Rosa Luxemburg), literary models (the bourgeois tragedies of Lessing and Hebbel), and private life (Heiner Müller's wife, Inge Müller).[13]

Instead of the five-act structure, *Hamletrash* is loosely constructed of ten juxtaposed scenes. In the prologue, which imitates the chorus of *Henry V*, the actor-narrator invites the audience to supply the poverty of scenery with the power of their imagination. His insistence on theater as theater recalls Brecht's alienation effects. A reference to "Brazil, tropical paradise" relocates the play from Denmark to Brazil. It is a reminder to the audience that the stereotyped narrow vision of the exotic, sensual land of carnival and samba, that has always fascinated Europeans and Americans, still survives abroad, representing Brazilian culture in an erroneous way.

In scene 2, Almeida inserts some topical elements into the reduced Shakespearean plot to throw into relief the corruption of the contemporary political reality. This scene speeds through fragments from the first five scenes of act 1, ending with the appearance of the Ghost demanding vengeance. The idea of rottenness is metaphorically conveyed by pigs "rolling in the mire," an image intended to remind the spectators of a version of *Hamlet* that was staged in Curitiba shortly before the impeachment of Fernando Collor de Mello. Its director, Marcelo Marchioro, decided to drown the stage in mire[14] in order to supply a concrete picture of the degradation of the state. Almeida's text suggests the setting of Marchioro's play:

> ... this country is drowned in mire in which we are all rolling ... we are all rolling in the midst of lies and hypocrisies ... even if they say we don't! ... but I, Hamlet, I shall fight to do away with American

imperialism—its fall shall result in the inundation of the "third world," where the fountains murmur, where I quench my thirst . . . where the moon plays . . . ah! this beautiful, wonderful, delightful country, it's a pity it's so poor. . . . There is something rotten in the state of Denmark. Something is rotten in this age of moon . . . there is something rotten . . . truly rotten—pinch me, tell me it's any place except . . . no! Do you mean to say this is not Denmark, what is it then? Brazil??? Oh, my God, was there no better place to be born in . . . (HT 1–2)

In this scene, the actor-protagonist shows an acute awareness of the failures of the Brazilian government and the ruling elite that are largely responsible for the existing cultural manipulation in supporting political and economic subjugation. He also mentions American imperialism as one of the determining factors in the ills that beset his country. Swearing vengeance, he reveals his desire to provide intellectual change that will liberate people from the fetters that enslave them.

In scene 3, Hamlet/Cesar Almeida communicates his complex sense of the precarious social reality. He expresses his anger and revolt at the brute facts of mass poverty and misery. He inserts into the text a fragment from a poem by Carlos Drumond de Andrade entitled "José", which helps him to evoke the capacity of the poor people in Brazil to survive despite the weight of unbearable deprivation. The repetition of the refrain ". . . e agora, José?" [What are you going to do now, José?] activates the backgrounded poem as a whole, so that there is no need to make any further statement about the stoicism of the persona: José, despite the enormous difficulties he has to transpose every day, does not curse his fate, but fully embraces strife engaging in the existential conflict. The quoting of a single fragment brings to mind the overall statement of the poem that emphasizes patient and uncomplaining endurance of suffering: "Mas você não morre, você é duro, José!" [But you won't perish, you are tough, José!] Through parodistic allusion, Almeida opens the text to its fullest signifying potential. As Laurent Jenny has aptly put it in *The Strategy of Form:*

> The allusion suffices to introduce into the centralizing text a meaning, a representation, a story, a set of ideas, without there being any need to state them. The source text is there, potentially present, bearing all of its meaning without there being any need to utter it. . . . This confers to the intertext an exceptional richness and density.[15]

Then in the midst of a sequence of well-known lines collaged from Shakespeare, the actor-narrator hints at the crisis of the Brazilian theater,[16] and the lack of popular enthusiasm for artistically serious drama compared with other forms of popular entertainment. In a jocoserious attitude, he questions the validity of the effort of the aspiring artist (Hamlet/Cesar Almeida) of staging a play that questions the validity of staging serious drama in an age dominated by cultural mediocrity. Here the main theme developed in the play is introduced: the dilemma of the serious creative artist, whose aspirations are paralyzed by the power of the cultural industry.

In the newspaper article already mentioned in the introduction, Almeida (1996, 22) draws attention to the fact that

> ... our cultural heritage has been debased and trivialized, having been transformed into a great amount of "trash." The vehicles of communication, in an attempt to adapt themselves to the circumstances imposed by the industrial revolution, started to demand a new speed even for the process of assimilation of the work of art by the spectator; there is no time to waste, everything assumes an absurd urgency in an age of consumism at its highest stage, so that not even Hamlet can remain unscathed.

These conjectures are reminiscent of Ezra Pound's analysis of the contemporary scene after the Second World War in the long poem *Hugh Selwyn Mauberley*. He criticizes the cheapness and trivialization of art and culture of the time by comparing the state of affairs to "an old bitch gone in the teeth."[17] Almeida's statements also recall the ideas developed by Adorno and Horkheimer in *The Dialectic of Enlightenment* (1977, 114). The German philosophers, who coined the term "cultural industry," make an ostensive criticism of the monopoly of culture held by the mass media, which has taken over the task of spreading an ideology destined to legitimate the trash it purposively produces. They argue that humanity is sinking into a new barbárie since there is a generalized preoccupation with profit rather than humanitarian values.[18]

Almeida's main target of irony is Globo Network Television, in his opinion the great villain that manipulates the audience by creating an aesthetics of consumption, with which the artist cannot compete since the growing incursion into the homes of people of different forms of cultural "trash" of no aesthetic value constitutes an invitation to mental laziness and accommodation, leaving little space for more demanding, thought-provoking theatrical events.[19]

The playwright realizes that, due to these adverse circumstances, he had to make Shakespeare more palatable in order to meet with popular success. Thus, he decided to integrate the very forms he intended to attack, weaving into the texture of his dialogue the most disparate elements disseminated by TV Globo for popular consumption, such as references to soap operas (*The Cattle King, The Next Victim*), popular television programs (*You Shall Decide*), as well as popular icons (Coca-Cola, Skol), and jingles. These bits of trash, as the playwright calls them, lend a semblance of actuality to the text since the references are well known and therefore immediately apprehended and appreciated by the audience, providing an opportunity for the author to make a critique of media culture in a covert and subtle way.

By the end of scene 3, the critical situation of the artist divided between the desire to be transformed into a machine liberated from pain and the temptation to become a prophet of the contemporary age is narrated off-stage:

> Hamlet mediates . . . Hamlet is a thinking-machine designed to accomplish vengeance—he has to fulfill the promise annotated on the tables of his memory—the idea of vengeance haunts him . . . Hamlet is perplexed (*the light darkens*). He needs the help of a psychiatrist . . . No, Hamlet prefers to drink a Coca-cola in the dark. (*The interminable sound of a Coke being poured into a glass is heard*). Ah! It's delightful! (HT 3)

This attitude of pleasure, delight, and forgetfulness associated with the escapist tendency[20] that Coca-Cola, one of the pop icons of the American consumer society implies, is later repudiated by the actor-protagonist. In scene 6, he makes fun of the glamorous images of the American way of life and playfully hints at the importance of being Hamlet in tropical setting when he chooses to drink "Hamleite—com sabor de frutas tropicais" [Hamletmilk—enriched with tropical fruit].

There is one extended non-Shakespearean scene in the play that dovetails Hamlet into an interactive TV program situation. In scene 10, the actress-character assumes the role of the presenter of a popular TV Globo program entitled *You Shall Decide*. People at home are encouraged to make telephone calls in order to choose between two alternatives to decide the outcome of the story. The actress-character mimicks the action of the TV program:

Ladies and gentlemen, we have now arrived at the crucial point in our story. We have seen our dear Hamlet obsessed by his desire of vengeance. His action has caused multiple deaths. Polonius and his daughter Ophelia have already been sacrificed, as well as other innocent victims . . . the next will be Ophelia's brother Laertes . . . You have seen that up to now Hamlet's mortal blows have not reached the target . . . vengeance is a terrible monster dragging everything along . . . now we have come to the moment of highest tension—the time has come for Hamlet to kill his uncle—the king—to set things right—unfortunately this is his cursed fate . . . But now you are given the opportunity to decide the ending of this interactive Hamlet. Either Hamlet stops procrastinating and kills his uncle—the king—or he continues being unable to make up his mind—he does not accept the challenge to duel with Laertes and is transformed into a vermin without dignity, not being worthy to breathe, not even this rotten air of Denmark! But today YOU SHALL DECIDE! (*She encourages the audience to interact*). (HT 10)

This interactive strategy causes disgust in Hamlet/Cesar Almeida, who has been watching the proceedings. He decides to warn the audience that the freedom of choice proposed is in fact illusory, since they are supposed to choose from a clear-cut two-dimensional pattern formulated by the either/or structure. Consumed by rage and fury, he professes his determination to defy cultural mediocrity, destroying everything that imposes limits upon him. He strikes the air in the manner of Bruce Lee. There follows a travestied version of the final catastrophe, and in the epilogue the actor-protagonist asks the few elected who have come to the theater to tell his story to posterity.

In *Hamletrash,* Almeida illuminates one of the most debated critical questions of the end of the millenium—the identity crisis of the creative artist, fighting for his space in an age dominated by globalization, which in the context of the play acquires a double meaning: on the one hand, it can be interpreted as a concept developed by economic structures to do away with artistic diversity in order to create a universal culture of low standards aiming at profit, and on the other hand, it can be understood as a direct reference to TV Globo, a dangerous cultural industry that has succeeded in destroying theatrical audiences through manipulation of mass taste and mass desire.

The theater of Cesar Almeida functions as a metacommentary on Brazilian society and culture. The spectators are encouraged to become aware of their condition of inertia and are induced to "take arms" against oppression, injustice, manipulation of aesthetic standards, and cultural mediocrity.

Almeida belongs to a group of playwrights of the nineties who experiment with form. Although he has not created a new form, since many playwrights have deconstructed Shakespeare in a similar way, his work is important because it can be included in the tendency that strives for an art liberated from the commercial pressures, initiated in Brazil by Denise Stocklos and Gerald Thomas, both of international renown, to whom he pays homage within *Hamletrash* by travestying them as queen-mother and gravedigger.[21] He shares with them the self-reflexive exploration of dramatic language, the metatheatrical approach, and the use of parody as an instrument of critical-ironical distancing.

Notes

1. M. Billington (in H. Kerr, 1996, 19). Also see p. 20 where the author provides an example of a production that has become a politically subversive weapon aimed at corrupt and decadent tyrannies: ". . . But proof that Hamlet is not just a specific text but a revolving metaphor was provided by Alexandra Tocilescu's remarkable production from Bucharest's Bulandra Theater. This was created in 1985 when the evil Ceausescu was still in power. But instead of taking the obvious line and showing Elsinore as a barbaric despotism, the production seemed to be set in a dusty museum on the point of collapse. Claudius and Gertrude may have been greeted everywhere by sycophantic applause and ritual anthems. But the court was a shabby relic full of wire-netted cases stuffed with skulls, armor, musical instruments, unread tomes. There was even an onstage piano player knocking out wistful nocturnes and waltzes in a mood of exhausted melancholy. I have rarely seen a production that caught so well the desolation and bankruptcy of tyranny. Ideas that seem a cliché in the West—such as portraying Fortinbras as a ruthless pragmatist who here had Horatio stabbed to death—also became chillingly appropriate for Romania. Seeing the production in 1990, I was reminded that Romania had recently witnessed not a political revolution but a brutally effective coup. In the West Hamlet still tends to be read as a study of an individual dilemma. In eastern Europe, it becomes something else: an echoing poem about the emptiness and vulgarity of absolutism."

2. According to Charles Marovitz the conservatives strive to preserve Shakespeare's integrity, which in fact is sheer arrogance because it is impossible to deduce the author's original state of mind; the moderates are willing to accept a change of period or a shift in emphasis; the radicals enthusiastically applaud the innovations which deliver new sensations to the spectator. (See Charles Marovitz, "How to Rape Shakespeare," in *Recycling Shakespeare* (London: Macmillan, 1991), 16–31.

3. Nelson de Sá defines the play as "a happening" based on images and dialogues from Hamlet. See *Divers/idade* (São Paulo: Hucitec, 1997), 25.

4. See Haroldo de Campos's essay "A M.O.R.T.E. e o Parangolé." S. Fernandes; J. Guinsburg (1996), 217–26.

5. See M. Silveira et al, "Luzes na Ribalta," *Manchete* (7 September 1991): 83.

6. See João Wady Cury's article "Bete Coelho Faz 'Ham-let' no Oficina," *O Estado de São Paulo* (9 October 1993): 2.

7. César Almeida, *Hamletrash*, unpublished Brazilian version. Henceforth quotations from the play will be indicated in the text by *HT,* followed by page numbers. All the translations are mine.

8. See Adélia Maria Lopes's article "Mensagem de Hamlet via Internet," *O Estado do Paraná* (15 August 1997): 19.

9. According to Friedrich dü Renmatt (Sander, *Friedrich Durrenmatt* [New York: Continuum, 1982], 258–59), parody offers the artist the possiblity of originality. He argues that original subject matter is practically nonexistent, what we have is preformed literary material, i.e., material which has already been given form.

10. The broad concept of parody formulated by Linda Hutcheon in *A Theory of Parody* will serve as a theoretical basis for the analysis of the play.

11. In Germany, Lessing initiated the tendency of the serious comedy, a mixture of *Lust u. Trauerspiel,* where certain vices of the bourgeoisie were exposed to ridicule. He makes the bourgeoisie laugh at their own vices, incorporating ridicule within their own class. This current of the serious comedy was fortified by J. M. R. Lenz (*Sturm und Drang*), who can be considered an early precursor of Hebbel, Ibsen, and Strindberg. His views on comedy are expressed in his *Rezension des Neuen Menoza,* where he defines *Komödie* as a genre tending towards tragicomedy—he turns tragedy into a parody of tragedy, a tendency which contemporary drama has followed. Lenz proposes that because society in his era exhibits barbaric as well as refined tendencies, it is content neither with mere comedy nor with pure tragedy. While tragedy tends to idealize its subject, comedy seeks to reproduce it realistically and in a socially critical manner: "Comedy is the image of human society, and when there are serious problems—this image cannot be solely laughable . . ." (See Lenz's "Theory of Tragicomedy," in L. P. A. Kitching, *Der Hofmeister* (Munich: Wilhelm Fink Verlag, 1976), 37–40.)

12. See J. Schleuter *Metafictional Characters in Modern Drama* (New York: Columbia University Press, 1997), 1–17.

13. See Ruth Röhl's analysis of scene 2 ("Das Europa der Frau") of *The Hamlet Machine* by Heiner Müller. She points out the sources the playwright used for his dramatic portrait of Ophelia, a composite character, representing all women who have confronted the social, legal, and psychological limits of gender roles. (Röhl, "Modernidade e Pós-Modernidade" (Ph.D. diss., University of São Paulo, 1994), 179–84.

14. See O. Gemba, "Hamlet—a Lama do Poder" *Gazeta do Povo,* (11 September 1992): 3.

15. L. Jenny, in T. Todorov, ed., *French Literarary Theory Today* (Cambridge: Cambridge University Press, 1982), 39–40. Also see Ben-Porat "The Poetics of Literary Allusion," *PTL* 1 (1976), 105–28.

16. J. C. Fernandes, "O Teatro em Crise?" *Gazeta do Povo,* caderno 6 (Curitiba), 22 March 1997, p. 1. In this article a group of actors, directors, playwrights, and theater critics discuss the crisis of the Brazilian theater, the waning of theatri-

cal audiences, and other problems on the occasion of the international theater festival that is held annually in March in Curitiba.

17. See E. Pound, "Hugh Selwyn Mauberley," in Ellmann and O'Clair, eds., *The Norton Anthology of Modern Poetry* (New York: Norton, 1973), 246.

18. Also see E. Morin, *Cultura de Massas no Século 20,* 2 vols. (Rio de Janeiro: Forense, 1986–87).

19. Some of the ideas developed in this paper have been discussed with the playwright himself, who agreed in participating in a public debate after one of the theatrical performances of *Hamletrash.*

20. J. Nachbar, et al., *The Popular Culture Reader* (Bowling Green, Tenn.: Bowling Green Popular Press, 1978), 6: "We may look at these images and artifacts as icons—objects that have special significance on both the individual and the collective level. These icons are often surrounded by folklore; who has not heard stories of the powers of Coca-cola? . . . how to get high by putting a couple of aspirin in a bottle of Coke? Doesn't it really have cocaine in it? . . ."

21. There is the hilarious scene where the gravedigger, with long, disordered hair à la Gerald Thomas digs the ground while pursuing philosophical meditations. He asseverates that our present involvement in history may be explained by uncovering the mystery of the various layers of shit accummulated by the successive civilizations. And in scene 10, a male and histrionic Gertrude with an enormous blonde wig provokes laughter among the audience because the stereotype suggests Denise Stocklos or Denise Stopa as the actor-narrator announces. These acts of reverence are included in the play, because Almeida wants to pay homage to these two figures who have obtained celebrity status in Brazil and abroad; they are the precursors of the postmodern tradition in Brazil, having influenced a number of playwrights and directors emerging in the eighties and the nineties including Almeida himself.

BIBLIOGRAPHY

Adorno, Theodor W., and Max Horkheimer. *Dialética do Esclarecimento: Fragmentos Filosóficos.* Trans. Guido Antônio de Almeida. Rio de Janeiro: Zahar, 1997.

Almeida, César. "Hamlet_Nascido da Sucata Trash." *O Estado do Paraná.* July 11, 1996. Curitiba.

Almeida, César. *Hamletrash.* Unpublished Brazilian version.

Bennet, Susan. *Theatre Audiences: A Theory of Production and Reception.* London: Routledge, 1994.

Ben-Porat, Ziva. "The Poetics of Literary Allusion." *PTL* 1 (1976): 105.

Cury, João Wady. "Bete Coelho Faz *Hamlet* no Oficina." *O Estado de São Paulo.* October 9, 1993. São Paulo.

Ellmann, Richard, and Robert O'Clair, eds. *The Norton Anthology of Modern Poetry.* New York: Norton, 1973.

Fernandes, José Carlos. "O Teatro em Crise?" *Gazeta do Povo,* Caderno G, March 22, 1997. Curitiba.

Fernandes, Sílvia, and Jacó Guinsburg, eds. *Um Encenador de Si Mesmo: Gerald Thomas.* São Paulo: Perspectiva, 1996.

Gemba, Oraci. "*Hamlet*—A Lama do Poder." *Gazeta do Povo,* Caderno G, September 13, 1992. Curitiba.

Hutcheon, Linda. *A Theory of Parody: The Teachings of Twentieth-Century Art Forms.* London: Methuen, 1985.

Kerr, Heather, et al., eds. *Shakespeare: World Views.* Newark: University of Delaware Press, 1996.

Kitching, Laurence P. A. *Der Hofmeister: A Critical Analysis of Bertolt Brecht's Adaptation of Jacob Michael Reinhold Lenz's Drama.* Munich: Wilhelm Fink Verlag, 1976.

Lopes, Adélia Maria. "Mensagem de Hamlet via Internet." *O Estado do Paraná.* August 15, 1997. Curitiba.

Marovitz, Charles. *Recycling Shakespeare.* London: Macmillan, 1991.

Marsden, Jean I., ed. *The Appropriation of Shakespeare: Post-Renaissance Reconstructions of the Works and the Myth.* London: Harvester Wheatsheaf, 1991.

Morin, Edgar. *Cultura de Massas no Século 20,* 2 vols. Rio de Janeiro: Forense, 1986–87.

Nachbar, Jack, et al., eds. *The Popular Culture Reader.* Bowling Green, Tenn.: Bowling Green University Popular Press, 1978.

Pallares-Burke, Maria Lúcia. *Nísia Floresta, O Carapuceiro e Outros Ensaios de Tradução Cultural.* São Paulo: Hucitec, 1997.

Röhl, Ruth Cerqueira de Oliveira. "Modernidade e Pós-Modernidade na Obra Teatral de Heiner Müller." (Ph. D. diss. University of São Paulo, 1994).

Sander, Volkmar, ed. *Friedrich Dürrenmatt: Plays and Essays.* New York: Continuum, 1982.

Sá, Nelson de. *Divers/idade: um Guia de Teatro dos Anos 90.* São Paulo: Hucitec, 1997.

Schlueter, June. *Metafictional Characters in Modern Drama.* New York: Columbia University Press, 1979.

Silveira, Mauro, et al. "Luzes da Ribalta." *Manchete.* September 7, 1991. Rio de Janeiro.

Todorov, Tzvetan, ed. *French Literary Theory Today.* Cambridge: Cambridge University Press, 1982.

Quotations from *Hamlet* in the Chronicles of Machado de Assis

SILVIA MUSSI DA SILVA CLARO

IN HIS NOVELS, STORIES, AND CHRONICLES,[1] MACHADO DE ASSIS delineates the Brazilian character. He did this not through the description of local landscapes but by a reading of the psychological makeup and social behavior of individuals. He shaped a differentiated language, steeped in citations in which the values of civilization would be offered as a term of comparison with national life. He was an observer of the daily facts and associated them with references to world literature. Through this process, he constructed a unique relation between the private and the universal.

This chapter is a part of the analysis of the quotations from Shakespeare's works in the chronicles of Machado de Assis. It seeks to clarify the meaning of the play *Hamlet* in the day-to-day experience of Rio de Janeiro in the nineteenth century, according to the interpretation of that city's greatest chronicler.

Machado de Assis was a drama critic who followed closely the performances given by national and foreign theater companies in Rio de Janeiro. The outstanding Shakespearean companies of his time were those of João Caetano dos Santos, the great Brazilian actor, and of the Italians Ernesto Rossi and Tommaso Salvini, actors on world tour during the period. Machado de Assis was also familiar with Shakespeare's works in textual form. Editions of Shakespeare in English, French, Italian, Spanish, and Portuguese could be found in the libraries of Rio de Janeiro that the author visited: the National Library, the Portuguese Reading-Room, the Rio de Janeiro State Library, the Ramos Paz Collection, as well as the author's private library.

My intention is to study the use that Machado de Assis made of readings and theatrical performances of *Hamlet*. The phrases and episodes from the play cited in the chronicles will here be examined in the sequence in which they appear in Shakespeare's text.

There are more things in heaven and earth, Horatio,
Than are dreamt of in your philosophy.

(1.5.168–69)

It was these words that Hamlet spoke to Horatio after his father's ghost revealed the cruel fratricide of which his prophetic soul had already had a premonition. This was a form of knowledge that could not be absorbed by the reigning philosophical systems of the era: "But he was bound to surmise after seeing and hearing the Ghost, that there are more things in heaven and earth than he and Horatio could have conceivably learned from the study of natural philosophy, the scientific curriculum at Wittenberg."[2]

The first citation of this utterance in the chronicles of Machado de Assis appeared in 1873:

> Hamlet is right. There are more things between heaven and earth than those of which our philosophy dreams. . . .
>
> The philosophers who take themselves off into the atmosphere in search of systems which usually do not survive the century always seem to me vain dreamers.
>
> Down here, gentlemen, come down here, open the newspapers, peruse the police pages and destroy greater difficulties than those that go about dreaming in the between-worlds of Epicurus.[3]

In the context of the author's work, it was a vain dream to build theories in the air that did not deal with reality. The philosophers should concentrate on the concrete facts that occur on earth and are printed in newspapers.

Machado de Assis did not translate the expression "There are more things in heaven and earth" literally, but as "There are more things between heaven and earth." The preposition *between* did not conform to the English original, nor was it suggested by the French translations of Guizot, Montegut, and François-Victor Hugo, those most accessible in the Rio de Janeiro of the last century, which read as follows respectively:

> *Hamlet.* Il y a plus de choses au ciel et sur la terre, Horatio, quí'il n'en est rêvé dans votre philosophie.[4]

> *Hamlet.* Horatio, il y a plus de choses dans le ciel et sur la terre, que n'en rêvé votre philosophie.[5]

Hamlet. Il y a plus de choses sur la terre et dans le ciel, Horatio, qu'il n'en est rêvé dans notre philosophie.[6]

In the translations of the play into Portuguese, one could not find an equivalent of "between heaven and earth" either: one always reads "no ceu e na terra' [in heaven and earth]. One might conclude that, by using the preposition *between,* the author intended to lend a specific meaning to Hamlet's phrase. Might it refer to the "between-worlds" of Epicurus, quoted in the chronicle, in which philosophers wander in search of hypothetical problems? For Epicurus, the between-worlds were empty spaces existing between celestial bodies which made their movements possible. The writer certainly did not believe that the answer to the greatest human questions was in a vacuum.

In 1888, Machado de Assis again quoted Hamlet's phrase in his chronicle *Good Days:*

"Agreed, but what is it that separates them?" [political parties]
"The principles."
"What principles?"
"There are no others: the principles."
"But Aquirás is a title, not a principle; Ibiapaba is also a title."
"There is between heaven and earth more accumulation than your philosophy dreams of . . ."
"Perhaps so, but that still doesn't explain to me the reason for this mixture or exchange of groups, as it would seem better if they fused at once with their old adversaries. Doesn't it seem to you?"[7]

The author asked the Senator Castro Carreira for an explanation about the equivalence of the political groups in the state of Ceará. He inquired about the specific characteristics of each group and the principles that joined or separated them. These questions, however, were in vain, since the Senator cared to answer them in a tautological way, invoking the principles of good politics—good manners and common interest in the good of the province—for the purpose of concealing the personal financial interests involved: There is between heaven and earth more accumulation than your philosophy dreams of. Aquirás and Ibiapabas were titles, understanding this term as a designation of nobility and of negotiable paper. And in the space between heaven and earth, the titles have transformed themselves into principles, and have begun to govern events.

"There are more mouths than your useless statistics can reckon with."[8] This variation on Hamlet's phrase in 1893 in a newspaper chronicle entitled *The Week,* on the subject of how a rumor was disseminated. The Senate had held a secret session and was looking for an explanation for how the rumor had spread. The chronicle supplied a logical cause: the secrets spread by word of mouth. But as the secretary insisted that all the doors had been closed, the hypothesis of occult activity was ironically raised. As in Shakespeare's *Hamlet,* logic and superstition ran along parallel lines. In this case, the statistics were useless to measure the rumor—from an infinite number of mouths—that was spread through proximity, mainly in a short and narrow street with the suggestive name of *Ouvidor*—Listener. The unit of measure was inadequate to the phenomenon that they wanted to evaluate.

In 1889 Machado de Assis put in the mouth of his friend João a parody of Hamlet's phrase: "There are between your and my age many more things than your vain philosophy dreams of."[9] Your and my age substitute the heaven and earth of the original. At the same time, this and the other world appear in a parallel way in the chronicle about skeletons in jovial poses exhibited in shop windows: "There are so many roguish things in this world, that it is not worth going to another to snatch away those who are sleeping."[10] The desperate cleaving to life was expressed the wrong way round in the macabre shop window exhibition of skeletons, shown in capering poses as if they were dancing. The dead, reduced to bones, became the actors in a grotesque spectacle. Would they be inviting passersby to dance with them? Machado de Assis seemed to take refuge from this frightening scene by resorting to the fictional world. The mazurka danced by the skeleton reminded him of a certain João, who also played the mazurka and finished it off with the version of Hamlet's phrase mentioned above. What paths would there be on the journey between the age of the author and that of his friend? There would surely be the author's endless walks or trolley rides through the streets of the city, while he reflected on ideas to pass the time until time brought death.

In 1894, Machado de Assis said that among the many things between heaven and earth was financial speculation:

There are two astronomies: of heaven and of earth. The first has stars and numbers, the second dispenses with stars but keeps the numbers. But there are also, Horatio, many more things between heaven and earth than vain philosophy dreams of. One of these things is, as I say, the vertigo of the figures.[11]

What is specified in this quotation is that which belonged to the dominion of heaven and earth and that which hovered in the between-worlds of Epicurus. In the astronomy of the heavens, the numbers measured the stars; in that of the earth, the numbers were valued for themselves. De Assis continued, "The imagination likes to dive into these abysses of numbers that never more have an end. It is a way that man has to make himself grow."[12] Machado de Assis was ironical in saying that perhaps this mechanism explained the speculation, the request to the Municipal Council for some eight thousand *contos*[13] in exchange for five hundred and some cattle. The writer recalled to this effect another fact that had occurred in the period of the great inflationary crisis of 1890–91: the popular imagination had multiplied nearly fifteen times the income of a certain man, which did not prevent him from dying in the poverty in which he had always lived. The needier levels of the population let themselves be excessively fascinated by astronomical numbers as a way of compensation for the strict limitations of their lives.

In 1896, Machado de Assis repeated the phrase "There are more things between heaven and earth than our vain philosophy dreams of" with respect to the unsolved theft of some dynamite:

> Therefore, do not marvel that the dynamite is still unfound. There are more things between heaven and earth than our vain philosophy dreams of. This thought of Hamlet's is old but is not thereby lost. I don't ask of truths that they always have white hair, all truths will serve, even those with white and gray hair. Now if there are many things between heaven and earth, the dynamite might well be there. There is a lot, I admit, but the space is vast and abundant. How shall we fetch it that high? The police, even the English police, who are said to be the best equipped, do not yet possess airborne detectives.[14]

It was easier to catch in the light of day a thief of scarves who confronted the masses of people than the thieves who secretly stole more valuable objects in the dark. The between-worlds of Epicurus sheltered even stolen dynamite. The author says with slight irony that the fact of the police not being able to catch the more refined pilferers did not mean that that institution was not necessary for the order and security of a city.[15] The police symbolized the carrying out of the law. "As far as the regulations, if we consider them in the light of the true philosophy (the false is my neighbor's) we shall recognize that they are no more than pure abstractions. There are more concrete causes."[16]

The advantage of keeping the theft in obscurity spoke louder than the abstract regulations. In this context, philosophy was seen as a subjective matter not exempt from the influence of individual interests.

In a chronicle of 1896, Machado de Assis agreed with Hamlet regarding the poverty of philosophy:

> We drank tea and spoke of nothing in particular. It was on Wednesday of this week. We opened a chapter of mysteries, and of obscure phenomena, and we agreed with Hamlet on the poverty of philosophy. Spiritualism itself had a few minutes of attention. I left the place surrounded by shadows.[17]

The philosophy of Wittenberg did not explain what occurred in the reign of Denmark. It was also inexplicable that a young woman named Inês had died during a crisis of sleepwalking after a spiritualist seance. As for the responsibility for this occurrence, the author would suggest the freedom of belief be invoked, supported by article 72 of the Constitution but restricted by article 157 of the Penal Code. The conflicting regulations thus prevented a solution.

The expression "poverty of philosophy," used by Machado de Assis, not only refers to Hamlet but possibly evokes Marx's *Misère de la Philosophie,* written as a reply to Proudhon's work *Philosophie de la Misère.* Proudhon preached a morally desirable social order, and Marx retorted in the sense that the arrival of a system that expressed the interaction of historical forces was inevitable. The very nature of capitalist production caused an economic instability whose immediate results were speculation, the concentration of economic power, and the exploitation of labor. Machado de Assis seemed to believe that revolution itself was absorbed by the capitalist system, according to his chronicle of October 20, 1895. He reported that Luiza Michel, the star of anarchy, was sponsored by the Americans to give talks throughout Latin America in the rhythm of "time is money:" *"Only the Yankee soul is capable of evaluating what a journey of speeches by that famous woman would profit it. . . ."*[18] In an interview, Luiza Michel declared she had not come to Brazil to make a revolution but to divulge ideas, and for this reason she was carrying out a contract signed with the Americans.[19]

Perhaps it is possible to say that the author's variant of Hamlet's phrase—"there are more things between heaven and earth than are dreamt of in your vain philosophy"—also establishes a connection between the preposition *between* and the sharing in the profits. From *inter-esse* (to be between) in Latin can be derived the word *interest*.

☙

> *Hamlet.* Ay, sir. To be honest, as this world goes, is to be one man picked out of ten thousand.
> *Polonius.* That's very true, my lord.
> *Hamlet.* For if the sun breed maggots in a dead dog, being a good kissing carrion—have you a daughter?
> *Polonius.* I have, my lord.
> *Hamlet.* Let her not walk i' th' sun. Conception is a blessing, but not as your daughter may conceive. Friend, look to 't.
> (2.2. 179–87)

> . . . .
> *Polonius.* What do you read, my lord?
> *Hamlet.* Words, words, words.
> 2.2. 192–93)

In *Hamlet,* Denmark was rotten, and words had been emptied of meaning. The yellow fever was described by Machado de Assis as the rottenness of home. It never disappeared once and for all, and it spread through the inaction of the sanitary authorities.

> The yellow fever is homely, it likes its own rooms and it doesn't demand that they be clean or large. The question is that they let it stay. Once they let it stay, they can discuss it, examine it, turn it upside down, write reports on reports, issue official statements, inquire and quote; "words, words, words," it says, in order to quote something too. And still quoting Hamlet: "If the sun can breed worms in a dead dog." . . . It will not be dead dogs that it lacks. As for the watery sheet, we will see it become an impressive sheet of paper. "Papers, papers, papers."[20]

The watery sheets fed the fever, which was fought with sheets of paper: "papers, papers, papers." The authorities did not leave the libraries for the streets, and their words—"words, words, words"—were not transformed into action. The phrase "words, words, words" was used as an epigraph to the chronicle published in 1868.

Periods and Commas
Words! Words! Words!
Shakespeare, *Hamlet*[21]

Machado de Assis criticized political counselor Victor Hugo for expressing concepts of a general character without using good sense to analyze the peculiarities of each situation. The French writer thought that the republic was the best form of government because it was equivalent to administrative probity, will, and freedom in government. He forgot that there were countries like Belgium and England which, while not being republics, governed themselves very well. *"Freedom as a magnet of annexations is simply a phrase,"* Machado de Assis said, echoing the "words, words, words" of Hamlet.[22]

In 1893, Machado de Assis gave Rio's version of "words, words, words":

> I, if I had put *Hamlet* into a language that is pure Rio de Janeiro, would translate the famous reply of the Prince of Denmark "words, words, words" like this: "rumors, rumors, rumors." In effect, there is no other phrase that best gives the meaning of the great melancholic. Words, rumors, dust, nothing, nothing at all.[23]

The word, which Hamlet used as a weapon in his struggle against the crumbling values around him, had been converted into an instrument of intrigue, being pulverized until it was reduced to the final silence.

Among the people of Rio, rumors produced conspiracies, dissensions, and explosions.[24] It was not then facts or qualities that were expressed in words, but the words that created reality. Vice and virtue were perhaps nothing but pure rumors. The very creation of the world would be a rumor invented by these times in their anxiety to obliterate immortal time. As for those who thought they existed, they were perhaps nothing but the very words of the rumor. It was not the man who expressed himself in words, but the word which invented the man. Creation was thus reduced to signs: the explosion of the Island of Mocanguê would be a comma, the bombardment a reticence, the disease a solecism, death a hiatus, marriage a diphthong, the parliamentary, electoral, and other struggles a cacophony.[25] What remains in this case is for Machado de Assis to constitute the word as the raw material of his art. "I am content with words. Words blooming in the heat of debate, or composed through study, daughter of necessity, derived from love to refinement, the work of chance; whatever may be its baptism certificate, here is what interests me in the history of men."[26]

Hamlet's soliloquy "To be or not to be."

(3.1.58–90)

Hamlet was a scholar recently out of the university who saw himself suddenly going through a labyrinth where at each crossing he had to stop and decide the best path to take. His seven soliloquies correspond to his deliberations, and the fourth one, in particular, occupies a central place in the play, since it prepares the set of measures to be adopted by the Prince relative to the circumstances of his return. Contrary to the other soliloquies, this one does not mention specific events or individuals. Doubt is a rhetorical process that controls the ideas: "The process of dubitation with its disjunctive "eithers" and "whethers" usually involves more choices than one."[27]

The expression "that is the question" appeared in a chronicle written on January 1, 1877:

> In this I hear an argument. To whom will belong the wealth that was found? To the State? To the leasers of the demolition work? "That is the question." Opinions are divided: some want it to belong to the leasers, others to the State, and many good reasons are brought forward from one side to the other.[28]

Hamlet's doubt, his *question,* is related to the reason for existence, the validity of this life, and the nature of the next. In the text of Machado de Assis, the question is *Whose?* and not *Why?* Possession comes first. The discovery of archeological matter of great importance to the community becomes less important than the commercial value of the element that was found: gold. The controversy thus became a dispute.

In 1877, too, Machado de Assis made a reference to the phrase "Ay, there's the rub," from the same soliloquy:

> After a long debate in the congress, if my doctor gives me a prescription for arsenic pills, how shall I be able to look at him in the face? What dost thou bring, pill? I shall speak in the form of a monologue; did the hand of the pharmacist slip on the arsenic? Dost thou bring life or death? Am I going to walk to the corner or to Cajú [a cemetery]? Pill, art thou a pill or a partner of the Funeral Enterprise? It is the rub....[29]

The scientific procedures of medicine and pharmacy frightened the writer since, through error, they could carry the patient off to the other world, in a pact with the funeral business. In this association of death and commerce comes the difficulty: the rub. Just as Hamlet did, the author puts his questioning in a monologue: "Pill, art thou a pill or a partner of the funeral enterprise?" These were questions raised by the idea of poison, as in *Hamlet.* And the answers in no case brought reassurance.

In a chronicle of 1878, a legal problem was personified as a gentleman with an interrogative bearing, a mixture of Hamlet and the sphinx of Thebes, who asked the councilmen: "Who has the obligation to remove the corrupt remains? It is the rub. Answer me or I devour thee."[30] The corrupt remains were the rotten goods left over after a fire in the Galeria das Mil Colunas, whose odor infected the air and aggrieved the neighborhood.

The inspector sought out the owners of the property and the insurance companies, but each attributed to the other the responsibility for removing the ruins. Through the suggestion of the alderman, the inspector decided to modify the way the question was put: "Who is not responsible for removing the ruins?" The answer, however, did not elucidate the problem. The alderman, after futilely attempting to divert the attention of the inspector, concluded that the question was neither easy nor difficult, or rather, was easy as well as difficult. The truth is that removing the rottenness was in the interests of neither the owners nor the insurers. In this situation, the city council decided to transfer the case to another authority: the bey of Tunis or the Carmelite cardinal. The former was impious and heathen, suspected of taking part in the scourges by which providence punished men. The latter must have prayed for the remains not to rot and the typhus not to spread.

Everything seemed to be settled when the councilmen observed that they had no way to communicate with the bey of Tunis or the cardinal. Thus, the best thing was to file the case. Offended, the problem turned into a dilemma[31] and decided to react, arranging to disturb the breast of the alderman, who, for his part, sneaked off, handing over the case to his lawyer. The Hamlet-sphinx was swallowed by the bureaucracy protective of shirking interests, and the ruins remained where they were.

In June, 1877, another passage of the "to be or not to be" speech was referred to by Machado de Assis. It was "the undiscovered country from whose bourn / No traveller returns." In Brazil, according to the author, the tavern has become the entrance to the grave:

> The tavern is always the gateway to something, whether the grave or the jailhouse. Yet up till now it has been only the latter establishment, rather unbecoming, it is true, but never definitive. One would go to the jailhouse as if one were going to Praia Grande—a boat ride. The grave is of easy access, but does not offer a way out to its guests. No one returned from that country, as Hamlet had pondered.[32]

At the end of the same year, the phrase that is the question once more expressed in the author's chronicles the dispute and not the doubt.

> Does Mr. Greenough have or not have a privilege? "That is the question." That is the point on which opinion is divided, not only the opinions of the contending parties, but those of all the civilized breathing beings beneath our sky.
>
> Naturally, Mr. Greenough takes an affirmative line, while his opponent inclines to the negative. From this point come a thousand demonstrations for and against privilege, and with such minute and discriminating detail, that they show how true it is that the Turks took Constantinople, since those articulating the arguments employ all their Byzantine shrewdness, which was expelled from the great city by the lieutenants of the Koran. The period is not long, but it is lovely.
>
> Placed between the two question-marks of Hamlet, Mr. Greenough prefers "to take arms against a sea of troubles"—in plainer language, to encroach upon his opponent. The latter does not allow himself to be encroached upon without returning the same. They grapple with one another. And there they are on the ground of the arena, and we see ourselves the bulls in the stands.[33]

The iron rails of Botafogo were the great, intricate, deep, obscure, and interminable question. "To be or not to be" in this case was equivalent to "which of the two contenders would have the privilege." Both the assistants and the involved parties differed considerably on this point. They chose and interpreted the legal decrees that served as a basis for the decision in accordance with their own advantage and interest.

What is certain is that the two opponents recognized their own intentions as legitimate and were determined to fight for their rights, "to take arms against a sea of troubles," that is, to contend with one another. The chessboard on which Hamlet and Claudius fought had turned into a bullfight arena.

In 1888 the alternative *esse aut non esse* was resolved in a synthesis made by the worms: *esse et non esse*. What took place was the familiarity of the opposites.

> "He is and is not buried!"
> "No. . . ."
> "Then it is the same grass that covers the others."
> "According to Sousa Lima, but, according to Bertini, it disinters."
> "Esse et non esse."[34]

For the love of truth, the writer had sought out the cemetery worms to learn of the whereabouts of Castro Malta, an unfortunate employee of Casa Laemmert, unjustly arrested by the police and tortured to death, without his family being able to see the body or learn the cause of death. The doubts to be clarified were many: some said Malta had died, others that he hadn't; some believed he had been buried, others that he had been disinterred. The circumstances of his death were a theme of argument.

The worms, in the meantime, were not interested in controversies or speculations. They had learned Latin by eating the Roman people and already they cast greedy eyes on the author. They were amused at the human need to resolve doubts, to check whether the Homerian grass had come from Siberia or Prussia. Perhaps it were a procedure if it helped to keep back the idea of death and give meaning to life.

Under the ground, the conjectures about "to be or not to be" did not matter. "To be" and "not to be" came to the same thing in the digestive process of the worms.[35] And the author should not be surprised, since above ground each thing was and was not at the same time. Rodrigues was dead according to Teodoreto, and Teodoreto was dead according to Rodrigues. It was not a case of the absurd, but of the familiarity of diverging opinions.

※

Hamlet. "Get thee to a nunnery: why wouldst thou be a breeder of sinners?" (3.1.123).

In this time, in which we shall have learned what we lack in order to be entirely acquainted with freedom, cries will not be heard such as those that are heard in the South, because a young woman from Porto Alegre left her father's house to become a nun. The papers say that it is religious fanaticism. It may be, but I would say also that it is an act of freedom. Gasparina is twenty-four years old, and from the time she was fifteen she has thought of going to the convent. It might have been the reading of *Hamlet* that gave her such resolution: "Get thee to a nunnery: why wouldst thou be a breeder of sinners?" Unlike Ophelia, Gasparina obeyed. If the ministry's dispatch of 1855 were still current, it would be impossible for Gasparina to even take the veil of a novice, but the dispatch is gone. Now there is full freedom, and freedom exists not only for that which is to our taste.

. . . .

Freedom is freedom. Look at the old English freedom. . . . I, for my part, thank the hand of Shakespeare for this term of comparison with our Ophelia of Porto Alegre. Good-bye.[36]

The unshakable decision of the Ophelia of Porto Alegre to go to the convent was inspired by the reading of *Hamlet*. Machado de Assis preferred to think of freedom in the light of the Shakespearean text. The parameters were English freedom and the freedom of art.

Hamlet decides not to kill Claudius when he sees him praying (3.3.73–96).

Hamlet is not the prototype of the avenger who attacks his prey without considering the multiple aspects involved in revenge. Upon seeing Claudius praying and possibly begging pardon for his sins, Hamlet did not wish to send him to heaven, as his own father had been murdered by surprise, without any time to purify the spirit which had spoken to the son in a tone of suffering.

In a chronicle of 1896, this episode of Hamlet was mentioned by Machado de Assis for the purpose of comparing the Prince's doubt about the opportunity to kill Claudius and the monolithic certainty which guided the arm of the Persian Shah's assassin:

> See what fanatic souls are. It was not the three hundred thousand contos worth of jewels that armed the arm of the murderer, but a religious motive. The Shah was just entering the sanctuary to pray. If the motive were another, it is likely that the assassin would have put off the deed, repeating with Hamlet the phrase "Not now; it would send him to heaven!" On the contrary, since the Shah was going to pray for his sect,

he would not go to heaven according to the assassin; it was a good occasion to send him to the devil. See what fanatic souls are.[37]

The author was astonished on discovering that in a distant place the life of a person would be taken by some other motive than money, understood as a value of exchange. In Persia, the fanatics of a religious sect would not give up their convictions; about them they had no doubts. On killing the Shah who prayed, the assassin was certain of sending him to hell, since heaven was foretold only for his own sect.

On facing this murder in the light of the episode from *Hamlet* just mentioned, Machado de Assis intended to make it aesthetically more agreeable. He would even suggest that the crime should be committed with a dagger or some other kind of weapon poetically associated with the Orient: "The tragedies kill with cold iron."[38] But the Shah had in fact fallen by a shot from a blunderbuss.

Laertes. Too much of water hast thou, poor Ophelia
And therefore I forbid my tears.

(4.7.158–59)

. . . but as to this continuous rain I don't know if it is more tiresome watching it fall than hearing it told of. Shakespeare puts this quibble in the mouth of Laertes, when he learns that his sister drowned in the river: "Too much of water has thou, poor Ophelia, and therefore I forbid my tears." Let us forbid the ink. The writing-inks made the sad showers of the spirit, and in such cases there are no canoes for navigation: one is to be beaten or to run away.[39]

Machado de Assis spoke in 1896 of the floods of water and paper money that had occurred in Rio de Janeiro periodically since the founding of the city. He asked if to pour out words to tell of the uninterrupted rain would not be as tiresome as watching the rain come down. The pair of water-tear of Shakespeare's character is transformed into water-ink in the author's text. He should be sparing in the use of words, with the consideration that they have the power to create situations.

The Gravedigger's Scene

(5.1. 1–179).

On saying, "Alas, poor Yorick" (5.1. 180), Hamlet externalized his deep emotion regarding the skull that had belonged to a court fool full of infinite grace and wisdom. The memory of Alexander the Great came to him, since he, like all mortals, had been reduced to dust, able to serve as a cork for a cask. It was demoralizing to contemplate pulverized human greatness when one was no longer able to find remains of the individual qualities that had once characterized each creature.

In the text of Machado de Assis, the phrase "Alas, poor Yorick" was pronounced by the worms.

> Alas, poor Yorick! We can know nothing; this here below is all anonymous. No one from here has a name. César or João Fernandes is for us the same dinner . . . We do not distinguish names or faces or opinions, whatever they are, political or not. Look, you sometimes beat one another in elections and some of you die. Here below, as no one has an opinion, all are limited to be equally devoured, and the taste is the same. At times, the liberal is better than the conservative, at others, it is the opposite: it is a question of age. The worms (not the gods, as the ancients say) love those who die young.[40]

Under the ground, names, opinions, and individual features do not matter. All were eaten indiscriminately as delicacies in a banquet. "Alas, poor Yorick!" was thus in the mouth of the worm a declaration of the end of individuality in death. On the lips of Hamlet, the same phrase echoed a lament for the fleeting character of existence.

For the second time in 1884, Machado de Assis referred to the graveyard scene:

> The judicial exhumation was announced for yesterday. The day dawned splendidly; the intense sun, the stifling air. On the other hand, to see cadavers disinterred, even though judicially, can be an interesting spectacle, but I prefer to see the graveyard scene, told both by today's newspapers and by Shakespeare: "I know him, Horatio. These holes . . . this hour . . ." In the book, al fresco, at home, it is delicious. In the cemetery, it must have been hell.[41]

The judicial exhumation of dead bodies was a spectacle that attracted many people. But this entertainment, this way of passing time, was felt by the author to be a direct and shocking confrontation with death. He preferred to filter this unbearable reality through the reports of newspapers and literary works. The news reports and the Shakespearean text were two sources of information he used together. The author read the report of the exhumation at home, at a distance, without having to smell the bad odor. And by evoking Hamlet and his emotion at seeing the skull of Yorick, he lived vicariously his distress in the face of the conflict of finite man's anxiety over eternity. With the catharsis over, the author could then say moderately: I concentrate on books, al fresco, and this is delicious. It was not the first time that literature mediated contact with reality, softening its impact.

Five years later, Machado de Assis would assert that he admired the respectful freedom with which Hamlet addressed Yorick's skull:

> I saw at the door of some houses human skeletons, set in jovial postures. You know my only defect is being fussy. I venerate the skeletons both because of what they are and because I am not that. I don't know if I have explained. I take off my hat to cadavers; I like the respectful freedom with which Hamlet speaks to the remains of the fool Yorick.[42]

The words of the Prince of Denmark to the remains of what had been the court fool were lightly touched with deep sadness and flowed with extreme spontaneity. Hamlet did not fear to touch the skull and fraternized with it in his condition as a mortal. Machado de Assis, on the contrary, put up the barrier of veneration between himself and the skeletons: "because of what they are and because I am not that." Irony was the defensive artifice used to avoid a direct confrontation with his mortal being.

In 1894 Machado de Assis wrote the chronicle for the *Gazeta de Notícias* called *The Graveyard Scene,* also composed from a fusion of Shakespeare's text with a newspaper item on the stock quotations.

The Graveyard Scene

> Do not mix unlike things is the best advice I can give to people who read in bed at night. As I infringed on this rule last night, I had a terrible nightmare. Listen, and you will not waste the five minutes it takes.
> As it happened, I had not finished reading the morning newspapers, and so I did this at night. I had little to read: three stories and the stock quotation. Morning news read at night always produces the effect of old-fashioned ways, from which I conclude that the greatest delight of the papers is the hour at which they appear. Even though the quotation

had the same features, I did not read it with equal indifference because of the memories it brought me of that terrible year (1890–91). I spent rather more time reading and rereading it. Finally, I put the papers aside, and it not being very late, picked up a book, which happened to be Shakespeare. The play was *Hamlet*. The page opened by chance to the graveyard scene, Act V. There was nothing to say to the book or the page, but this mixture of poetry and stock quotations, of dead people and living money, could not result in anything good. It was the mixing of unlike things.

What happened was to be expected: I had a nightmare. At first, I couldn't sleep; I would toss from one side to another, seeing the figures of Hamlet and Horatio, the gravediggers and skulls, hearing the song and the conversation. After a long while I fell asleep. If only I hadn't! I dreamt I was Hamlet, I wore the same black cape, and breeches, doublet and hose of the same color. I don't know if you still remember Rossi and Salvino. I was a like figure, but rather more, as I had the same soul as the Prince of Denmark. Up to this point there was nothing to scare me. Nor did it frighten me to see, at my feet, dressed as Horatio, my faithful servant José.

I thought everything quite natural and he did not think it less. We left the house for the cemetery. We crossed a street that looked like the Primeiro de Março and entered a space that was half cemetery, half room. In dreams, there are such confusions, double or incomplete imaginations, a mixture of opposite things, dilacerations, inexplicable unravelings, but, in short, since I was Hamlet and he Horatio, all that must have been a cemetery. So much so that we soon heard from one of the gravediggers this stanza:

> It was a new title,
> Worth more than eight-hundred
> Now that it's old
> It's not worth two-hundred.

We went in and listened. As in the tragedy, we let the gravediggers talk to one another while they dug Ophelia's grave. But the gravediggers were, at the same time, stockbrokers, who dealt with bones and papers. One of them I heard proclaim had thirty shares of the Promotional Company of Economic Potatoes. The other replied that he would give five-thousand reis for them. I thought this very little and said as much to Horatio, who answered me in the mouth of José: "My lord, the potatoes of this company were prosperous as long as the bearers of the titles did not plant them. The economics of the noble institution consisted precisely in not planting the precious tuber; once they planted it, it was a certain indication of decadence and death."

I didn't understand too well, but the gravediggers, digging up skulls from the soil, were making jokes and proclaiming titles. They spoke of banks, the Only Bank, the Eternal Bank, the Bank of Banks, and the respective titles were sold or not, according to whether seven nickle or two silver coins were offered for them. They were not precisely titles or skulls: they were both things at once, a fusion of aspects, promissory notes with eye-holes, teeth for signatures. We took a few more steps till the gravediggers saw us. They were not surprised but went on with their work of digging and selling.—A hundred of the Balsam Company!—Three thousand reis.—They're yours.—Twenty-five of the Savior Company!—A thousand reis.—Two thousand reis! Two thousand, one hundred, two hundred, five hundred!—They're yours.

I went up to one to talk to him, when I was interrupted by the man himself: "Prompt Relief! Gentlemen! Ten from the Prompt Relief Bank! You give nothing, gentlemen?—Prompt Relief! Gentlemen, how much? Twenty cents? Oh no, no, they're worth more! Prompt Relief! Prompt Relief!" Finally, the man was quiet, not without hearing from the other gravedigger that as a relief the bank could not have been more prompt. They made puns, like Shakespeare's gravediggers. One of them, hearing seven shares of the Punctual Bank being proclaimed, said that such a bank was really punctual till the day on which it went from punctum to points of omission. As wit, it was no great thing: hence, a shower of tibias that fell upon the author. The scene was, at the same time, both gay and lugubrious. The grave-diggers laughed, the skulls laughed, the trees, bending in the winds of Denmark, seemed to bend with laughter, and the open graves laughed in the expectation that there would be weeping over them.

Many other skulls or titles arose. Fifty-four of the Beyond-the-Tomb Exploration Campaign appeared, which were sold for ten reis. The aim of this campaign was to purchase for each shareholder a lot of thirty square meters in Paradise. The first titles, in March, 1891, rose to one conto, but if there is nothing safe in this known world, can there be in the unknown? This doubt entered the spirit of the campaign treasurer, who took advantage of a transatlantic ship to consult a European theologian, taking with him everything that was most known among the valuables. It was a gravedigger who told me of this company incident. At this point, however, a voice came out of the bottom of the grave they were opening. A debenture! A debenture!

It was already something else, a debenture. I went up to the gravedigger and asked him what was it he was saying. He repeated the name of the title. A debenture! A debenture! Let me see, my friend. And, taking hold of it, like Hamlet, I exclaimed, filled with melancholy:

Alas, poor Yorick! I knew him, Horatio. It was a magnificent title. Those eye-holes were diamond, sapphire, and opal numbers. Here, where the nose was, there was a promontory of old engraved ivory.

From this mouth came the most sublime promises in an elevated and noble style. Where are now the fine words of another time? Eloquent and fertile prose, where do the long periods, the gallant phrases stop, the art with which you made people see noble steeds with silver horseshoes and golden harness? Where are the crystal chariots, the satin cushions? Tell me, José Rodrigues.

"My lord . . ."

"Do you believe that a promissory note of Socrates here is in the same condition as this paper?"

"Surely."

"—Such that, an I.O.U. from the noble Socrates will not today be more than a broken down debenture?"

"The very same."

"How far down can we go, Horatio? A note of Socrates can come to have the saddest uses in this world: to clean shoes, for example. Perhaps it is worth less than this debenture."

"You should know that I would give nothing for it."

"Nothing? Poor Socrates! But wait, let us be silent, there comes a burial."

It was the burial of Ophelia. At this point, the nightmare was becoming more and more disturbing. I saw the priests, the king and queen, the attendants, the coffin. Everything made me cloudy and confused. I saw the queen lay flowers on the dead woman. When young Laertes leaped into the grave, I did too; right there, we fought, struck one another. I sweated, I killed, I bled, I screamed . . .

"Wake up, boss, wake up!"[43]

The author's nightmare turned into a narrative where dead people and living money were mixed together. The oneric mechanisms were tranferred to the process of the composition of the piece: confusions, double or incomplete imaginings, a mixture of opposite things, dilacerations and inexplicable unravelings. The complete identification of the author with Hamlet in the dream occurred through the mediation of Rossi and Salvini, the Italian actors who had performed in Rio and whom the author had seen and admired twenty-four years earlier. Horatio, faithful friend of the Prince, was now José, faithful servant of the boss.

The space of the scene was the combination of a stockbrokers' floor and a cemetery. The gravediggers were brokers who disinterred titles-skulls as well—notes with eye-holes and teeth for signatures—and they sang ballads that told of the devaluation of money after the inflationary crisis of 1890–91. One gravedigger told of an incident concerning the Beyond-the-Tomb Exploration

Campaign, which sold lots of thirty square meters in Paradise and whose treasurer, in doubt about the security of the business of this world and the next, had skipped with this world's money.

The author took in hand the debenture that the gravedigger had found in the grave and addressed to this title of dischargeable debt his "Alas, poor Yorick!" He discovered that the numbers and promises of wealth associated with it were now reduced to discredit. In the same way, a promissory note of the noble Socrates would at that moment be no more than a crumpled, worthless piece of paper.

Machado de Assis's text is full of word-play just as is Shakespeare's graveyard scene. The names of the company banks suggest balsam, quick relief, eternity. But the true evil for which there was no balsam or quick relief was the devaluation of negotiable paper that had already gone to the cemetery. In the nightmare, the author was a character and as such he sweated, bled, killed. Awakened to reality, he returned to his task of observing and giving the facts, without involving himself in them.

"The rest is silence."

(5.2. 310)

> The question of suicide does not now come under discussion. The old theme is reborn whenever a man does away with himself, but it is soon buried with him, to be reborn with another. Old question, old doubt. It has now come under discussion, as the act of Raul Pompéia inspired in all an extraordinary haunting sensation. Pity has come to intensify the act, with that single, two minute memory of the deceased, in requesting the mother to succor the sister, victim of a nervous fit. What answer will be given to the old theme? The best is still the one given by the young Hamlet: "The rest is silence."[44]

The writer Raul Pompéia was a man of struggle, interested in the abolitionist campaign and in political questions, which made him countless enemies. On the occasion of the death of the nationalistic former president Marshal Floriano, everyone knew that Pompéia would make a violent speech, exalting the dead man. On October 18, journalist Luis Murat insulted Pompéia in an article entitled "A Madman in the Cemetery." Raul Pompéia, a hypersensitive person, suffered terribly, but he reacted by sending two replies, which were not published, to the newspapers for which he wrote. Feeling demoralized, he retired to his house, where his mother and sister tried to comfort him. It was Christmas Eve, and Pompéia, completely vanquished, put an end to his life with a shot from a revolver, after writing to the newspaper *A Notícia* that he was a man of honor.[45]

The question of suicide was rhythmically repeated at the beginning of two paragraphs of Machado de Assis's text. And for this old theme the author could only find the answer given by the young Hamlet: "The rest is silence."

Hamlet's last words, before he enters the silence from which he has previously recoiled, are as rigorous as the final proposition in the *Tractatus Logico-Philosophicus:* "Whereof one cannot speak, thereof one must be silent."[46]

When the word is not efficacious, silence imposes itself. Then *not to be* is preferable to *to be*. Horatio will tell the story of the Prince to posterity, so that his honorable deeds will be known. Raul Pompéia wished to claim the same honor in his last note to the newspapers.

Hamlet and his melancholy

Asserting that he was the most melancholy of men,[47] Machado de Assis pointed to another kind of melancholy as another specific feature of Hamlet's personality.

> But, let us leave this melancholic assumption to go to another not less melancholic, it is true, but of another kind. Many are the kinds of melancholy of this world. Saul's is not like Hamlet's, Lamartine's not like Musset's. Perhaps our own, dear reader, are different, and one can say that in this variety resides the grace of the feeling.[48]

Melancholy was not the same thing for all people. The Prince of Denmark's was related to the melancholy of life and surrounded by death, according to Machado de Assis.[49]

Although he was inclined to self-annihilation, Hamlet was desolate before the ruin to which death reduces human greatness.

In another chronicle, Machado de Assis avoided the direct confrontation with death, speaking of health and disease. Each time had its own diseases and when the human engine discovered remedies for some of them, man became weary of his physical well-being and invented new ills nearly as perfect as the natural ones.[50]

Another variation of the author on the theme of death treated the question not of dying but of paying dear for the costs of the burial. In the end, there would be no reason for profit and melancholy to be irreconcilable.

> A gravedigger in Hamlet says that the position of gravedigger, as it is Adam's, is the noblest of the world, but it is necessary to remember that the Funeral Business had not been invented either in the time of Adam or of Hamlet.
> However so, what is certain is that the Funeral Business, as sad as it can be, is no less lucrative. There is no incompatibility between melancholy and profit: they are two phenomena that conciliate and complete one another.[51]

Machado de Assis constantly evoked Hamlet when he reflected on the precariousness of human existence: "When we cannot imitate the great men, we can at least imitate the great fictions."[52]

The vision of life derived from Shakespeare's play carries on a dialogue with daily events in the chronicles of Machado de Assis in the years 1868–99. It is the dialectic of history and philosophy, in which the latter is brought up to date in the former, in which the meaning of each thought is tested and adjusted to the facts. The philosophical questions are revealed as social and economic.

The literary quotations, especially those from *Hamlet,* function in Machado de Assis's text as a mechanism for distancing reality in order to relativize it and soften its impact on the author himself. In some way, they work as a filter of reality and a privileged place of observation. Without doubt, words are for Machado de Assis, as they are for Hamlet, an instrument of struggle in facing the turbulence of the world. The newspaper is the tribune where the author plies his foil.

Departing from the most well-known soliloquy of the play, our author develops the process of doubting and the taste for the yoking of opposites which end up being destroyed in a distinct way—indiscriminately eaten by worms.

Notes

1. I.e. *Crônicas,* a Brazilian literary genre, short essays on topical subjects, often published in newspapers.
2. Harry Levin, *The Question of Hamlet* (New York: Viking Press, 1967), 41.
3. *Semana Illustrada* [Illustrated Weekly] (Rio de Janeiro, February 23, 1873),

5090–91, Machado de Assis, *Contos e Crônicas* [Stories and Chronicles], ed. Raimundo Magalhães Jr. (Rio de Janeiro: Editora Civilização Brasileira, 1958), 243. All quotations from Machado de Assis are here translated by myself.

4. William Shakespeare, *Oeuvres Complètes,* trans. M. Guizot, vol. 1 (Paris: Didier, 1862), 165.

5. William Shakespeare, *Oeuvres Complètes,* trans. M. Emile Montegut, vol. 3 (Paris: Hachette, 1870), 488.

6. William Shakespeare, *Oeuvres Complètes,* trans. M. François-Victor Hugo, vol. 10 (Paris: Alphonse Lemaire, n.d.), 46.

7. Machado de Assis, "Bons Dias," (May 4, 1888) in *Obra Completa,* vol. 1 (Rio de Janeiro: Editora José Aguilar, 1962), 487.

8. *Gazeta de Notícias* (Rio de Janeiro, July 1893), Machado de Assis, *A Semana,* vol. 1 (Rio de Janeiro: W. W. Jackson, 1938), 332.

9. Machado de Assis, "Bons Dias" (January 21, 1989) in *Diálogos e Reflexões de um Relojoeiro* [Dialogues and Reflections of a Watch-maker], ed. Raimundo Magalhães Jr. (Rio de Janeiro: Editora Civilização Brasileira, 1956), 196.

10. Ibid., 195.

11. *Gazeta de Notícias* (Rio de Janeiro: February 11, 1894), Machado de Assis, *A Semana,* vol. 2 (Rio de Janeiro: W. W. Jackson, 1938), 39.

12. Ibid., 38.

13. Brazilian monetary unit of the period, equivalent to one thousand *cruzeiros.*

14. *Gazeta de Notícias* (Rio de Janeiro: December 20, 1896), Machado de Assis, *A Semana,* vol. 3 (Rio de Janeiro: W. W. Jackson, 1938), 371.

15. Ibid., 368.

16. *Gazeta de Notícias* (Rio de Janeiro: February 11, 1894), Machado de Assis, *A Semana,* vol. 2 (Rio de Janeiro: W. W. Jackson, 1938), 39.

17. *Gazeta de Notícias* (Rio de Janeiro: October 20, 1895), Machado de Assis, "A Semana" in *Obra Completa,* vol. 3 (Rio de Janeiro: Editora José Aguilar, 1962), 682.

18. *Gazeta de Notícias* (Rio de Janeiro: October 20, 1985), Ibid., 679.

19. Ibid., 681.

20. *Gazeta de Notícias* (Rio de Janeiro: October 18, 1896), Machado de Assis, *A Semana,* vol. 3 (Rio de Janeiro: W. W. Jackson, 1938), 315.

21. *Semana Illustrada* (Rio de Janeiro: December 23, 1868), 3338–39, Machado de Assis, *Contos e Crônicas,* ed. Raimundo Magalhães Jr. (Rio de Janeiro: Editora Civilização Brasileira, 1958), 143.

22. Ibid., 145.

23. *Gazeta de Notícias* (Rio de Janeiro: April 23, 1893), Machado de Assis, *Obra Completa,* vol. 3 (Rio de Janeiro: Editora José Aguilar, 1962), 582.

24. Ibid.

25. *Gazeta de Notícias* (Rio de Janeiro: October 29, 1893), Machado de Assis, "A Semana" in *Obra Completa,* vol. 3 (Rio de Janeiro: Editora José Aguilar, 1962), 586.

26. *Gazeta de Notícias* (Rio de Janeiro: March 12, 1893), Machado de Assis, "A Semana" in *Obra Completa,* vol. 3 (Rio de Janeiro: José Aguilar, 1962), 579.

27. Harry Levin, *The Question of Hamlet* (New York: Viking Press, 1967), 69.

28. *Illustração Brasileira* (Rio de Janeiro: January 1, 1877), Machado de Assis, *Chronicas,* vol. 3 (Rio de Janeiro: W. W. Jackson, 1938), 167–68.

29. *Illustração Brasileira* (Rio de Janeiro: June 1, 1887), Machado de Assis, *Chronicas,* vol. 3 (Rio de Janeiro: W. W. Jackson, 1938), 223.
30. *O Cruzeiro* (Rio de Janeiro: June 9, 1878), Machado de Assis, *Chronicas,* vol. 4 (Rio de Janeiro: W. W. Jackson, 1938), 28.
31. Ibid., 70.
32. *Illustração Brasileira* (Rio de Janeiro: September 1, 1844), Machado de Assis, *Chronicas,* vol. 3 (Rio de Janeiro: W. W. Jackson, 1938), 253-54.
33. *Illustração Brasileira* (December 1, 1884), Machado de Assis, *Chronicas,* vol. 3 (Rio de Janeiro: W. W. Jackson, 1938), 286-87.
34. *Grazeta de Notícias* (Rio de Janeiro: December 12, 1884), Machado de Assis, *Crônicas de Lélio,* ed. Raimundo Magalhães Jr. (Rio de Janeiro: Editora Civilização Brasileira, 1958), 188.
35. Ibid.
36. *Gazeta de Notícias* (Rio de Janeiro: November 24, 1895), Machado de Assis, *A Semana,* vol. 2 (Rio de Janeiro: W. W. Jackson, 1938), 48-49.
37. *Gazeta de Notícias* (Rio de Janeiro: May 3, 1896), Machado de Assis, *A Semana,* vol. 3 (Rio de Janeiro: W. W. Jackson, 1938), 169-70.
38. Ibid., 170.
39. *Gazeta de Notícias* (Rio de Janeiro: February 2, 1896), Machado de Assis, *A Semana,* vol. 3 (Rio de Janeiro: W. W. Jackson, 1938), 103.
40. *Gazeta de Notícias* (Rio de Janeiro: December 24, 1884), Machado de Assis, *Crônicas de Lélio,* ed. Raimundo Magalhães Jr. (Rio de Janeiro: Editora Civilização Brasileira, 1958), 187-88.
41. *Gazeta de Notícias* (Rio de Janeiro: December 24, 1884), Machado de Assis, *Crônicas de Lélio,* ed. Raimundo Magalhães Jr. (Rio de Janeiro: Editora Civilização Brasileira, 1958), 200.
42. "Bons Dias" (Rio de Janeiro: January 21, 1889), Machado de Assis, *Diálogos e Reflexões de um Relojoeiro,* ed. Raimundo Magalhães Jr. (Rio de Janeiro: Editora Civilização Brasileira, 1956), 195.
43. *Gazeta de Notícias* (Rio de Janeiro: June 3, 1894), Machado de Assis, *A Semana,* vol. 2 (Rio de Janeiro: W. W. Jackson, 1938), 114-20.
44. *Gazeta de Notícias* (Rio de Janeiro: December 29, 1895), Machado de Assis, *Obra Completa,* vol. 3 (Rio de Janeiro: Editora José Aguilar, 1962), 691-92.
45. Raul Pompéia, *O Ateneu* [The Athenian], ed. Ivan C. Proença (Rio de Janeiro: Edições de Ouro, 1969).
46. Harry Levin, *The Question of Hamlet* (New York: Viking Press, 1967), 98.
47. *Gazeta de Notícias* (Rio de Janeiro: July 16, 1893), Machado de Assis, *A Semana,* vol. 1 (Rio de Janeiro: W. W. Jackson, 1938), 338.
48. *Gazeta de Notícias* (Rio de Janeiro: June 30, 1895), Machado de Assis, *A Semana,* vol. 2 (Rio de Janeiro: W. W. Jackson, 1938), 413.
49. *Gazeta de Notícias* (Rio de Janeiro: November 19, 1893), Machado de Assis, *A Semana,* vol. 1 (Rio de Janeiro: W. W. Jackson, 1938), 430.
50. Ibid.
51. *Gazeta de Notícias* (Rio de Janeiro: June 30, 1895), Machado de Assis, *A Semana,* vol. 2 (Rio de Janeiro: W. W. Jackson, 1938), 413.
52. *Gazeta de Notícias* (Rio de Janeiro: November 19, 1893), Machado de Assis, *A Semana,* vol. 1 (Rio de Janeiro: W. W. Jackson, 1938), 430.

Staging Practices in the Elizabethan Theater: *Titus Andronicus* at the Rose

Maria Clara Versiani Galery

The discovery and excavation of the foundations of the Rose in 1989 revealed what constitutes by far the most concrete evidence regarding an Elizabethan playhouse for which Shakespeare wrote his plays. The Rose was an outdoor theater of an irregular polygonal structure, built in 1587 by Philip Henslowe, a prosperous impresario who introduced theater to London's South Bank, an area free from the interference of city authorities and notorious for providing entertainment in the form of brothels, bowling alleys, and bearbaiting rings. Transportation across the Thames to the South Bank was not a problem, as boats were readily available to move the city's traffic from one side of the river to the other, delivering audiences to landing stairs within short walking distance of the grounds where Henslowe's playhouse stood.[1] The lifeline of the Rose may be divided into two distinct phases, delimited by its refurbishment and expansion in 1592.[2] The remains of this theater throw some light upon the context in which early English Renaissance plays were performed. Yet, while the measurements of the stage and other fairly precise facts have been concluded, other aspects of its proportions cannot be very accurately determined, partly because sections of the playhouse were destroyed in the 1950s, when an office building was constructed on the site where it had stood.

The excavations show the Rose to have been much smaller than anticipated, with a diameter of approximately seventy-four feet. This discovery suggests that the Globe may also have been smaller than scholars had previously imagined, if it was built according to the same scale and architectural principles as the Rose. It is indeed a matter of great difficulty to determine what part of the evidence at the excavation is representative of Elizabethan theaters in general and what part is unique to the Rose. The remains of this theater appear to attest that perhaps Elizabethan playhouses were far more different from each other than had been previously assumed.

The aim of this chapter is to provide a discussion of how theater was produced and performed in Elizabethan times. I look into conjectures drawn from the staging demands of *Titus Andronicus,* one of Shakespeare's earliest plays, for which there is evidence of a *mise en scéne* at the Rose. The stage directions in *Titus Andronicus* provide information about the kind of scenic resources the Rose might have offered, thus complementing what the remains found at the excavation site can teach us about the conditions of Elizabethan staging.

In his book *Shakespeare at the Globe,* B. Beckerman defines staging as "an art of illusion, but its illusion, unlike that of acting, deals not with being but with time and space."[3] In the theater, the factor that characterizes the time and place presented before an audience is its otherness, its fictional or theatrical nature in relation to the real time and space shared by the spectators who are watching the play. The question to be discussed in relation to staging in the Shakespearean era is how that fictional other world was conveyed to the spectators. The Elizabethan theater was nonillusory, in the sense that no proscenium arch separated the world of the players from that of the members of the audience. The actors were very close to the spectators. There is no evidence that devices such as painted perspective scenery were employed, although several props are listed in Henslowe's inventory of the Rose.[4]

While there is a general agreement among scholars that no significant changes occurred in the stagecraft practiced in the private halls and in the public outdoor playhouses, the determination of how scenic location was conveyed in the Elizabethan theaters remains largely conjectural. Some controversy exists surrounding the possibility of simultaneous staging, in a sort of continuation of the medieval practice of using "mansions" to represent the various locations required in the play, thus leaving the stage occupied by more than one setting at the same time.[5] The nonillusory character of Elizabethan theater would make it easier for audience members to accept the violation of realistic distance and the use of simultaneous settings. E. K. Chambers believed that simultaneous staging was distinctive of Court performances while sequential staging characterized the public playhouses. However, that conjecture is no longer accepted: scholars have found evidence to confirm that the occurrence of simultaneous settings in outdoor theaters like the Red

Bull or, to a lesser extent, the Globe, was not uncommon. While Henslowe's inventory list for the Rose registers a "wooden canepie" and a "sittie of Rome," structures that may have been used on stage much like the medieval mansions, the dimensions of the stage at the Rose would present a limit to the size of the properties which could be placed on it.[6]

Because the polyscenic juxtaposition of mansion staging is primarily a feature of medieval theater, the acceptance of its use during the Renaissance period finds some resistance among scholars who would like to think in terms of an evolution in staging conditions.[7] It is necessary to remember, however, that there is no such thing as complete rupture from one period to another; there is, rather, a continuation of some elements along with the evolution of others. As Hattaway phrases it,

> Elizabethan drama was derived from so many sources that it is not surprising to find these devices that were both "Renaissance," in that they resembled those used in mythological entertainment, and "medieval" in that they functioned like the simultaneous scenic decors of the mystery plays.[8]

The use of freestanding structures that might have been present on stage throughout the entire performance would meet the staging requirements of some Renaissance plays, especially those containing "discovery scenes," in which a stage hanging might be lifted in order to reveal a scenic tableau. These discovery scenes led scholars of a past generation to conjecture the existence of a so-called inner stage in the Elizabethan theater, "a sort of prototype of the proscenium-arch stage, a curtained acting area located behind the platform and capable of being pre-set with scenery.[9] This theory is now challenged due to lack of reliable evidence, but because several Elizabethan plays require enclosurelike spaces, it is possible that some theaters would have had a sort of semipermanent structure that would allow the staging of these enclosed scenes. In a description of a performance at the Curtain Theatre in 1590, the Swiss traveler Thomas Platter mentions the use of "tents" on stage.[10] Battle scenes in some plays, such as *Richard III*, indicate that tents could have been erected on stage during performance. However, the size and complexity of the sort of three-dimensional structures required for some plays, and described in the accounts from the Revels Office, shows it to be improbable that such properties were brought on stage only during certain scenes or moments of the performance.[11]

Elizabethan stage directions can be quite timid when it comes to the description of space and movement. However, Scott McMillin, in his study of the promptbook manuscript *Sir Thomas More,* calls the attention of his readers to a direction that explicitly indicates a discovery scene, revealed by the parting of a curtain: "An Arras is drawne, and behinde it (as in Sessions) sit the L. Maior, Justice Suresbie, and other Justices, Sheriffe Moore and the other Sherife sitting by, Smart is the Plaintife, Lifter the prisoner at the Barre."[12] McMillin believes *Sir Thomas More* to be a play representative of the theater in which it was performed. As the original version of the play seems to have been intended for the Rose, then one may deduce that this theater was equipped for the staging of scenes like the one above. This can be verified by looking at the stage directions of another play, *Tamburlaine, Part 2,* staged at the Rose in 1588, where an arras or stage hanging is also used to disclose a tableau. The directions for the opening scene of this play read as follows: "The Arras is drawn, and Zenocrate lies in her bed of state, Tamburlaine sitting by her; three Physicians about her bed, tempering potions. Theridamas, Techelles and Usumcasane, and the three sons."[13] A structure such as a curtained pavilion, placed against the wall of the tiring-house, would meet the conditions necessary to produce such a tableau. The tiring-house was the offstage area where the players changed costumes and waited for the cues to make their entry. This sort of pavilion was versatile enough to stage a wide variety of scenes. It may have been a common device in Elizabethan playhouses and could have been used to convey scenes such a Malvolio's "dark room" in Shakespeare's *Twelfth Night,* in which the stage directions "within" could refer to the use of such space.

Along with this discovery space, McMillin points out the need for a raised acting area on the Elizabethan stage, which he believes might have been met by the use of a scaffold. However, a drawing of another Elizabethan theater, the Swan, made by Johannes De Witt, shows that the gallery behind the stage could have served for the same purposes.[14] Gallery staging would have been cheaper and more practical than a freestanding structure like a scaffold, that occupies space on a small stage and would need to be removed for subsequent scenes. Like the enclosed space, a raised area created what McMillin calls a "divided stage technique," which was used in conjunction with the platform stage that projected into the auditorium.[15] Another feature of this divided use of the stage was the trapdoor, the need for which can be found in early plays like Marlowe's *Doctor Faustus,* which played at the Rose in 1594. The raised space, the platform, and the trap together formed a multileveled acting area that was explored by contemporary playwrights with a varied degree of frequency.

The appearance of the tiring-house wall is a controversial aspect of the Elizabethan stage.[16] While the drawing of the Swan shows an essentially bare playing area and unlocalized tiring-house façade, very little is actually known about what the tiring-house wall looked like. Foakes affirms that the "stage façade was highly decorated."[17] There is evidence that some plays made use of tapestry or other types of hangings to provide a setting or background. It is possible that curtains with painted symbolic motifs were used. For instance, lines from *A Warning for Fair Women,* which possibly dates from 1590, suggest that the color of the hanging indicated, symbolically, the nature of the play: "The stage is hung with black and I perceive / The auditors prepared for tragedy."[18] But there is no additional contemporary evidence that other colors were used for comedies.

With regard to the use of props to convey scenery, Hattaway interestingly points out that the nature of props in the Elizabethan theater was "metonymic rather than representational," suggesting perhaps that minimal props may have been used to indicate a larger dramatic context and location than the one immediately depicted on stage.[19] The use of functional props such as banquet or council tables, as well as beds and thrones which could be discovered or brought on stage provide an effective means of conveying temporary scenic locations. Against an unlocalized tiring-house façade, a bed represents a chamber, for example. These functional props are convenient, especially in plays where there is frequent alternation between indoor and outdoor scenes. In the staging of such plays, a nonrepresentational tiring-house wall is an asset, for the clearing of actors and properties from the stage automatically cancels any suggestion of place, as the characters move from one scene to another.

Beckerman believes that scene changes were indicated to the public primarily through the presence and movement of the actors. Although performances made use of the practice of continuous staging, with no intervals between acts, changes of scene could be accomplished without any awkwardness. Transition from one locale to another did not require too much reliance on scenic indications of a physical sort. Beckerman insists that "the stage was a fluid area that could represent whatever the author wished. . . . The actors did not regard the stage as a place but as a platform from which to project a story, and therefore they were unconscious of the discrepancy between real and dramatic space."[20] In spite of recognizing that Elizabethan staging maximized the presence of the actors, the long-shared view, based on the Swan drawing, that the stage was bare and that few resources were used is no longer accepted by some scholars, who insist that the playhouses "offered their public colour, spectacle, and richness."[21]

Scenic location may also have been conveyed by placing the actors in formal groupings. Beckerman points out that "space, though flexible, was not amorphous, and that there were some patterns in the physical arrangement of actors on stage."[22] The grouping of characters on stage would form the setting, thus reducing the need for backcloths or other forms of scenic façades. He suggests, for instance, that attending characters would remain in the background, near the tiring-house, while the active characters would come forward and speak where they could be seen and heard well by the spectators. According to Beckerman, there was not much variety in the blocking and design of the groupings, which tended towards symmetry. Established formal patterns in stage groupings have the advantage of allowing the companies to present even large-cast plays with a minimum of rehearsal; it is important to keep in mind the basic conditions of production, which demanded that the actors learn their parts and mount a multiscene play in a period that usually did not exceed two weeks.

Of course, the description of scenery by the characters is an efficient and widely used means to convey location. Characters in Elizabethan plays are frequently required to explain what they are doing in a certain place, how they got there, and where they are going. Entrances and exits are announced. It is not the setting but the presence of the actors that dominates the scene. As Beckerman affirms, ". . . in the Elizabethan drama, particularly in the Shakespearean, a character enters not into a place but to another character. Where he enters is of secondary importance—to whom he enters or with whom he enters is of primary interest."[23]

I will now discuss the staging of *Titus Andronicus,* keeping in mind the presence and movement of the actors in an attempt to find out how a stage as small as that which the excavation of the Rose uncovered could be used effectively to stage this tragedy.[24] *Titus Andronicus* may be the earliest extant piece of writing by Shakespeare. Although its authorship has been disputed by some scholars, the external evidence designating Shakespeare as author of this play is greater than that indicating otherwise. *Titus Andronicus* was published in the Folio, in 1623, by John Heminge and Henry Condell, who were senior partners in the same company of players as Shakespeare, giving credibility to Shakespeare's authorship of the play:[25] it is unlikely that they would have included the play in the Folio if they believed it to be spurious. Francis Meres also recorded the play in his *Palladis Tamia* of 1598, a review of English literature from Chaucer to the author's own day, where *Titus Andronicus* is noted among the tragedies chosen by Meres to prove Shakespeare's genius.[26] There is, however, a generation of critics who refuse to believe it was written by Shakespeare, mainly because of Edward Ravenscroft, who was born twenty-five years after Shakespeare's death and who wrote an adaptation of the play. In Ravenscroft's version, a note tells the reader that Shakespeare was not the original author, he "only gave some Master-touches to one or two of the Principal Parts or Characters."[27] This is the only piece of evidence that challenges Shakespeare's authorship, but it has been used by some scholars, who shun the violent character of the play, to claim that Shakespeare could not possibly have written anything so bloody. In the twentieth century the tendency has been to believe in the authenticity of the play as being Shakespeare's; this belief has been confirmed by recent critical studies of the text, including computer analysis and comparison of lines.

Titus Andronicus appears to have been very popular when it first came out. The earliest reliable reference to this tragedy can be found in Henslowe's *Diary,* which records performances by the Earl of Sussex's Men. According to Henslowe, "*titus & ondronicus*" played from December 26, 1593, to February 6, 1594. A note at the margin says *ne,* which is usually taken to mean new or newly entered. It is thus safely assumed that *Titus Andronicus* premiered at the Rose, where it played with the atypical frequency of three days out of six and earned Henslowe the highest receipts of the season.[28] In the first page of the earliest published version of the play, a quarto copy printed by John Danter in 1594, the following information is given: "The Most Lamentable Romaine Tragedie of Titus Andronicus: As it was Plaide by the Right Honourable the Earle of

Darbie, Earle of Pembrooke, and Earle of Sussex their Servants."[29] So it would appear that the text of this first Quarto, Q1, is the version most closely approximate to the one used for the performances at the Rose since it was published the same year as the performances recorded by Henslowe. The two subsequent Quarto editions of the play contain slight variations, while the Folio version of *Titus Andronicus* has more explicit stage directions in regard to use of space, as well as a whole scene that is omitted from the Quartos.

The stagecraft of what may constitute Shakespeare's first tragedy is a fascinating piece of study not only because it contains elements which prove Shakespeare's early theatrical expertise, but also because it provides a "dramatic inventory of the resources at the disposal of an Elizabethan theatre company."[30] Shakespeare's willingness to experiment with various parts of the stage informs a great deal about the kind of theater he worked for and how the physical conditions of that theater may have influenced his writing. The play makes extraordinary use of contemporary theatrical resources: "Its mastery of space, movement and grouping is characteristic of Shakespeare's, resembling his mature use of these devices as dramatic metaphors for theme and meaning."[31]

It is interesting to observe how the three levels of the stage are used. Most of the action occurs on the platform. However, the gallery (or raised space) as well as the trap are used for important scenes rather than for brief effects. In this sense, Shakespeare's use of stage space is innovative and experimental. The need for a raised level is designated in the stage directions by the expressions *aloft* or *above* and occurs already during the opening scene of the play, called for in the following stage directions: "*Enter the* Tribunes *and* Senators *aloft: And then enter* Saturninus *and his followers at one dore, and* Bassianus *and his followers, with Drums and Trumpets.*"

The entrance of the figures of authority at the raised level creates a visual metaphor of power, for they are placed in the commanding position above Saturninus and Bassianus. The gallery would have to be large enough to accommodate the actors representing the Tribunes and Senators.[32] Q1 does not make it clear whether Saturninus and Bassianus are to use different doors when making their entrance. However, the directions that appear in the Folio clearly establish that the two brothers, with their respective groups, should make use of distinct doors. If the Folio version comes from a prompt-book depicting the actual use of space made in performance, then the tension between the two factions would be increased by each group's use of different colors as well as by their processions on stage. Entrances at doors at opposite ends of the stage would portray the conflict of the two brothers, in what constitutes an effective choice in use of space to inform the audience of the antagonisms present in the play. Such grouping is indicated in the more explicit directions, where the clash of two blocs is interestingly illustrated in the Q1 column arrangement of the directions, which also provide evidence of the existence of separate entrances:

Enter the Emperor, Tamora and her two sonnes, with the Moore at one doore.	*Enter at the other doore Bassianus and Lauinia, with others.*

But the stage directions in Q1 are laconic in the description of this other entrance: *"Marcus Andronicus with the Crowne."*

It is not made clear where Marcus Andronicus should make his entrance although the directions in the Folio specify that it should be *aloft,* thus once more identifying the gallery with power, for it is from this raised space that Marcus Andronicus addresses the common people of Rome. In the Folio there are more explicit directions for the use of the gallery than in Q1. But in any case the play makes extensive use of this resource, which is an index of the suitability of the gallery behind the stage at the Rose for such scenes. Directions also point to the movement of the actors from the platform to the gallery, indicating that the stage may have been left for a few moments while they reached the gallery through the stairs behind the wall of the tiring-house: *"They goe up into the Senate house."* The raised level is used to symbolize power and command in another moment of act 1 scene 1, when Saturninus is made ruler, as these directions show: *"Enter Aloft the Emperor with Tamora and her two sonnes and Aron the moore."*

Much later in the play the gallery is used to designate a part of Titus's house. Tamora, Demetrius, and Chiron come to visit him in their allegorical disguises representing Revenge, Murder, and Rape. The location of Titus's study can only be in the raised area, from where he speaks to Tamora. Evidence for the use of the gallery is not found in the stage directions but in their dialogue, where Tamora asks Titus to "come downe." Titus's lines "Oh sweete Reuenge, now doe I come to thee" could also indicate that he is about to leave the gallery and go down to the platform to greet Tamora, whose lines beginning with "This closing with him fits his Lunacie," commenting on Titus's apparent madness and loss of reason, make more sense if he is not seen on stage. The possibility that Titus was in the gallery is reinforced by the eleven lines spoken by her, which would give him time to exit and come down from the gallery. Just before he appears, she says, "See here he comes, and I must plie my theame."

Shakespeare also innovates in his use of the trap, a space that was more or less sparingly employed in the early 1590s, by making it the focal point of act 2, scene 3. In this long and important scene, Tamora's sons, Chiron and Demetrius, murder Bassianus before the rape and mutilation of Lavinia. Much of the dramatic development in the play arises from this scene, including the death of Titus's two sons, Quintus and Martius. The pit, inside which Bassianus's body is thrown, the "abhorrèd pit" obsessively described by loathsome and dark terms "evocative not only of death and hell but also of the threatening female sexuality that is embodied in Tamora," can only have been a trap door, especially since the evidence at the Rose excavations indicate the possibility of its existence.[33] The reference to the pit as a "subtle hole" also reinforces the use of this device. It is likely that the trap door remained open for the duration of this scene and was disguised by branches or other means, for Quintus says that its opening was "coverred with rude-growing briers." Quintus and Martius fall inside the pit, where they get Bassianus's blood all over themselves and are consequently accused of murdering him. The action centered around the trap door results in the unfolding of violence and treachery, thus setting the tone that predominates in the play.

The following directions for act 3 indicate an unusual exploration of stage space: *"Enter the Iudges and Senatours with* Titus *two sonnes bound, passing on the Stage to the place of Execution, and* Titus *going before pleading."* Allardyce Nicoll has suggested that *"passing on the Stage"* could imply that the actors made their entrance from the yard and then mounted the stage, crossing it horizontally before descending to the yard again.[34] In view of the small dimensions of the Rose's tapered stage, the procession of the judges and senators would have to take place upstage, fairly close to the tiring-house wall. Titus and Lucius would be placed downstage, from where they would deliver their comments, positioned fairly close to the groundlings.

The representation of the Andronicus family tomb in the first scene of the play could have been accomplished through different means, such as the use of stage props. Henslowe's inventory list includes a "tombe," so it is plausible that such property could have been employed. Other possibilities include draperies or cloth hung across the tiring-house façade. If the stage of the Rose had a third entrance like the one shown in Fludd's *Ars Memoriae* drawing, this central door could have been used for the tomb. A pavilion, placed against the tiring-house wall, the sort that could also serve for discovery scenes in other plays, might have been adapted for the representation of the tomb. The trap door of the Rose is another possibility that would serve for the staging of this scene. The trap would be effective in conveying a spatial metaphor, as the space below the stage would carry unpleasant connotations for the spectators throughout the play. In this sense, it is interesting to look at how the three vertical levels in this stage can be reminiscent of medieval mise en scène: the highest level, which would be occupied by God in the passion plays also appears in *Titus Andronicus* as an allegory of power, substituting the divine authority with an earthly representation in the form of Roman leaders. Likewise, the lowest acting space, used to convey the pit and the tomb, is the realm of death and suffering, which can only be linked to hell.

Verbal description is used to paint the forest scene when Titus enters with "*his three sonnes, making a noise with hounds & hornes.*" The audience is informed that they are going hunting when Titus says: "The hunt is vp the Moones is bright and gray, / The fields are fragrant, and the woods are greene...." In a similar fashion, Tamora describes her surroundings when she is alone with Aaron:

> My louelie Aron, wherefore lookst thou sad,
> VVhen euerie thing dorh make a gleefull bost?
> The birds chaunt melodie on euerie bush,
> The snakes lie rolled in the chearefull sunne,
> The greene leaues quiuer with the cooling winde,
> And make a checkerd shadow on the ground.

It is not known how much the audience members would have to rely on descriptions such as the one above to be informed of where the action was taking place. But as far as theatrical signifiers are concerned, a word must be said about costume. It is known from Henslowe's *Diary* that a great deal of money was spent to create spectacular costumes. Specific evidence for the kind of costumes that may have been worn during a performance of *Titus Andronicus* is provided in a document known as the *Longleat manuscript,* which may be a representation of an actual performance of this play. The document is a pen and ink drawing captioned by the lines "*Enter Tamora pleadinge for her sonnes going to the execution,*" followed by a dialogue attributed to Titus, Tamora, and Aron. The dialogue is an odd condensation of Shakespeare's tragedy, blending moments from the beginning and end of the play into one single composition, so it cannot be regarded as the portrayal of a distinct scene on stage. The *Longleat manuscript* is believed to have been produced in 1595, but it could have been created as late as 1615.[35] At any rate, it is the only existing illustration of what may have been an Elizabethan performance. Even if the artist had not himself seen the play, it is an illustration of how an Elizabethan viewed a performance, and it tells something about the costumes used in the production of plays. There is some attempt in portraying historically accurate Roman costumes, but, on the whole, there is a great mixture of styles. Titus wears a Roman tunic, while Tamora's dress is not really distinctive of any particular time; the soldiers standing behind Titus are dressed in Elizabethan attire with halberds. The men kneeling behind Tamora as well as the coal black Aaron are dressed in a sort of Roman costume. Although the combination of styles is eclectic, the use of Roman fashion by some of the characters tells the audience where the action is taking place. With regard to the use of costumes in the drawing, Hattaway makes the following observation: "The conventions of the costuming remind us that the play is a myth, [reinforcing] the double awareness of the audience that what they are watching is of the past and of the present."[36] Costumes would thus carry the function of being informative not only of where the action of the play occurred, but also what sort of play it was.

What was uncovered when the foundations of the Rose were excavated takes one back to the ritual of the Elizabethan plays that were once performed in that playhouse. The pieces that were left of Henslowe's theater tell something about the resources that the Rose offered for the production of plays; they also serve as clues that inform us of what the performances were like. The remains at the site of the Rose can be used as reliable evidence in the study of early Elizabethan plays, especially when confronted with the internal evidence provided in the text and stage directions of plays.

Titus Andronicus is a remarkable play for the study of the staging potential of the Rose. Its extraordinary use of space provides information regarding the resources offered by the Elizabethan playhouse. When used in conjunction with other evidence, such as the inventory lists in Henslowe's *Diary,* this piece of drama can throw some light upon the conditions of theater production in Renaissance England, offering a direction so that the conjectures can get closer to a factual reconstruction of those performances which took place four hundred years ago.

Notes

1. Carol Chillington Rutter, ed., *Documents of the Rose Playhouse* (Manchester: Manchester University Press, 1984), 1.
2. In 1660 Henslowe built another theater, the Fortune, on the other side of the city. The Fortune was meant to replace the Rose, which was pulled down sometime in 1605, after Henslowe's lease expired.
3. Bernard Beckerman, *Shakespeare at the Globe, 1599–1609* (New York: Macmillan, 1962), 157.
4. Henslowe's *Diary,* in which he kept careful records of the finances related to his theater, is one of the most valuable historical documents of Elizabethan stage practice.
5. Medieval staging is characterized by the juxtaposition of scenic locations or "mansions," grouped around the staging area. In the medieval plays depicting the stories of the Bible, for example, the most important mansions are those that represent Heaven and Hell, which were traditionally situated opposite each other in the acting area.
6. Michael Hattaway, *Elizabethan Popular Theatre* (London: Routledge and Kegan Paul, 1982), 38–39.
7. R. A. Foakes is one who makes a point about the Elizabethan theater having developed away from the practice of simultaneous staging typical of medieval theater. He affirms, for instance, that "the use of three-dimensional structures or 'houses' placed in different parts of the stage, or along the rear, to represent different localities, gave way as a general principle to successive staging for audiences that loved romances, histories, and tragedies." See Foakes, "Playhouses and Players," in *The Cambridge Companion to English Renaissance Drama,* ed. A. R. Braunmuller and Michael Hattaway (Cambridge: Cambridge University Press, 1990), 21–22.
8. Hattaway, *Elizabethan,* 40.
9. Scott McMillin, *The Elizabethan Theater and the Book of Sir Thomas More* (Ithaca: Cornell University Press, 1987), 98.
10. Hattaway, *Elizabethan,* 38.
11. Ibid.
12. Qtd. in McMillin, *Elizabethan Theater,* 97.
13. Qtd. in Foakes, "Playhouses," 20.
14. Johannes De Witt, a Dutchman who visited London around 1596, sketched the inside of the Swan Theater. This drawing remains the only identifiable record of the interior of an Elizabethan playhouse.

15. McMillin, *Elizabethan Theater,* 106.
16. Hattaway, *Elizabethan,* 24.
17. Foakes, "Playhouse," 21.
18. Qtd. in Hattaway, *Elizabethan,* 24.
19. Hattaway, *Elizabethan,* 36.
20. Beckerman, *Shakespeare,* 164.
21. Foakes, "Playhouses," 21.
22. Beckerman, *Shakespeare,* 164.
23. Ibid., 174.
24. The stage at the Rose tapered from thirty-seven feet, six inches at the junction with the inner frame to twenty-four feet, nine inches in the arena, and was about fifteen feet, six inches deep.
25. Alan Hughes, introduction to *Titus Andronicus,* by William Shakespeare, ed. A. Hughes (Cambridge: Cambridge University Press, 1994), 10.
26. Ibid., 14.
27. Qtd. in Hughes, introduction, 11.
28. Rutter, *Documents,* 78.
29. William Shakespeare, *Titus Andronicus: The First Quarto, 1594,* reproduced in facsimile (New York: Charles Scribner, 1936). All stage directions and lines are taken from this "edition" of the First Quarto, which does not divide the play into acts or scenes.
30. Hughes, introduction, 154.
31. Ibid.
32. If the Swan drawing is taken as evidence of use of gallery space, then the actors would have to line up beside each other, making the best of what must have been a dark and shallow stage space. But the sort of gallery space shown in the stage façade depicted in Robert Fludd's *Theatrum Orbis* (1623), from his *Ars Memoriae* would work well for the staging of the raised scenes in *Titus Andronicus,* allowing for a greater variety in the grouping of the actors who must make their entrances "aloft."
33. Jonathan Bate, introduction to the Arden Shakespeare edition of *Titus Andronicus,* by William Shakespeare (London: Routledge, 1995), 9.
34. Allardyce Nicholl, "Passing over the Stage," *Shakespeare Survey* 12 (1959): 53.
35. Bate (London: Routledge, 1995), 30.
36. Hattaway, *Elizabethan* (London: Routledge and Kegan Paul, 1982), 194.

Homo/Vir: The State of Man and Nature in *Macbeth*

THOMAS LaBORIE BURNS

THE UNNATURAL REPLACES THE NATURAL WHILE MACBETH RULES. The murder of Duncan, like any murder, is unnatural in the sense that the king has not been allowed to live out the span of his natural life: Macbeth himself uses the expression "live the lease of nature" (4.1. 115). It is unnatural, too, in the sense that the king is the state, both symbol and executor of the body politic, and killing him makes for a headless state and so upsets political equilibrium, smooth government, and the state of peace. The pathetic fallacy notwithstanding, the state of nature may be seen as an echo or reflection of the human world in *Macbeth,* for the world of phenomena and nonhuman creatures has meaningful signs. The first scene has a storm: nature is disturbed. The foul weather during the day's battle that the Thane of Cawdor refers to in act 1, scene 2, is a reflection of the day's "bloody business," and yet with the victory of the loyal forces the outcome is fair. Coupling the two terms, fair and foul, he unconsciously takes up the initial chant of the witches and sets the program of action in which good and evil, in this unnatural state, seem interchangeable.

As nature shows disturbance through the warring elements in the heavens, the king wages war against a treasonous rebellion on earth, a connection made explicit in the simile by the sergeant, who mentions "shipwrecking storms" and "direful thunders" (1.2. 26–27). When Macbeth hears the fatal prophecy on the heath, he says,

> My thought, whose murder is yet but fanstastical,
> Shakes so my single state of man that function
> Is smothered in surmise, and nothing is
> But what is not.
>
> (1.3. 138–41)

His metaphor for his psychological imbalance, the murder of thought, manifests what yet lurks beneath his conscious mind, the thought of murder. The state of man he refers to means his condition of living, thinking person, but perhaps also with the implied Elizabethan metaphor as its warring elements, and, even further, in the context of the play, a miniature reflection of the political state of Scotland, torn by a rebellion he himself has just helped repress but that will yet groan under his own future tyranny.

As the state of the natural world appears throughout the play's complex layers of imagery and has been amply explored in the critical literature, I shall discuss it more briefly than the state or condition of manhood, which seems to me to have received less attention but to which the idea of nature is also connected. Natural phenomena are invoked by Macbeth in the first act to aid him in his unnatural deed: he calls on the stars (1.4. 52–53) not to reveal his black desires and the earth not to hear his footsteps (1.7.56) as he moves stealthily to Duncan's chamber; and in the third act he calls on the night to "scarf up the tender eye pitiful of day" that he might more easily dispose of Banquo (3.2. 48). The light and dark motif occurs, and with the same meaning of concealment, when Ross and the Old Man, discussing recent nocturnal events (2.4), note that darkness entombs the earth, an association of darkness with death that reflects the murder of Duncan in his sleep. The natural elements themselves seem to react to this dire deed: "the heavens, as troubled with man's act, / Threaten his bloody stage" (2.4. 5–6). The pervasive motif of blood, the vital force of nature in the body, here stands for violent death on the stage of the world, the bloody backdrop, as it were, for human action. Once spilled, blood may corrupt nature herself, as when Macbeth, after murdering Duncan, asks despairingly:

> Will all great Neptune's ocean wash this blood
> Clean from my hand? No. This my hand will rather
> The multitudinous seas incarnadine,
> Making the green one red.
>
> (2.2. 58–61)

The world of animals is also strangely disturbed. A falcon, hunting bird of the nobility, has been killed by a mousing owl, a nocturnal predator used to lesser prey. The king's horses have turned wild, that is, gone back to a state of nature when they break out and eat each other. These extraordinary and unnatural events may be signs of human discord. If the falcon and the owl are, respectively, Duncan and Macbeth (Lady Macbeth hears an owl shriek right before the murder), the subsequent action may reveal the cannibalistic horses as the fratricidal Scottish thanes.

In the scene before the murder is discovered (2.3), Lennox describes the night as "unruly," a word usually applied to human misbehavior and lack of control. He reports "lamentings heard in the air, strange screams of death," clamorings of the "obscure bird" (i.e., the owl), and even an earthquake, a natural phenomenon known to cause commotion in animals even before it occurs, and which has its biblical prototype in the earth-shaking and tomb openings of Matthew 27, 51–52 (Macbeth's response to all this commotion—"Twas a rough night"—seems comically inadequate). The biblical notion seems to be taken up by Macduff, who discovers Duncan's body, when he refers to it as a sacred object, "the Lord's annointed temple" (2.3. 67). The assassination represents not only political disequilibrium; it is a defilement, a sacrilegious crime against an entire people. If the night was unruly, "confusion now hath made his masterpiece" (2.3. 65), for which the unnatural disorders served as portents.

Finally, the disturbed natural world is present in the motif of planting and growth. The grateful Duncan rewards his valiant cousin thus: "I have begun to plant thee, and will labour / To make thee full of growing" (1.4. 28–29), but Macbeth as progenitor, as he learns to his dismay from a later prophecy, is destined to bear no fruit. Ready for the climactic attack on the tyrant's castle (4.3), Malcolm says that "Macbeth / is ripe for shaking" (4.3. 239–40), as if he were an apple ready to drop, and it is clear that the natural order of the state, represented by the legitimate heir—Malcolm is called "the sovereign flower" (5.2. 30)—will be restored only when that bad apple has fallen. At the end of the play, Macduff hails Malcolm, who answers in his condition of restored ruler of Scotland, that he will accomplish what "would be planted newly with the time" (5.11. 31).

The plant also appears in the form of a tree in the third apparition, a crowned child holding a tree in his hand, prophetic of the future king advancing on the castle with the English army camouflaged behind branches of Birnham Wood, an advance which spells Macbeth's military defeat. The natural world of plants in the apparition is linked to the cultural world of man: the child is man at an early stage of growth, and the crown and the tree are figures for kingship and family, two institutions Macbeth assaults by murder. The vision suggests that nature will reassert itself with the demise of him Macduff calls the "usurper" of the natural order of the state. And there may be a bit of black comedy here, as well, when the messenger (5.5), upon informing Macbeth that Birnham Wood is advancing, is answered that if he is lying he will hang from the nearest tree!

The play's imagery, then, presents nature as confounded, confused, profoundly disturbed. Anarchy or disarray in the human world is paralleled by disorder and violence in the natural world. "Let the frame of things disjoint," Macbeth pronounces, afflicted by terrible dreams of guilt. As is seen in the examples, nature is consistently invoked as personal. Macbeth's invocation of natural phenomena as if they were malevolent spirits confirms how anxious he is to become king by the unnatural path of assassination, to "o'erleap" Malcolm's natural succession. By the fourth act, he has become totally dependent on the prophecies of the weird sisters and his own violent impulses, a corruption of his former self. His speech to the witches (4.1), ordering them to conjure up a dream of his future is itself an imprecation against nature: "though the treasure / Of nature's germens tremble all together, / Even till destruction sicken" (4.1.74–75), he must know his fate. The images in this speech—wind and wave, sinking ship and toppling castles, destroyed crops and trees—recall the natural violence in the first act and mingle the human and natural objects and phenomena in an apocalyptic vision of ruin.

Lady Macbeth's first speech, while reading the letter from her triumphant husband, characterizes her relation to her husband and her view of herself: "Yet do I fear thy nature. / It is too full of the milk of human kindness / To catch the nearest way" (1.5. 14–16). Macbeth now has the opportunity to satisfy his ambition, but his wife fears he is too good a man to achieve the prize by the shortest route, foul play. She vows to herself to give him the needed boost to do the deed, and by this, it may be noted, she assumes that she could not actually kill Duncan herself but only convince her husband do so. For this purpose, however, she must first call on evil spirits to make her more—or less—than a woman:

> Come, you spirits
> That tend on mortal thoughts, unsex me here,
> And fill me, from the crown to the toe top-full
> Of direst cruelty. Make thick my blood,

> Stop up th'access and passage to remorse,
> That no compunctious visitings of nature
> Shake my fell purpose, nor keep peace between
> The effect and it. Come to my woman's breasts,
> Wherever in your sightless substances
> You wait on nature's mischief.
>
> (1.5. 39–49)

Apart from the interesting physiology of this passage, in her invocation of evil spirits, she asks nothing less than to be unsexed, since her husband, who is no coward or stranger to violence in a righteous war, as witness his valor and "smoking" sword in the battle with the rebels, may actually lack the will to murder, as implied by her perception of him as "too full of the milk of human kindness." This metaphor, especially in connection with the lines just quoted and its parallel with blood, implies that while violence may be natural to a man, cruelty and lack of remorse are neither a part of the nature of this particular man nor of women in general; hence, she asks to be neutered, the gentleness natural to her sex to be neutralized. Blood must be stopped up in the veins to prevent the natural flow of remorse in human conscience, and the milk of human kindness, which her husband has imbibed in excess from his own mother, must be turned to bitter gall in her own breasts. She mentions nature twice. The "compunctious visitings of nature" seems to mean the natural pangs of conscience a human being would normally feel at the thought of committing murder and treason. Such a deed is not natural to people, even less so to a woman, who carries in her body the analogue of blood, the life-sustaining substance of milk. The second reference, "nature's mischief," alludes to deviations from the natural course of events, especially those caused by human interference through the invocation of evil but efficacious spirits.

In his first speech of the following scene (1.7), Macbeth shows himself to be the basically decent fellow his wife fears him to be, for he talks himself out of committing the murder with arguments based on the essential unnaturalness of the act: it would be parricide, go against human hospitality, and be unwise, that is, be offensive to nature, society, and good sense. When he tells his wife that he will therefore go no further in this business, she scoffs at him by undermining his manhood, comparing his previous ambition to the words of a drunken braggart who awakes the next morning with nothing more to show for his brave words than a hangover. She offers him to choose between the crown or life as a miserable coward in his own eyes, which is rather incredible when we remember she is addressing a war hero. In his own defense, he protests that he "dare do all that may become a man, / Who dares more is none" (1.7. 46–47), which I take to mean that he will do only what is proper and right for a human being, "man" as *homo,* that is, like the old joke, man as embracing woman, man as opposed to the beasts, who might kill without human scruple.

In her reply, Lady Macbeth turns this conception of manhood on its head:

> What beast was't then
> That made you break this enterprise to me?
> When you durst do it, then you were a man;
> And to be more than what you were, you
> Would be so much more the man. Nor time nor place
> Did they adhere, and yet you would make both.
> They have made themselves, and that their fitness now
> Does unmake you.
>
> (1.7. 48–54)

In the mention of beast, she may seem to have accepted his notion of man as opposed to animal, but she subtly changes this notion in the course of the speech: when you made your promise and expressed hope for success you were then a man, but now, when time and place are actually propitious, you quaver at the thought, "their fitness now / Does unmake you" (read *unman* you). He is not a real man, that sexual being who backs up his words with action, but an idle boaster who cannot live up to them, as would not be the case if he were actually more the "man" than he claims to be.

Lady Macbeth's notion of manhood therefore seems more restricted, that of man as distinct in sex and behavior from woman: that is to say, not *homo,* but *vir,* root word of both *virile* and *virtue,* referring to those creatures who are supposed to be ever willing to go beyond idle talk. She pushes him toward action, in other words, by questioning his masculinity. That she is clearly setting up a sexual opposition is shown by the astonishing words immediately following, in which she says that she herself would snatch her baby from her breast and dash out its brains before making such a false promise. The exaggeration and violence of the image point up her extreme anger at what she feels is her husband's unmanly hesitation (we can only imagine what she would say to Hamlet), but the image is also implicitly saying that if she, a woman, would do something so unnatural for a mother, what does that make him, a man, for whom violence is supposed to be second nature? This may be hitting below the belt, but it effectively wins the match. When he tells her to "Bring forth men-children only, / For thy undaunted mettle should compose / Nothing but males" (1.7. 72–74), he is effectively accepting her binary argument and even, in a sense, acknowledging her superior masculinity, and, paradoxically, doing so in terms of motherhood. This is the psychological turning point for Macbeth, and it is accomplished by his accepting his wife's definition of manhood against his own good nature. Henceforth, he too will cast aside scruples, human decency, and his expressed personal regard for his kinsman and king, in order to "bend up / Each corporal agent to this terrible feat" (1.7. 79–80), turn himself figuratively into a taut bow, a weapon.

Fatherhood also takes part in this defining of manhood. Once king, Macbeth finds his way to contentment blocked by Banquo, who is to be "root and father to many kings," an image that combines paternity and plant growth. (Macbeth's "barren sceptre" is the phallic but sterile image of his own power.) He becomes obsessed with eliminating his comrade-in-arms, whose "royalty of nature" is shown in his courage and wisdom, traditional kingly virtues. Macbeth and his wife may have had children, if one takes her expression of giving suck as alluding to her own motherhood, but the children, if any, are dead, as Macduff bitterly notes that [Macbeth] "has no children" (4.3. 17). Macbeth's main impediments, Banquo and Macduff, however, have visible families whom Macbeth is determined to destroy.

Curiously, given her earlier assumption that her husband will do the actual killing, Lady Macbeth's remark after the murder that she would have killed Duncan herself except that he resembled, when he slept, her own father, is a slip into the feminine sentimentality she accused Macbeth of giving in to. Fathers and sons make frequent appearances in the plot: when Duncan is killed, his sons escape for their lives and are conveniently blamed for the crime. Macbeth has Banquo murdered, but Banquo's son Fleance escapes and is thus able to fulfill the prophecy. Reversing this pattern, Macduff escapes and his son is murdered in his stead.

Fatherhood is mentioned as early as Macbeth's speech of loyalty to Duncan after the initial battle (1.4), where he compares the duties of a subject to those of children and servants. Duncan, although Macbeth's cousin, has a paternal affection for him. After the murder, Macbeth gives the bad news to the real son, Malcolm, telling him "the fountain of your blood is stopped," which connects the literal and figurative meanings of blood. After becoming king, Macbeth is most tormented with the idea of wearing a "fruitless crown," and his obsession with obliterating Banquo's rival line is a result of the effective sterility of his own manhood in contrast to the flagrant fatherhood of his perceived enemies. When he sees the apparitions conjured up by the witches, he eagerly misreads their meaning, except for the final one, the dumb-show of kings pointed to by the engendering Banquo. About this apparition, he makes no mistake but refuses to see more, a moment, to sustain the virile imagery, of unmanly weakness, and precisely at a time when he has decided to be bolder and more resolute.

Even Lady Macduff, a benevolent version of Lady Macbeth, discourses on the nature of fatherhood (4.2): "He wants the natural touch," she tells Ross, unconvinced of the motive for Macduff's precipitous flight for his life, even while Macduff is unaware that Macbeth will go so far as to put his family to the sword. Lady Macduff tells her son, without fully realizing what she is saying, that although the boy is fathered, yet he is "fatherless," and their dialogue rings changes on the need of a son to have a proper father and of a woman to have a proper man.

Yet, the idea of manhood is not exhausted by considerations of fatherhood. To circumvent fate, Macbeth employs men who do not seem to be professional assassins so much as men who have had a hard lot in life and are therefore ripe for manipulation. In convincing them of the need for revenge on Banquo for his alleged crimes against them, Macbeth compares their professions of manhood to a motley catalogue of creatures all going by the name of dogs (3.1). If you are "not in the worst rank of manhood," he tells them, then kill Banquo, using the following argument: if you do not merely go by the name of man (i.e., human being) in the same way that greyhounds, mongrels, curs, and demiwolves go by the generic name of *dog,* take up your knives and show yourselves to be real, that is, virile, violent men.

This attribution of violence to the masculine sex occurs again and again in the play. Right before the murderers enter to kill her son, Lady Macduff acknowledges this notion in her bitter lament at having no guarantee of safety: "Why, then alas, / Do I put that womanly defense to say I have done no harm?" (4.2. 77–78). In the following scene, Macduff in exile tries to persuade Malcolm to return to Scotland to recapture the throne. Suspecting he is a spy, Malcolm tests his loyalty by suggesting that he, Malcolm, has a base and unworthy character. His first vice is "voluptuousness," which hardly fazes an old soldier like Macduff, who grudges that his country has "willing dames enough" for the future king to indulge any excess of virility and this trait may even be considered normal for a powerful man, who should be able to "devour as many as will to greatness dedicate themselves." Sex and manhood, then, are not in question, but later in the same scene, the notion of manhood reflects the meaning it had in Lady Macbeth's early speeches. Ross arrives to give Macduff the news of his family's slaughter, to which the latter reacts with speechless shock and grief. Skillful politician that he is, Malcolm here perceives an opportunity to turn this grief to good acccount: "blunt not the heart, enrage it" (4.3. 231), he tells Macduff, "Dispute it *like a man*" (4.3. 221, emphasis added). For Malcolm, a man is the violent avenger he requires in his service.

Macduff recognizes the need but also the proper motive for retribution. To feel his crime "as a man," he says (note the change from *like* to *as,* indicating a natural way of behavior, not an imposed performance) is to act as any man would who feels natural affection towards his family and perceives, too late, his wife and children as unprotected victims. Malcolm, using the argument that a man is someone capable of violent action, succeeds, finally, in stirring his countryman to righteous wrath. Macduff says, "O, I could play the woman with mine eyes / And braggart with my tongue!" (4.3. 232–33) but bring the tyrant within sword's length and action will speak for words, which recalls Lady Macbeth's comparison of the drunken but ineffectual braggart in her similarly successful attempt to stir Macbeth to action. Satisfied with this response, Malcolm concludes: "This tune goes manly" (4.3. 237).

Right after Duncan's murder, Macbeth is overcome with the enormity of what he has done and rambles on about voices, prayers of the king's sons, and the sleep he has murdered. His wife is impatient at this display of moral conscience, which she predictably interprets as weakness: "you do unbend your noble strength to think / So brain-sickly of things" (2.2. 42–43). When he refuses to return to Duncan's chamber to plant the false evidence of the grooms' daggers, she chides him again for being "infirm of purpose." The imagery of disease is yet another motif connected to nature, illness bieng a pathological condition in which the normal equilibrium of the body or mind has been disturbed. As early as the prophecy on the heath, Banquo wonders: "have we eaten on the insane root / That takes the reason prisoner?" (1.3. 82–83). We have seen Lady Macbeth's worry over what she calls the illness or wickedness necessary to carry out one's ambition. When Macbeth finally commits the murder, it is clear that he has assumed an illness in ways unsuspected. Racked by a bad conscience, he is unable to sleep, insomnia itself being a subspecies of illness, an organic disturbance.

Macbeth's subsequent psychological deterioration is frequently recorded in organic terms. When he learns of Fleance's escape from the murderers, he cries: "Then comes my fit again" (3.4. 20). In the banquet scene, he becomes publicly deranged on seeing the bloody ghost of Banquo. Significantly, as soon as the ghost gives him a respite by disappearing, he announces to the astonished company that he is a man once again, not the quivering creature who says he would rather face tigers or bears than the unsettling sights of his imagination. With a timely intervention, his wife explains this bizarre behavior as a momentary fit, an infirmity he has had since youth. His true "illness," of course, is not only recent but incurable and progressive, and although she has led him to it, she cannot now control it with advice to be calm. She has evidently forgotten that his lack of control could be beneficial, at least to explain why in a supposed rage he killed the grooms, who would have been the only witnesses to his crime. As the play progresses, he becomes at once both more determined and more reckless. When he has Macduff's family murdered without any political motive, or, indeed, any personal one but rage, he has gone beyond even the pretense of control. As he recognizes (3.4. 135–37) with brutal self-perception, "I am in blood / Stepped in so far that, should I wade no more, / Returning were as tedious as go o'er."

Macbeth the sick tyrant has his healthy counterpart in King Edward of England, a saintly man with alleged powers of healing, a sort of white magic along with this strange virtue magic to counteract the black magic of the witches. And Edward along "with this strange virtue / . . . hath a heavenly gift of prophecy" (4.3. 157–58). By contrast, Macbeth, who kills rather than cures his subjects, corrupts the state with his tyranny, and unable to prophesy depends on prophecies that are not heavenly in origin but inspired by hell. The state, as well as the individual, may be sick and require healing. Ross comes to England to report on the sorry state of Scotland, where "good men's lives / Expire before the flowers in their caps / Dying or ere they sicken" (4.3. 171–73). The news of the demise of Macduff's family prompts Malcolm to ask Macduff to "make medicines" of their revenge, "to cure this deadly grief." It is ironic, given her manipulation of what she insisted was her husband's weakness in the beginning, that Lady Macbeth should be the one to succumb to madness at the end. Her obsession with washing out the "damned spot" of blood from her hands (5.1) parallels her rational reaction to her husband's similar affliction after Duncan's murder. In his case, "a little water" would clear him of the deed, but now "All the perfumes of Arabia" will not serve the same purpose. Her malady, as the doctor points out, is spiritual, and Macbeth's impatient reply to the medical report is desperate and contains its own answer: "Canst thou not minister to a mind diseased?" (5.3. 42) The pathology, as the doctor says, results from the fact that "Unnatural deeds / Do breed unnatural troubles" (5.1. 68–69). Macbeth wishes as well that the doctor could restore health to his diseased country, but a "purgative drug" cannot cleanse Scotland of its foreign invaders because the real disease is internal. Like Oedipus, Macbeth is the source of his country's contagion.

One final point with respect to nature in the play must be considered—the role of the supernatural. If the unnatural is a deviation from what is healthy, right, and just, the supernatural may supercede or intervene in the natural course of things. It might be benevolent, a *deus ex machina* of later Greek tragedy, or malevolent, like the witches in *Macbeth,* but in either case it is an interference in nature. The weird sisters discuss such interferences (1.3), when they dub themselves "posters of the sea and land." Banquo warns Macbeth that "the instruments of darkness" will "betray's in deepest confidence," but Macbeth is too rapt in his dreams of power to pay heed. He does, however, confess to an unnatural fear:

> Why do I yield to that suggestion
> Whose horrid image doth unfix my hair
> And make my seated heart knock at my ribs
> Against the use of nature?
>
> (1.3. 133–36)

These symptoms of fear, even terror, also stir in his soul a strange excitement, the beginning of conflicting impulses that will wrack his "single state of man" until he rejects his own good nature and turns himself into a monster.

The problem of free will and fate in relation to Macbeth's "vaulting ambition" is a tension between how much he is indebted to each. If Shakespearean tragedy is primarily a tragedy of will rather than fate, the supernatural interference in Macbeth's life is important—this being the most Aeschylean of Shakespeare's tragedies—but not decisive to his fall. If the prophecies have a supernatural origin, they also function in the plot as signs, which Macbeth willfully misreads. He cannot therefore be seen so much a victim of an infernal conspiracy, as I have argued here, as a potentially good man who foregoes his true manhood, his humanity, and willingly chooses evil by giving in to delusions of power, a familiar enough notion to our own time.

The Taming of the Shrew: Shakespeare's Theater of Repetition

Maria Lúcia Milléo Martins

CRITICAL READINGS OF *THE TAMING OF THE SHREW* TEND TO BE divided into two antagonistic positions, one arguing that the play is a romanticized assertion of patriarchal dominance, the other that it is an ironic representation undermining such power. Involved in those discussions is not only the play itself, but such matters as whether Shakespeare was a male chauvinist and, thus, should be condemned or forgiven; whether he was a feminist ahead of his time; or, regardless of ideology, simply a genius. If, after years of "unrelenting oratory" about these issues, you think I have come up with the key, I am sorry to disappoint you. My interest lies exactly in the ambivalence of the play and how it farcically presents the ambivalence of strained gender relations in the actual world. Critics and historians acknowledge the ambiguities of the Elizabethan period and explain them as the advent of significant cultural changes in the following century. Ambivalence is at the core of the so-called crisis of order, in its essence a crisis of power revealing, on one side, the struggle of the patriarchal system to keep its dominance, and, on the other, the disturbing force of women's rebellion against their oppression.

To argue that Shakespeare's play simply mirrors these contradictions may seem to assert its status as conservative comedy, at clear disadvantage in regard to John Fletcher's play, *The Woman's Prize or the Tamer Tamed,* a more liberal proposition for the gender debate. If so, genius would be in innovation rather than in repetition. My argument will be to attempt to prove the opposite in a discussion of Shakespeare's text as repetition of the inconsistencies of its time and as repetition restaged to new cultural contexts in theater and film productions. Finally, in the comforting light of some theories of our most praised contemporary gurus (and this is maybe the most ambitious part of this work), I expect not to close the debate on *The Shrew,* but rather to leave an additional suspicion that Shakespeare was perhaps an untimely-born postmodern genius.

As *The Shrew* opens, the ambivalence of roles in command is immediately put into play. The notion of male authority recognized in early modern England as natural or divine gains a curious configuration. The Induction suggests the construction of male authority as fiction in two ways: in the creation of Sly's identity as a lord, and in the enactment of the play itself as metatheater—"a kind of history" of how to exercise power. Sly, a poor drunkard, yet sober enough to remember his lineage and occupation, only becomes convinced of his identity as a lord when he is told that he has a wife:

> Am I a lord, and have I such a lady?
> Or do I dream? Or have I dream'd till now?
> I do not sleep: I see, I hear, I speak.
> I smell sweet savors, and I feel soft things.
> Upon my life, I am a lord indeed,
>
> (Ind., 2. 67–71)

The existence of such a lady with no identity—a "madam, and nothing else"—is what confirms Sly's identity, ironically reversing the Elizabethan order, that is, the concession of identity and status to women by their husbands, through marriage. Aware of his lordship and in full command of his senses, Sly is ready to impose his authority and demand from his wife immediate sexual obedience. "Madam, undress you, and come now to bed" (Ind., 2. 114). With a submissive excuse, however, Sly's wife deauthorizes the exertion of his power, subtly suggested as dependent on female will. If the induction inverts traditional practices, the two marriage proposals offer a complete inconsistency of two opposite measures applied to the same social situation. "If I get your daughter's love, / What dowry shall I have with her to wife?" (2.1. 120–21) Petruchio asks Baptista, implying not only the ironic dependence of the whole transaction on Kate's will, but also his self-confidence in his gifts of persuasiveness. Baptista specifies the dowry and reinforces the condition imposed. "Ay, when the special thing is well obtain'd / That is, her love; for that is all in all" (2.1. 128–29). Conversely, in the case of Bianca, Baptista ignores her approval and, confronted with the dispute between Gremio and Tranio, offers "Bianca's love" to the "greatest dower." (2.1. 339) While in the first proposal the dowry depends on love, in the second, love depends on the dowry. Considering a cultural context in which marriage contracts were made much more on the basis of business transaction assuring rights of land property than taking into account emotional links, the inclusion of "love" in both discussions can only be taken ironically.

Inversion of conventional modes or ambivalence of measures are not the only inconsistencies which Shakespeare ironically represents in *The Shrew*. After striking Petruchio, who swears to "cuff" her, Kate wittily articulates the absolute incongruity of two male codes: the code of male authority imposed through violence and the code of chivalry: "So may you loose your arms. / If you strike me, you are no gentleman, / And if no gentleman, why then no arms" (2.1. 119–21). The law at the time assured men the right to beat their wives as well as their children and servants but, in the double position as lords and gentlemen, they were to some extent supposed to be chivalrous. One could say that in this passage Kate establishes the code for Petruchio to tame her, a code which Lynda Boose defines as "domination with an aura of romantic bravado bound up with the mock chivalry" (193)[1]. As Petruchio starts his policy of domination, an inversion of roles is again put into play. Instead of Kate who, as bride, should be the center of the spectacle, Petruchio takes this place. In the extravagance of Petruchio's attire, Shakespeare not only deprives Kate of her conventional centrality but he ridicules this centrality in a burlesque paradigm. The farcical representation of this episode gains deeper implications if extended to the degrading exposure of woman's body at the center of a mocking parade in rituals of punishment.[2]

Another of Shakespeare's intricate inversions of roles happens at the scene of the wedding dinner when Kate, ignoring Petruchio's will in not staying for the dinner, commands: "Gentlemen, forward to the bridal dinner. / I see a woman may be made a fool, / If she had not a spirit to resist" (3.3. 94–99). As Petruchio knows a man can as well be made a fool for the same reason, he does not yield to his wife's insistence but, rather, ironically subverts Kate's discourse to assert his own authority:

> They shall go forward, Kate, at thy command.
> Obey the bride, you that attend on her.
> Go to the feast, revel and domineer,
> Carouse full measure to her maidenhead,

>   Be mad and merry, or go hang yourselves;
>   But for my bonny Kate, she must with me.
>
>   (3.3. 94–99)

In this alternation of roles in command, Shakespeare ironically plays with power tensions in gender relations. On one side, there is Kate's speech to be obeyed (yet with the exclusion of Petruchio), which can be read either against the conventional silence associated with women's obedience or their rebellion through language. On the other, there is Petruchio not deauthorizing such discourse but, rather, as Karen Newman suggests, "deliberately misunderstanding and reinterpreting [Kate's] words to suit his own ends." Newman explains that, as a receiver of Kate's messages, Petruchio "simply refuses their meaning; since he has material power to enforce his interpretations," and concludes that "it is his power over language that wins."[3]

I would not argue, as Newman does, that it is male dominance over female language that wins, for the problem here would be to define in what terms Kate's language can be taken as female. If it is difficult to distinguish Kate's speech from Petruchio's in rhetorical terms, as some critics have observed, it is yet more complex to conciliate in a single notion Kate's discourse while she can still "tell the anger of [her] heart" and after it is subverted to "be it the moon, or sun, or what you please." Newman explains the subversion of Kate's language as "mimetic" (in Luce Irigaray's sense of female mimeticism) and gives a sensible account of the underlying contradictions in such a representation of gender, which she calls the "female dramatizable." Nevertheless, what still remains unresolved is what role Kate's "earlier language of revolt and anger" plays in this female dramatization. In this way, one is left wondering which language has male dominance won (if it ever did). Rather than claiming a possible winner, I would call attention to the intricate web of power relations which language conveys, or, in other words, to the negotiations of power through linguistic strategies—rhetoric, punning, mimeticism, irony, repetition—blurring the ultimate resolution of who in fact is in power.

In a similar way to Petruchio's subversive use of her language to suit his own purposes of domination, Kate too appropriates his rhetoric to impose her will. Petruchio's *will you, nill you, I will marry you* (2.1. 265) becomes in Kate's version: "Love, or love me not, I like the cap / And it I will have, or I will have none" (4.3. 84–85).

Negotiations of power get far more intriguing after Kate is "bedazzled with the sun," or the moon, radically changing her strategy:

> Then God be blessed, it is the blessed sun,
> But sun it is not, when you say it is not;
> And the moon changes even as your mind.
> What you will have it nam'd, even that it is,
> And so it shall be still for Katherine.
>
> (4.6. 19–23)

Under the apparent affirmation of Petruchio's power over the universe (or his naming the universe), Kate is punning on the double meaning that the reverse of her expression "the moon changes . . . as your mind" suggests. For, as it is suitably observed in a note on this passage in the Riverside edition, "the moon was thought to govern the moods of a lunatic." Petruchio's lunacy is emphasized a few lines later in the ironic association of *sun* and *son* in Kate's excuse for her "mistaking eyes . . . so bedazzled with the sun." The expression *son* previously appears in Petruchio's inflamed proclamation of his power when he says: "Now by my mother's son, and that's myself, / It shall be the moon, or star, or what I list" (4.6. 6–7). This passage illustrates in its irony, punning, and subversive repetition how language is used both as a device to assert power and as a device to undermine it. The anxiety resultant of such an ambivalence can be particularly sensed in the hundreds of responses to Kate's final discourse attempting to define who in fact is in power.

One of the most significant responses to this debate came out in 1613: *The Woman's Prize or the Tamer Tamed,* by the dramatist John Fletcher. Fletcher, who did not believe that Kate had ever been tamed, opened his play years after her death with the scene of Petruchio's second marriage to a young woman named Maria. A seventeenth-century version of a highly politicized feminist, Maria not only had the responsibility to tame Petruchio but also to organize a massive manifestation of women's revolt against male dominance. Molly Easo Smith aptly observes the connection of Maria to Marion, the historical figure of May Day celebrations, suggesting the allusion to actual riots in the sixteenth and seventeenth centuries.[4] Fletcher's theatrical representation of women's rebellion marching up the streets with pots and ladles, reveling with ale and music, invoked two other farcical Renaissance manifestations: charivaris or skimmingtons and carnivalesque processions, ideal events for gender inversions and political criticism.

The undeniable link of Fletcher's play with such traditional masquerades and actual riots questions the very notion of boundaries between life and theater as separate realms. In this respect Smith points out that

> audiences of the seventeenth century would have seen the tactics adopted by the women and the nature of the rebellion, not as an entirely farcical improbability simply to be enjoyed within the artificial confines of the theatre, but as a genuine possibility similar to numerous such revolts that occurred and were occurring in Renaissance England. (43)

This reading of Fletcher's play as "possibility" invites a rereading of Kate's final discourse, challenging the assumption that an ironic view of Shakespeare's indoctrination was impossible for Elizabethan audiences. The possibility that Fletcher's play suggests was already a fact two decades earlier when *The Shrew* was first presented. The historical confirmation of women's rebellion in the domestic sphere and in public riots would not even be necessary if one considers simply the "need" for indoctrination. Sermons and homilies emphasizing the duty of wives would not have been so popular at the time if women's behavior was not at risk. Kate's final discourse farcically represents this need for indoctrination. Elizabethan audiences certainly did not ignore the threat of women's rebellion behind the sermons as they would not ignore it behind Kate's speech. Shakespeare subtly counterposes this threat to Kate's lesson of obedience by contrasting it with the silence of Bianca and the Widow, women who refuse to obey—in its essence an ironic inversion since silence was a code for obedience and discourse a form of transgression. I am not suggesting here the exclusion of a literal reading of this passage by early audiences, but contesting the idea that an ironic reading was unthinkable.

Ambivalent responses to Shakespeare's play, either viewing it as moralizing repetition of an old cliché or as its subversion, seem to be a natural consequence of the contradictions presented by the text itself as a mirror of these same contradictions in the actual world. Critics and historians acknowlede the inconsistencies of this period and explain it as the advent for significant cultural changes in the following century. Smith observes that this process of change may account for "major differences between Fletcher's play and Shakespeare's more conservative comedy." In a Foucauldian perspective, she considers that one may even argue that in Fletcher's play "we witness the prior enactment in the theater of a cultural change that would reach the record books only considerably later." (57) As evidences of cultural change, Smith points out the following: a proposal of a legislation to prevent husbands to use violence against their wives in *The Parliament Scout* in 1644; the gender inversion in skimmington practices in the late seventeenth and early eighteenth centuries with the mockery of male agression instead of female rebellion; and the disappearance of scolds from record books after the midseventeenth century.

If Fletcher is due the recognition for a more liberal perspective of the gender debate or a visionary insight of cultural changes, what would be left for Shakespeare? The merit of a "more conservative comedy," a mere repetition of old platitudes? Let us consider repetition. But first I suggest a brief reflection on what Gilles Deleuze has to tell us about the theater of repetition:

> The theater of repetition is opposed to the theater of representation, just as movement is opposed to the concept and to representation which refers it back to the concept. In the theater of repetition, we experience pure forces, dynamic lines in space which act without intermediary upon the spirit, and link it directly with nature and history, with a language which speaks before words, with gestures which develop before organized bodies, with masks before faces, with specters and phantoms before characters—the whole apparatus of repetition as a "terrible power." (10)[5]

Deleuze's notions of the theater of repetition not only apply to Shakespeare's act of repeating in his text the anxieties of his time about the old axiom of male dominance but also to the innumerable times his text has been and will be repeated in the theater. As Deleuze observes, theater is in its essence "movement," but not a repetitive movement in the sense of return to the "same," but "one which selects, one which expels as well as creates, destroys as well as produces" (11).

From this infinite cycle of repetition, I have chosen two productions to illustrate how the anxieties of Shakespeare's text have been restaged or adapted to new cultural contexts. The productions in question are Franco Zeffirelli's cinematic adaptation of *The Shrew* in 1966 and Charles Marowitz's version in 1974. The reason for such a choice is the contradictory way in which these performances reshape *The Shrew,* confirming the urge to resolve what Shakespeare's text leaves open.

In Zeffirelli's version, *The Shrew* becomes a carnivalesque spectacle celebrating sensuality and legitimizing familial myths. By locating the image of the shrew in Elizabeth Taylor's body, an icon of femininity and desire, Zeffirelli establishes from the start an aura of romanticism through which the audience can anticipate the terms of her taming. As Barbara Hodgdon observes, "Taylor's body language overmatches Burton's facility with Shakespeare." She explains that, whereas "Petruchio owns the words, silence codes his wife's presence until the play's end, when Kate talks and talks and talks" (545).[6] Interestingly, silence—a code for obedience in the Elizabethan context, or possible transgression as in the case of Bianca and the Widow listening to Kate's indoctrination—here becomes a code for voyeurism inviting complicity with the fantasy that the text itself does not provide. Hodgdon calls attention to the way silence is visually concentrated in Taylor's famous violet eyes and how close-ups privilege Kate's point of view. Hodgdon pinpoints two key passages to illustrate that: one is the close-up of Kate's eyes at the window while Petruchio boasts of his victory to the other men. "Kate sinks into a thoughtful pose," describes Hodgdon, "and a smile crosses her face as the sound track's soft, romantic music expresses her private pleasure, inviting spectators of either gender to share and, perhaps, extend her fantasy" (545). The other passage is at Bianca's wedding dinner, when, after exchanging glances with Petruchio, Kate's eyes are driven to several children playing. The scene insinuates both sensual intimacy and familial instinct, codes which the audience easily recognizes, minutes later, in Kate's final discourse.

To read Zeffirelli's adaptation of Shakespeare's text against the cultural context of the 1960s is to be confronted with a curious shift of opposite forces. What seems to be at stake is no longer patriarchal dominance versus women's rebellion but familial institution versus sexual license. In Zeffirelli's version, body language and silence serve to accommodate such a conflict in a promise of a model of marriage in which eroticism and familial virtues can partake of the same bed. With the exclusion of the Induction, Zeffirelli removes one layer of fictionality. This omission added to his choice of Taylor and Burton as protagonists—a couple in real life as well as on the stage—makes the lines between reality and fiction less distinct.

While Zeffirelli associates male dominance with sensuality and pleasure, Marowitz privileges sadism and brutality. Alternating scenes from the original text with scenes of a stereotyped modern couple, Marowitz refashions Shakespeare's debate into a gender and class issue. In his final collage, Marowitz blends Sly's discourse with Petruchio's who, embracing Kate, says "Madam, undress you and come now to bed." As Kate repeats Sly's wife's excuse, Baptista enters the stage and exclaims: "O monstruous arrogance!" Narrating the continuation of the scene, Hodgdon tells us that:

> Kate is backed over to the table and thrown down. While the servants and Baptista hold her wrists, Petruchio looms up behind her and whips up her skirts ready to do buggery. As he inserts, an ear-piercing, electronic whistle rises to crescendo pitch: Kate's mouth is wild and open, and it appears as if the sound issues from her lungs. (539)

In the following scene, after a blackout, Hodgdon informs us that Kate delivers her final speech hesitantly, as if the words were not hers. Towards the end of Kate's speech, the modern couple dressed in wedding clothes enter the scene, smile, and pose for a wedding picture. The physical violence which Shakespeare's text silences but that circulates in the surrounding culture emerges in Marowitz's postmodern version as a confirmation of its omnipresence or eternal return. By juxtaposing violence with the emblematic picture of the modern couple at the end, Marowitz effaces the possibility of pleasure which Zeffirelli privileges, leaving in its place hypocrisy dissimulating brutality.

In both productions it is worth pointing out the singular impact that female presence represents on the stage in opposition to the "boy actresses" who used to occupy such space in the Elizabethan theater. Kathleen McLuskie disagrees with the notion that cross-dressing was a convention accepted without ambivalence. She explains this ambivalence in Shakespeare's comedies by the way cross-dressing seemed *to invite* "and at the same time [deny] a metatheatrical awareness of the identity of the actor playing the woman's part" (123–24).[7] McLuskie also points out the implications of boys playing women being viewed as trangressors of "the primary boundary between male and female" (120). The reason for the reference to cross-dressing is not only to demonstrate how such an ambivalence is dissolved, but to draw the attention to how female presence becomes crucial in modern productions, as it is mostly the case in Zeffirelli's.

The anxiety to respond to Shakespeare's text that we have seen in these three examples confirms the "terrible power" which Deleuze attributes to the theater of repetition. In fiction or in the theater, heroes and heroines not only challenge old patterns when they subvert them as did Maria, Fletcher's heroine, but also when they passively repeat them. Their silence or their submissive discourse are disturbing presences urging on the audience an immediate need to respond. Audiences in general reject the doubleness of repetition and tend to interpret it either as a mere portrait or an ironic disguise. The leading debate on *The Shrew* confirms that.

Thus, the old dilemma of *The Shrew* becomes what one could call the postmodern anxiety of repetition. Deleuze attempts to resolve this dilemma by distinguishing between the repetition of the "Same" and the repetition that includes difference. The first, he says, is

> explicable by the identity of the concept or representation; the second includes difference and includes itself in the alterity of the Idea, in the heterogeneity of an "a-presentation." One is negative, occurring by default in the concept, the other affirmative, occurring by excess in the Idea.... One is inanimate, the other carries the secret of our deaths and our lives, of our enchainments and our liberations, the demonic and the divine. One is a "bare" repetition, the other a covered repetition, which forms itself in covering itself, in masking and disguising itself. (24)

However, toward the end of Deleuze's analysis, the two kinds of repetition intertwine:

> The clothed lies underneath the bare, and produces or excretes it as though it were the effect of its own secretion.... It is always in one and the same movement that repetition includes difference (not as an accidental and extrinsic variant but at its heart, as the essential variant of which it is composed...). (289)

The importance of repetition goes far beyond what is "dreamt of in your philosophy"; it can decide whether Shakespeare was a male chauvinist, a feminist ahead of his time, or a postmodern genius.

If, in a postmodern anxiety, we still read *The Shrew* as "bare" repetition, Shakespeare is a male chauvinist and we have only to decide whether to condemn or to forgive him. If, on the other hand, we are not convinced of the bareness of *The Shrew* or suspect of her "clothes," there you may find "the secret of Shakespeare's liberation." Finally, if we are exhausted by this recital of equivalences and divisions, Foucault has the solution. The whole problem is in fact "good sense." Good sense, says Foucault,

> "is the world's most effective agent of division in its recognition, its establishment of equivalences, its sensitivity to gaps, its gauging of distances, as it assimilates and separates. And it is good sense that reigns in the philosophy of representation."[8]

Foucault's suggestion is also mine: "Let us pervert good sense and allow thought to play outside the ordered table of resemblances." In such a perspective we would be less anxious about clothing *The Shrew* or accepting her in her bareness, and could, perhaps, experience "the pure forces, the dynamic lines in space" of this theater of repetition, the theater of that untimely-born postmodern genius

NOTES

1. This and subsequent quotations of Boose are from "Scolding Brides and Bridling Scolds: Taming the Woman's Unruly Member," *Shakespeare Quarterly* 42 (1991): 179–213.

2. For a detailed account of punishment practices in the Renaissance see especially Lynda Boose's article.

3. Karen Newman, "Renaissance Family Politics and Shakespeare's *The Taming if the Shrew, English Literary Renaissance* 16 (1986): 95.

4. This and further references to Fletcher's play are essentially based on a recent study by Molly Easo Smith entitled "John Fletcher's Response to the Gender Debate: *The Woman's Prize and The Taming of the Shrew,*" *Papers on Language and Literature* 31, no. 1 (1995): 38–61.

5. Gilles Delleuze, *Difference and Repetition,* (New York: Columbia University Press, 1994).

6. This quotation is taken from Barbara Hodgdon's essay "Katherina Bound; or, Play(K)ating the Strictures of Everyday Life," part of a broader study on how theatrical, cinematic, and televisual versions of Shakespeare reproduce cultural debates. *PMLA,* 107, no. 3 (1992): 538–54.

7. Kathleen McLuskie, "The Act, the Role, and the Actor: Boy Actresses on the Elizabethan Stage," *New Theatre Quarterly* 3 (1987): 120–30.

8. Michel Foucault, *Language, Counter-Memory, Practice: Selected Essays and Interviews,* ed. Donald F. Bouchard (Ithaca: Cornell University Press, 1977), 183.

BIBLIOGRAPHY

Boose, Lynda. "Scolding Brides and Bridling Scolds: Taming the Woman's Unruly Member." *Shakespeare Quarterly* 42 (1991): 179–213.

Deleuze, Gilles. *Difference and Repetition.* New York, Columbia University Press, 1994.

Foucault, Michel. *Language, Counter-Memory, Practice: Selected Essays and Interviews.* Ed. Donald F. Bouchard. Ithaca: Cornell University Press, 1977.

Hodgdon, Barbara. "Katherina Bound, or, Play(K)ating the Strictures of Everyday Life." *PMLA* 107, no. 3 (1992): 538–54.

McLuskie, Kathleen. "The Act, the Role, and the Actor: Boy Actresses on the Elizabethan Stage." *New Theatre Quarterly* 3 (1987): 120–30.

Newman, Karen. "Renaissance Family Politics and Shakespeare's *The Taming of the Shrew.*" *English Literary Renaissance* 16 (1986): 95.

Smith, Molly Easo. "John Fletcher's Response to the Gender Debate: *The Woman's Prize* and *The Taming of the Shrew.*" *Papers on Language and Literature* 31, no. 1 (1995): 38–61.

Shakespeare's *Hamlet,* Salman Rushdie's "Yorick," and the Dilemmas of Tradition

ADELAINE LA GUARDIA NOGUEIRA

> *Art is a passion of the mind. And the imagination works best when it is most free. Western writers have always felt free to be eclectic in their selection of theme, setting, form; Western visual artists have, in this century, been happily raiding the visual storehouses of Africa, Asia, the Philippines. I am sure that we must grant ourselves an equal freedom.*
>
> Salman Rushdie

IN HIS ARTICLE ENTITLED "THE EMPIRE WRITES BACK," IYER CALLS attention to the fact that Britain's former colonies "have begun to capture the very heart of English literature, while transforming the language with new colors, strange cadences and foreign eyes" (1993, 46). He suggests that the Empire has begun to write back in the sense that it is now able to confront the European past—both historical and literary—in order to review and supplement it.

Bombay-born British writer Salman Rushdie stands as an exemplar of the vigor of a generation of postcolonial writers, whose production originates in his "in-between" condition within the cultures he inhabits or through which he circulates, belonging neither to an Indian nor an European tradition, but rather to a hybrid culture. Iyer also enumerates, among the virtues of writers such as Rushdie, the capacity to bring "a foreign punning liberation to the English language. As Rushdie himself has argued, however, writing in the language of the colonizer also means an exploration of the condition of "translated men," those who, by their own status as "not quite" or "outsiders inside" can only view the world not as a whole, offering instead a "stereoscopic vision." Such a condition, he points out, comes not as a loss—something traditionally attributed to translations in general: "I cling, obstinately, to the notion that something can also be gained" (1991, 17). His attitude towards the English language inevitably leads to a remaking of it, because of or despite his ambiguity towards it, which can only reflect a conflict, a linguistic struggle both inside the man as well as outside, in the real world.

In *Imaginary Homelands,* Rushdie also raises the important issue of the consequences for the "polycultural" or "amphibian" writer "of refusing to make any concessions to Western ideas and practices," or "of turning away from the ones that came here with us" (1991, 18). The author states that there is no definitive answer to such a dilemma, or, at least, he does not attempt to prescribe principles of literary conduct. Rushdie's anxiety can, in part, be translated in the terms postulated by Harold Bloom (1973), according to whom the writer fears that the works of his predecessor assume priority over his own writing. Bloom explains that the "strong poet" must engage in a fierce literary battle with his precursors, a warfare similar to an Oedipal struggle, through which a man is made a writer by destroying his literary father(s).

In Rushdie's case, however, the problem becomes further complicated by the fact that, as a polycultural heir, he is placed within the impossible condition in which he must decide precisely who his literary and cultural fathers are before he can effectively "kill" them. The writer's position, therefore, reminds one of the condition of Prince Hamlet, who has lost a father and is faced with the challenge of having to murder his own stepfather. *East, West* is a witness to what T. S. Eliot once postulated about the writer's talent: his readings, when carried alive in his mind, make of his conception of poetry (or, for our purposes, his literary conception) a "living whole" of "all that has been written." "Yorick" constitutes one among a number of short stories in *East, West*—itself composed of three parts, wherein the texts are grouped as belonging to an Eastern or a Western tradition, and finally, through the mixture of themes and the new treatment of language, a third term that transcends polarities is proposed in the hybrid East/West category of texts. Thus, an apparent unrelatedness or a jagged brokenness of styles seems to prevail throughout the book, but that is part of a rather calculated textual scheme that attempts to overcome cultural/literary boundaries by assuming instead a more conciliatory stand, first through the juxtaposition of Eastern and Western literary styles and eventually through the blurring of such boundaries. Therefore, the whole work demands a comprehensive study of the strategies explored and their significance in the total scheme. The relevance of such study would be in that Rushdie's readers and critics would be better equipped to evaluate the new paths this literature on the threshold of cultures is treading. Hence, the aim of this study is limited. I shall consider it a fragment of a possible answer, which awaits enlarged readings and further critical inquiry.

In the Ruins of Tradition

First published in 1994, *East, West* includes among its short stories the dramatic narrative entitled "Yorick," a remarkably self-conscious piece of work in which Shakespeare's *Hamlet* is rewritten. Therefore, it is possible to examine the intertextual practice therein so as to reveal the modes through which the new text is produced, the processes of appropriation, absorption, integration, and/or rejection of the elements belonging to the source material or style(s) being imitated. By so doing, further inferences can be made regarding the writer's relation to the Western canon, how he deals with the questions of influence, and the dilemmas of tradition in literature.

Rushdie's choice of Shakespeare may have obvious reasons. Being the fountainhead of all wisdom, the Bard's texts have a prescriptive force that gives that writer the position of preeminence shared by other great figures of the pantheon, such as Sophocles, Homer, or Cervantes. However, the fact that Shakespeare's texts continue to exercise such long-term effects wherever they are read is due not only to their obvious quality but also to the fact that the texts have been brought into constant connection and articulation with other texts, "socially and politically mobilized in different ways within different class practices, differentially inscribed within the practices of educational, cultural and linguistic institutions and so on." (Drakakis 1991). In short, their inherent openness and dialectical nature have allowed for a plurality of rewritings and interpretations, thus offering a multitude of exploration possibilities for both readers and writers.

Hamlet comes as specially fruitful material for someone seeking to overcome the so-called anxiety of influence since it is, first and foremost, a story of parricide, the story of a man's desire to kill his father and his inability to carry out his design. Rushdie's choice falls upon that moment in the play in which the truly demotic voices are heard, those of the clowns in act 5, scene 1, as they comment upon the dubious legitimacy of Ophelia's burial and thus demystify the aristocratic death ritual. In other words, Rushdie rewrites *Hamlet* from a particular point in which the oppressed group in the play, those located in a liminar position (which may reflect the writer's own situation), are allowed to remake the world through the word. Built mainly from such fragments within Shakespeare's tragedy, Rushdie's text reflects a sort of excavation proces' within the ruins of Western literary tradition, from which certain productive elements will be retrieved or, to use T. S. Eliot's words, where "the living in the dead" may be found.

Act 5, scene 1 is permeated with what Bakhtin defines as "a carnival sense of the world" and "a joyful relativity," typical of carnivalistic genres. The liminar space of the cemetery works as a stage upon which a familiar, comic, and profane dialogue on the threshold *(Schwellendialog)* takes place between the clowns and Hamlet. In the passage, the prince is found contemplating the skull of Yorick, the old King's Fool, whereupon Hamlet comments on him as "a fellow of infinite jest, of most excellent fancy: he hath borne me on his back a thousand times" (H 5.1. 180–82).

In such extraordinary context, a profound word is provoked through laughter, which exposes the inconsistencies of human nature and social conventions, while celebrating insanity, naiveté or nonsense as valid human attributes. While preparing Ophelia's grave, the two clowns comment, lightly and humorously, on the law that affords nobles who commit suicide the privilege of a Christian burial: ". . . and the more pity that great folk should have count'- nance in this world to drown and hang themselves more than their even Christian" (5.1 26–29). The clown's words seem to insist on an order in which nobles and commoners can be one of a kind, as in death. Their dialogue also contains parodic references to the Bible, which bring its serious tone and religious content down to a human, familiar context, consequently destroying its solemnity or rigid authority. No ceremony is awarded the dead by the clowns, which allows for a more concrete and realistic view of death and, from such behavior, an awareness of the illusions and vanities that surround the living is aroused. Death levels us all, the passage suggests, but that is also a call for social equality. Shakespeare's text may be satirical or even cynical, but it is undoubtedly the result of the author's terrifying clairvoyance.

As he explicitly avoids any moral or ethical prescriptions, Shakespeare endows the reader with the power to contemplate the comedy of life which places men in their roles as "poor players."

Whether dead or alive, high or low, inside or outside, the play celebrates the relativity of all planes. Naturalistic aspects linked to death, degraded language, and observation from unusual points of view lend the passage its comic aspect, as in ritual laughter, which seems to insist on change or a shift of authorities and truths. Thus, its scope within *Hamlet* goes beyond the mere "refreshment" of an intermezzo, touching upon social issues and profound human questions through a carnivalistic sense of the world. Those are the aspects that appeal to the contemporary writer and which will be exhaustively explored in his rewriting.

The Yorick motif has inspired writers throughout the centuries. Poised between life and death, Yorick's skull is a powerful visual representation of limen. The audience that faces the death mask is faced by it in turn as a mirror of life's transience, the futility of all human pretensions to power, to social and economic ascension, to intellectual notoriety, to all sorts of illusions that human beings construct to celebrate the apparent materiality of being. As such, it acquires a particular significance in the hands of writers such as Salman Rushdie, who wish to convey a sense of being on the threshold of cultures and literatures.

Laurence Sterne adopted Yorick's name as a pseudonym in *A Sentimental Journey,* and in *Tristram Shandy* he turned it into the figure of the lively, witty, and heedless parson of Danish extract, a probable descendant of *Hamlet*'s Fool. The narrator in *East, West* claims the Yorick tale has been brought down to him from the nineteenth-century writer—a transgressive attitude towards the "original" source which serves to affirm a literary legacy. By claiming that the Yorick motif comes not from an original father, the narrator significantly camouflages the idea of source and disregards literary paternity. In the contemporary version, Hamlet's confusion of his father's name or his failure to recognize him as such also reinforces the theme of parricide. Such an "unfilial gesture" suggests that the writing practice in "Yorick" belongs first and foremost to the carnivalistic lineage of modern writers such as Sterne, while it explicitly parodies the Shandean style:

> Yorick's saga . . . that same ancient account which fell . . . into the hands of a certain—no, a most uncertain—Tristram, who . . . was neither triste nor ram, the frothiest, most heady Shandy of a fellow; and which has now come into my possession. . . . Truly a velluminous history!—which is my present intent not merely to abbreviate, but, in addition, to explicate, annotate, hyphenate, palatinate & permanganate. (64)

As Ostovich (1992) affirms, *Tristram Shandy* plays on the notion of Madam Reader as hobby-horse. Rushdie explores this idea through the visual representation of young Hamlet astride Yorick's back. And just as it happens in *Tristram,* the contemporary text plays reductive games with the reader, creating a literary image of folly and stimulating a response on various interpretive levels. An acute awareness of the hermeneutical function of the text is found in Sterne and Rushdie as both address the "audience" directly as a physical presence or through appealing devices that "spur the hobby-horsical reader trotting along."

If Rushdie adopts Sterne's style—its constant interruptions, flourished digressions, and wayward typographic marks—he does so with the same concern found in Sterne's *Tristram Shandy,* which is to call the reader's attention to the writing practice itself: the artifices it adopts, the illusions it conveys, its vain pretension at depicting "real life" in minute detail. However, critical distance towards Sterne's style and tone is established as the contemporary writer inserts self-deprecating comments like: "O *******! let me say the text begins to ramble, listing in gruesome detail all the crimes committed by the *prince* . . . in brief, a most lamentable lack of brevity, which we shall rectify here without delay (71).

Similarly, Shakespearean diction, despite its variety, does not go unscathed, especially when it assumes the usually serious tone of tragedies:

> *Yor.(awakes)* O, a! What whoreson Pelion's this, that, tumbling down from Ossa, so interrupts my spine? . . . I interrupt myself, for there occurs to me a discordant Note: would any man, awakened from deepest slumber by the arrival on his back of a seven-year-old princeling, truly retain such a command of metaphor and classical allusion as is indicated in the text? (67)

The story is built upon the assumption that the narrator has come upon an old parchment that once belonged to Laurence Sterne. The presentation of material evidence such as letters or documents, which constituted a cliché in the eighteenth-century literary tradition intended to lend credibility to the account, is parodied by Rushdie. And as happens in *Tristram Shandy,* the text as a physical object is represented through the figure of the "strong vellum."

This metaphor pervades the text, as the following quotation indicates: ". . . itself the tale of a piece of vellum,—both the tale of the vellum itself and the tale inscribed thereupon" (64). The metaphor suggests that this is the story of how a text came to be or, generally speaking, of how texts come to be. In other words, it is through the telling of a specific story that the writer self-consciously will treat the question of how texts come to be. It therefore implicates the question of origin, of originality versus copy.

It could also be read as the story of the circuit involved in the reading process, as it implicates the reading of both a story and of its origins, as well as the writing process itself, being a representation, or the representation of a representation—a technique also employed by Shakespeare as he inserts a theatrical performance within *Hamlet*. The palimpsestic quality of the text and, consequently, of the writing practice itself is here indicated as well.

Rushdie's story can also be read as the history of literary cultures, as they cross time and space, become immortalized by the fact that they are reworked again through various processes of appropriation and rupture which, though destructive, guarantee the renewal of traditions, hence an almost mythical practice. Such procedure is not too far from the postmodern recycling process, defined in "Yorick" in the following terms:

> [F]or the existence upon our earth of the material known as strong vellum, which, like the earth upon which I have supposed it to exist . . . this noble stuff endures—if not for ever, then at least till men consciously destroy it . . .—for it's a true fact that men take an equal pleasure in annihilating both the ground upon which they stand while they live and the substance (I mean the paper) upon which they may remain, immortalized. (63)

The materiality of writing is recalled by the word *vellum*, as a whole economic history of writing involving East and West is synthesized in such reference, for the vellum, a parchment originally made from calf skin, came as a substitute to the papyrus made in the East, after an embargo of the product by the Greek city of Pergamon. Destruction, therefore, is not restricted to the writing practices, but affects the whole economy which involves and controls the writing and reading activities.

The plot in "Yorick" relies on a series of carnivalistic inversions, mésalliances, and decrownings. Hamlet is depicted as a merry seven-year-old who rejoices in harassing old Yorick—though the boy is already cursed with insomnia and "a mother-loving passion." The jester is married to young Ophelia and they have a baby child. The heroine is less than half the jester's age and "more than twice his looks." The romantic element is especially ridiculed through the heroine, who is plagued with "the rottenest smelling breath on earth," which made men run away from her instantly except, of course, the jester who "courted her with a peg on his nose." Such parodic treatment of Ophelia is similar to that afforded by Shakespeare to his dark lady in Sonnet 130, in which the whole tradition of feminine characterization is placed in check as the poet declares:

> My mistress' eyes are nothing like the sun;
> Coral is far more red than her lips' red.
> If snow be white, why then her breasts are dun;
> If hairs be wires, black wires grow on her head.
> I have seen roses damasked, red and white,
> But no such roses see I in her cheeks;
> And in some perfumes is there more delight
> Than in the breath that from my mistress reeks.

The stereotypical image of women in Elizabethan and Petrarchan sonnets is thus reviewed as they address the beloved one as fair-haired, fair-eyed, blessed with rosy cheeks, and delicate manners: true goddesses that walk in invariably perfect beauty, leaving behind them a trail of the sweetest scents.

In Shakespeare's *Hamlet,* Ophelia embodies an extremely "feminine" weakness. She becomes the symbol of Oedipal repression being divided between the authority of her father and the love she secretly cherishes for Hamlet. As John Drakakis points out,

> she is an "object" of masculine authority and control, subject to the patriarchal law of her father; his death, and Hamlet's rejection of her produce a crisis in her own subjectivity and the psychological fragmentation and death that result register the danger produced by that deprivation. (1991, 46)

Only in madness can the heroine assume her own desire, manifested through a language richly drenched in sexual connotation:

> By Gis, and by Saint Charity,
> Alack, and fie for shame!
> Young men will do't, if they come to't,

> By Cock, they are to blame.
> Quoth she "Before you tumbled me,
> You promised me to wed."

Unlike Shakespeare's Ophelia, Rushdie's heroine is endowed with clear-sightedness as well as an ability for feigning—as can be observed through her frequent asides. She plays the role of a narrator/commentator who sheds light upon the story:

> *Oph. (aside)* My husband never loved this prince; a spoiled brat, and cursed with sleeplessness, which plague he passes on to us. Here's how we wake each morning, with royal fists a-tearing at our hair, or heir-apparent buttocks jig-jogging on our necks. Were he my child . . . good morrow, sweet my prince! (68)

The world in "Yorick" is pervaded by an acutely Rabelaisian sensibility and a joyful celebration of whatever is impure, unhealthy, degraded, decaying, or putrefying. Thus, "something is rotten in the state of Denmark" (1.4.67) is rephrased and extended in Rushdie's text to qualify the heroine's breath as

> the rottenest-smelling exhalation in the State of Denmark, a tepid stench of rat's livers, toad's piss, high game-birds, rotting teeth, gangrene, skewered corpses, burning witchflesh, sewers, politician's consciences, skunk-holes, sepulchres, and all the Beelzebubbling picklevats of Hell! (66)

To those low, naturalistic details others are added of a more anatomic and cannibalistic nature, which reflect the writing practice in Rushdie's text, as it seems to thrive on the flesh of other texts. The new writer's literary hunger is as large as the old imperial gluttony, a truly Rabelaisian banquet:

> Picture a banquet at fabulous Elsinore: boar's heads, sheep's eyes, parson's noses, goose-breasts, calves' livers, fish-roes, venison haunches, pig's trotters. . . . Tonight Horwendillus and his Gertrude are feasting FORTINBRAS, hoping to stay his territorial greed by satisfying his belly's equal liking for expansion. (73)

Political disorder is depicted in Shakespeare through the same "gluttonous excess" in the imagery of oceans eating the land with "impetuous haste" and "riotous heads" to announce Laertes's entrance in the kingdom as a threat to Claudius and the established order (Drakakis 1991).

The question of originality and authenticity is challenged in "Yorick" through the author's reference to the prince's "unfilial mistake" in believing the ghost's name to be Hamlet, which, he claims, contradicts the facts narrated in Saxo Grammaticus's *History of the Danes*. In fact, the year in which Shakespeare wrote *Hamlet* has given rise to much discussion.

The first version of the play appeared in 1599, was completed in 1601, and first staged in 1602. References by Nash, Lodge, and others indicate that a play on the same subject, now lost, preceded Shakespeare's, and it was presumably a source. For Malone, this may have been Thomas Kyd's *Hamlet* or even the old prose *Hystorie of Hamblet*. Dr. Bell suggests the source may have been Hans Sach's *Hamlet*, a version in German, which appeared in 1558. Shakespeare's chief nondramatic source was Saxo Grammaticus's narrative in his *Historiae Danicae* as retold by Francis de Belleforest, a French gentleman. Belleforest's *Histoires Tragiques* is a collection of original and nonoriginal novels translated chiefly from Bandello's texts. Its first volume came out in 1564, and each new tome was published successively for some five years. The fifth volume has this title: *Avec quelle ruse Amleth, qui depuis fut roy de Dannemarch, vengea la mort de son pere Horveundille, occis par Fengon son frere, & autre occurence de son histoire* (Furness 1963).

Rushdie is aware of Shakespeare's sources and suggests, through the reference to Horwendillus (a name similar to that of Hamlet's father in Saxo Grammaticus's text), that the sources for *Hamlet* are vague and various, thus that the original text was the product of successively transgressive operations, which substantiates the possible claim that new authors are not in debt with their fathers from tradition, since all creative acts result from similar "trickeries." T. S. Eliot, through his reading of J. M. Robertson, correctly calls attention to the fact that *Hamlet* is a "stratification," representing the collective efforts of various authors, "each making what he could out of the work of his predecessors" (1965, 99).

Shakespeare's *Hamlet* is given a new temporal dimension through Rushdie's reworking of the play. Time is stretched backwards, as the story comprises the prince's childhood and Yorick's life—and it also encompasses the events described in Shakespeare's play. By setting his story in an anterior time, the author again toys with the concept of originality and source while reversing their positions—as much as he toys with the idea of a linear time. Thus, Rushdie's story becomes a pre-text that anticipates Shakespeare's tragedy, sending from the present a new light upon which the text from the past may be read in a fresh way.

In Shakespeare, Hamlet seems to question the very foundations of language. The prince plays havoc with the signifying chain, allowing for an ineluctable "free sliding" of the sign which baffles his interlocutors as the extract below exemplifies:

> *Ros.* What have you done, my lord, with the dead body?
> *Ham.* Compounded it with dust, whereto 'tis kin.
> *Ros.* Tell us where 'tis, that we may take it thence
> And bear it to the chapel.
> *Ham.* Do not believe it.
> *Ros.* Believe what?
> *Ham.* That I can keep your counsel and not mine own. Besides, to be demanded of a sponge—what replication should be made by the son of a king?
> *Ros.* Take you me for a sponge, my lord?
> *Ham.* Ay, sir; that soaks up the King's countenance, his rewards, his authorities. But such officers do the King best service in the end. He keeps them, like an ape an apple in the corner of his jaw, first mouth'd to be last swallowed. When he needs what you have gleaned, it is but squeezing you, and, sponge, you shall be dry again.
> *Ros.* I understand you not, my lord.
> *Ham.* I am glad of it. A knavish speech sleeps in a foolish ear.
> *Ros.* My lord, you must tell us where the body is, and go with us to the King.
> *Ham.* The body is with the King, but the King is not with the body. The king is a thing—
> *Guil.* A thing, my lord?
> *Ham.* Of nothing. Bring me to him. Hide fox, and all after."
>
> (4.2. 4–30)

Rushdie's Hamlet preserves such linguistic qualities, as he is depicted as the prince whose speech is poisonous. However, the incantatory power of his words, as in Plato's pharmacy, is turned into a deadly medicine which annihilates its own user:

> **What was the princely poison?**
> Only solve your own riddle, Reader, and you'll know . . . there, never mind, I'll solve it for you. It was SPEECH. O deadliest venene! Being insubstantial, though very serpentine, it knows no antidote. . . . (78)

In Rushdie's text Hamlet persuades his father's fool that Horwendillus and Ophelia had an affair. The whole tradition around the theme of treason and jealousy, such as one finds in *Othello,* is evoked through the canonical prototypes represented by the handkerchief or billet-doux, and parodied in "Yorick" through the golden nose plugs cruelly brought forth as proofs by the young boy against the virtuous heroine. In *Othello,* unreasoned jealousy is produced by Iago's shrewd and persuasive words, which themselves become the strongest evidences of adultery. The narrator in "Yorick" refers to the "deadliest, unsubstantial venene" represented by speech as a powerful device used by Hamlet to produce a false reality; the same tool is explored for carnivalistic purposes:

... no, I cannot say that terrible word of doing, when in truth was nothing done!—And possibly (the vellum is smudged, at this point, by ancient tears or other salty fluid) the cruel boy brought "proofs":—a pair of golden nose-plugs, wrapped in a forged billet-doux? Or was it a handkerchief? No matter. The damage is done, and Yorick is multiply a fool: always a Fool by trade, he has become a doubled Dolt for being the Prince's gull, and (in his own eyes, for, as he sees it, seeming a Fool in the lovers' eyes) an Ass as well, an Ass most Foolish in appearance, because of the cuckold's horns between his ears" (79).

The prince whose speech is poisonous eventually drinks from a poisonous cup. The same dynamic principle is present in the idea of the strong vellum, as both the tale of a parchment and the tale inscribed in it. Dynamism and reversion can also be seen in the fact that the man who performs the role of a fool becomes a fool in "real life" and is thus turned into an even more tragic figure than that character in Shakespeare's *Hamlet.* As an effect of such reversibility the cheerful possibility emerges of destroying dualities as fixed entities. To be or not to be is not a question in Rushdie's text, since the polarities present/past, life/death or writing/reading, can be reverted one upon the other.

The paradox of death as life is also part of the narrative logic. Yorick's skull, retrieved from Shakespeare's tragicomic scene, is provided with life and endowed with reproductive powers. Yorick's child, the seed/product metaphor, emerges for immortality, as it outlives the deaths of its predecessors and is disseminated throughout the world.

East, West ostensibly pays homage to different texts, styles, and motifs from East and West, as it eventually proposes a fusion of both or the abolition of the very idea of a Western or an Eastern literary tradition. In its concern with cultural traditions, it is built as a double voiced text in which various texts or writing practices are examined from the perspective of their influence and the possibility of their renewal through destruction. In other words, the books' relevance cannot be fully appreciated through a mere relation to a short story per se, but through the richness of its references. If the text celebrates influence, however, it does not imply this is a passive reception, but rather a productive encounter with the other text that excludes hierarchies based on claims of precedence or originality. In fact, the text testifies to what Bakhtin described in the past as an intertextual practice that he called dialogism. Rushdie produces a radical comment upon Shakespeare's tragedy, contesting both its "original" status, established meanings and authority.

Rushdie's enterprise in "Yorick" indicates that the value of a work of art lies not only in the invention of forms, but also in its unusual combination of old forms, its discovery of unknown worlds or unexplored zones and possiblities—where its fertility and originality reside. The break with the linear succession that "Yorick" imposes upon *Hamlet* also testifies to what Octavio Paz has described as "an art of conjugation," one in which the reader's coparticipation is demanded, an art that counts on the combination, dispersion, and reunion of languages, spaces, times, and cultures.

Salman Rushdie works in the preservation factory by rearranging the sequences, stretching and compressing time, or reorganizing its elements. The tumpty-tum stylistic recourse explored by the narrator in "Yorick" draws one's attention to the storytelling process, or the rhythmic, linear sequences that punctuate the Western writing tradition, which the contemporary writer makes a point of disrupting. The reader is invited to participate as a coworker, by assuming, as Linda Hutcheon (1985) suggests, a more dynamic role during his reading time—or, as the narrator humorously declares, by "exercising one's dog," one's freedom of reading and creating, exactly what Rushdie proposes in the epigraph above.

Reading, as the text suggests, should not be an evaluative measurement between different works. If the author does not prove to be too faithful to the "original," it is because sources are always questionable, or because he believes stories exist to be told in different ways, for the sheer freedom and pleasure of writing and rewriting, telling, listening to, or reading them: "[S]o let the versions of the story coexist, for there's no need to choose" (81). Yorick's seeds, dispersed as they are through the world, seem to insist on the idea that all versions of the story are legitimate. Fathers can rest in peace, since their children-texts, like language itself, belong nowhere, are nobody's property, but constitute a universal heritage.

Like the Argentine writer Jorge Luis Borges in "Kafka and Its Precursors," Rushdie forces us to reread the works belonging to the Western literary tradition not as a source or influence for the contemporary writer, but rather as instigating works in view of the fact that the contemporary writer exists for them. Borges believed that each writer creates his own precursors in the sense that his work modifies our conception of the past as it will modify the future. In Rushdie's words that means the following:

> ... [A]nd multicoloured generations follow, ending (I'll now reveal) in this present, humble AUTHOR; whose ancestry may be proved by this, which he holds in common with the whole sorry line of the family, that his chief weakness is for the telling of a particular species of Tale, which learned men have termed chanticleric, and also taurean. (83)

For the author, tradition is turned into a question of reading, but as readings become different in time so does tradition, when viewed as a constant process of review and change. No longer in debt to it, the new text can be inscribed in the pre-existing order, as Eliot argued, altering its arrangement. The contemporary writer can also inscribe himself as a truthful heir to that carnivalistic lineage in which Shakespeare, Sterne, Melville, Machado de Assis, and others participate as Rushdie himself acknowledges in *Imaginary Homelands*.

In conclusion, one should recall, once again, T. S. Eliot's statement on the marks of a mature poet, or, for our purposes, the fiction writer, as one who not merely restores a tradition which has been in abeyance, but one who is able to fuse together as many straying strands of tradition as possible (Matthiessen 1950). Eliot's literary principles, which have been applied to reinforce the notion of a European literary canon, acquire their fullest richness in Rushdie's text, for through the larger scopes of writers on the borderline of traditions the canon can be forced to recognize the value of very special texts, including non-European ones.

The straying strands are thus recovered, like Yorick's skull or his seeds, which are disseminated throughout East and West. Shakespeare's legacy, itself the legacy of forgotten or lost fathers, is passed on to Sterne and now to Rushdie, representing the work of the present and the past, of East and West, fused together, to examplify not abeyance to tradition, nor mere imitation of it, but a rediscovery of the new in the old—or the old in the new—a task which could only be achieved by master writers such as Rushdie and Shakespeare, who truly depict an individual talent.

BIBLIOGRAPHY

Bakhtin, Mikhail. *The Dialogic Imagination.* Trans. Michael Holquist and Caryl Emerson. Austin: University of Texas Press, 1981.

———. *Problems of Dostoevsky's Poetics.* Trans. Caryl Emerson. Minneapolis: University of Minnesota Press, 1985.

Bloom, Harold. *The Anxiety of Influence.* New York: Routledge, 1973.

Boehmer, Elleke, *Colonial and Postcolonial Literature.* Oxford: Oxford University Press, 1995.

Borges, Jorge L. "Kafka y sus Precursores." In *Otras Inquisiciones.* Madrid: Alianza Editorial, 1981,

Bullough, Geoffrey. *Narrative and Dramatic Sources of Shakespeare.* London: Routledge and Kegan Paul, 1962.

Drakakis, John. "Myth, History and *Hamlet.*" *Anais do XXIII SENAPULLI* (February 1991): 39–47.

Eliot, T. S. *Selected Prose.* Ed. John Hayward. Harmondsworth, England: Penguin, 1965.

Furness, H. H., ed. *Hamlet: A New Variorum Edition of Shakespeare.* 2 vols. New York: Dover Publications, 1963.

Gottschalk, Paul. *The Meanings of Hamlet.* Albuquerque: University of New Mexico Press, 1972.

Holderness, Graham. " 'What Ish My Nation?' Shakespeare and National Identities." *Anais do XXIII SENAPULLI* (February 1991): 19–28.

Hutcheon, Linda. *Narcissistic Narrative: the Metafictional Paradox.* London: Methuen, 1985.

Iyer, Pico. "The Empire Writes Back." *Time,* February 8, 1993), 46–51.

Levin, Harry. *The Question of Hamlet.* London: Oxford University Press, 1978.

Matthiessen, F. *The Achievement of T. S. Eliot.* London: Oxford University Press, 1950.

Ostovich, Helen. "Reader as Hobby-Horse in *Tristram Shandy.*" In *Tristram Shandy: Contemporary Critical Essays,* ed. Melvyn New. London: Macmillan, 1992.

Paz, Octavio. *Signos em Rotação.* Trans Sebastião Uchoa Leite. São Paulo: Perspectiva, 1972.

Resende, Aimara da Cunha. "Remythologizing Shakespeare: The Bard as Cultural Product," *Anais do XXIII SENAPULLI (February 1991): 87–90.*

Rushdie, Salman. *East, West.* London: Vintage, 1995.

———. *Imaginary Homelands.* Ed. John Hayward. Harmondsworth, England: Penguin, 1992.

"*Uhuru!*": Césaire's and Shakespeare's Uncontainable Calibans

José Roberto O'Shea

This chapter has a twofold division. The first part addresses Shakespeare's *The Tempest,* first performed in 1611, and first published in 1623, mainly in terms of a critical discussion of the play's traditional versus revisionist readings; the second focuses on *Une Tempête,* a play by the Martinican writer Aimé Césaire, first published in 1969, as a radical Caribbean rewriting of Shakespeare's analogue.

Traditional readings have rendered *The Tempest* mainly as a pastoral tragicomedy with the themes of nature, art, and reconciliation at its center. In the words of Peter Hulme, "fully and confidently Mediterranean, moving majestically to its reconciliatory climax with hardly a ripple to disturb its surface" (1986, 105). Audiences in traditionally envisaged productions have too often been invited to see *The Tempest* as a drama of magic, magnanimity, and forgiveness, and in many classrooms students are still asked to consider the play merely as part of "the romance tradition" in English literature, or urged to concentrate on the play's undeniable aesthetic value—all prioritized over the imperial theme.

In fact, traditional readings have excluded the imperial theme from the play, by promoting Prospero and attempting to make the spectators identify with him (instead of Caliban), by drawing attention to the magical effects produced by Prospero, so that the Calibans in the audience might be, as it were, awed into complicity with the colonial closure that is part of the play's enterprise (Loomba 1989, 146–47). To be sure, in idealist, essentialist readings and productions, Prospero has invariably been presented as an exemplar of timeless human values, praised for the way in which his hard-earned magical powers enable him to teach the shipwrecked Italians a moral lesson, to heal the civil strife, and, more importantly, to triumph over his own vengefulness by forgiving his enemies (Skura 1989, 42).[1]

For now, one implication of idealist readings needs to be foregrounded: the relationship between savagery, slavery, and civility. Surely, the Aristotelian notion of slavery as the necessary stage between savagery and civility is a common seventeenth-century topos (Norbrook 1992, 38). Surprisingly, however, the notion is picked up by twentieth-century critics, for example, Hallett Smith and Frank Kermode, who, respectively, see Caliban as "beyond the lower limits of the human race" (1607) and as a "natural slave" (xliii).

The cast list included at the end of the play in the 1623 Folio, whether authorial or interpolated by Ralph Crane, does describe Caliban as a "salvage and deformed slave" (Yale Facsimile 19), and, for Kermode, this means that Caliban is to be taken as Aristotle's "natural slave," incapable of civility. Drawing on book 1 of The Politics, especially chapters 3 through 6, Kermode argues that if Aristotle is right in surmising that men who are inferior to others, as the body is to the mind, are "slaves by nature," and that it is advantageous for such men to be always under government, then, "the black and mutilated cannibal must be the natural slave of the European gentleman, and *a fortiori,* the salvage and deformed Caliban of the learned Prospero" (xliii).

But is Kermode's reading of Aristotle sensible? For one thing, it has been argued that Aristotle does not really prove the naturalness of slavery, that apart from the flimsiness of the argument, from analogy, Aristotle himself admits that nature, while making obvious and visible the distinction between humans and animals, has not done so for free men and slaves. Aristotle's point is merely that in any society there must be "hewers of wood and drawers of water" and that such labor should be done by those best fitted by nature—physically—for menial tasks (Sinclair 34–35).

However, Prospero and Miranda do see Caliban as a natural slave and as an inferior; Prospero refers to Caliban several times as "slave", **his** slave (1.2.311, 316, 347, etc.), and he admits to Miranda:

> ... as 'tis,
> We cannot miss him. He does make our fire,
> Fetch in our wood, and serves in offices
> That profit us.
>
> (1.2.313–16)

Miranda, on her part, famously, claims:

> When thou didst not, savage,
> Know thine own meaning, but wouldst gabble like
> A thing most brutish, I endow'd thy purposes
> With words that made them known.
>
> (1.2.358–61)

As David Norbrook has aptly stressed, if Sycorax died before Caliban was of the age to speak, Miranda's claim may be literally true; but, more importantly, the claim reflects the standpoint of colonialists who considered Indian languages intrinsically debased (1992, 40).

Be it as "natural slave," an inferior "beyond the lower limits of the human race," or, in Prospero's curse "a born devil on whose nature / Nurture can never stick" (4.1.188–89), traditional readings have rendered Caliban, monolithically, in terms of his alleged inferiority, cultural incapacity, ungratefulness, and ultimate submission to Prospero's power.

Yet, Caliban is more than that. As Alden and Virginia Vaughan have demonstrated, particularly outside the hegemonic Anglo center, there is something about the Caliban metaphor that has an overwhelming appeal, something that continues to elicit revision and appropriation:

> There is no denying the power of the Caliban metaphor on the Third World, even if its impact on political and cultural consciousness defies precise measurement. . . . That Caliban served so many masters surely reflects Shakespeare's unmatched universality and *The Tempest*'s adaptability to colonial contexts, whether seen from the imperialist's or the native's perspective. (1991, 171)

Ahistorical notions of universality have become the object of increasing objection, but the Vaughan's stress on the appeal of the Caliban metaphor can be attested, and not only in the periphery but in the center as well, although, no doubt, the former has been more vocal about such appeal.[2]

However, as might be expected, it is in the periphery that revisionist appropriations of *The Tempest* have been more daring. In 1878 Ernest Renan published his drama *Caliban: suite de "La Tempête."* In Renan's work, although Caliban is the incarnation of the people presented in their worst light, this time his conspiracy against Prospero is successful, and he does achieve power—which only ineptitude and corruption prevent him from retaining. In Renan, a revengeful Prospero lurks in the darkness and Ariel disappears.

Then, in 1900, the Uruguayan José Enrique Rodó publishes, at the age of twenty-nine, one of the most famous works of Latin American culture: *Ariel,* written in direct response to the 1898 American intervention in Cuba. North American civilization is implicitly presented there as Caliban, while Ariel would come to incarnate—or should incarnate—the best of what Rodó does not hesitate to call more than once "our civilization," that is, Latin America (viz. Retamar 1989, 11).

From Renan and Rodó, slowly but surely, particularly in the periphery, new readings and appropriations of *The Tempest* begin to coalesce. And what largely takes the place of canonized interpretation—especially since George Lamming's pioneering essay of 1960, *Pleasures of Exile*—is the reading that moves colonialism, and therefore, the New World, the Atlantic material, to the center of the play (Hulme 1986, 106). And since my foci here are Caribbean appropriations of *The Tempest,* I must stress Lamming's work, the first fully fledged Caribbean appropriation of Shakespeare's analogue. Lamming is also considered the first Caribbean writer to champion Caliban (Nixon 1978, 565).

And Bob Nixon is right in arguing that the era from the late 1950s to the early 1970s was marked in the Caribbean (and in Africa) by a "rush of newly articulated anti-colonial sentiment associated with the burgeoning of both international black consciousness and localized nationalist movements" (558). Nixon reminds us that between 1957 and 1973 the vast majority of African and the larger Caribbean colonies won their independence. This period was distinguished among African and Caribbean intellectuals by a "pervasive mood of optimistic outrage."

These individuals comprised the first generation from their regions "to call collectively for a renunciation of Western standards and a refutation of the bequeathed values of the colonial powers" (ibid.). Thus, in the context of the challenges to an increasingly discredited European colonialism, dissenting intellectuals choose to resort to Shakespeare's *Tempest* as "a way of amplifying their calls for decolonization within the bounds of the dominant cultures" (Nixon 557–58).

However, some time before the emergence of Caribbean new

readings of *The Tempest,* there appeared in Paris, in 1950, Octave Mannoni's *Psychologie de la colonisation.* Significantly, the English translation (1956) was to be entitled *Prospero and Caliban: The Psychology of Colonization.* To approach his subject, Mannoni formulates the Prospero complex, defined, in Retamar's paraphrase, as the sum of those unconscious neurotic tendencies that delineate, at the same time, the paternalist colonial and the racist whose daughter has been the object of an (imaginary) attempted rape at the hands of an inferior being (12). Mannoni's understanding of the psychological climate of colonialism is articulated through an opposition between the Prospero (or inferiority) complex and the Caliban (or dependence) complex. Still according to Mannoni, Europeans in Madagascar (site of his investigation) typically displayed the need, common among people from a competitive society, to feel highly regarded and to dominate. The Madagascars, on the other hand, were found to be marked by a Caliban complex, a dependence on authority allegedly characteristic of a people forced out of a tribal society, into the competitive hierarchies of Western culture (Nixon 563).

Mannoni's assessment of *The Tempest* has been found simplistic and reductive. He values the play most highly for what he takes to be Shakespeare's dramatization of two cultures' mutual sense of a trust betrayed: Prospero is a dissembler, Caliban, an ingrate. For Mannoni, Caliban does not complain of being exploited; he complains of being betrayed. Caliban's conspiracy is an action, in Mannoni's words, "not to win his freedom, for he could not support freedom, but to have a new master whose 'footlicker' he can become"; and Mannoni concludes: "It would be hard to find a better example of the dependence complex in its pure state" (qtd. in Nixon 562–63).

As might be expected, a strong reaction against Mannoni ensued. His views were refuted by African and Caribbean intellectuals who, already in the 1950s, sensed the imminence of large-scale decolonization in their regions. Besides, the insinuation that, as a native, Caliban is incapable of surviving on his own and does not even aspire to independence causes considerable affront and spurs appropriations of *The Tempest* that, in effect, rehabilitate Caliban into a heroic figure (Nixon 564).

One of the first such refutations came from Frantz Fanon. The theory that Caliban suffers from a dependence complex that leads him neurotically to require and naturally accept the presence of

Prospero as colonizer is squarely rejected by Fanon in chapter 4 of *Black Skins, White Masks* (1952), blatantly entitled *The So-Called Dependence Complex of Colonized Peoples.*

Like Frantz Fanon, Aimé Césaire finds Mannoni's utter disregard for economic exploitation disturbing and charges him with reducing colonialism to an encounter between two psychological types with complimentary dispositions who, at least for a while, find their needs mutually satisfied (Nixon 564). All in all, by the end of the 1960s, new readings of *The Tempest* became hegemonic in the Caribbean. In 1969, in Retamar's words, "Caliban is taken up with pride as our symbol" by three Antillian writers, each expressing himself in one of the main colonial languages of the Caribbean. In that year, Césaire published, in French, *Une Tempête: D'après La Tempête de Shakespeare—adaptation pour un théâtre nègre;* the Barbadian Edward Brathwaite brought out his book of poems *Islands,* in English, and Retamar himself published the famous essay, in Spanish, "Cuba hasta Fidel," which discusses the identification of Latin Americans with Caliban (Retamar 1989, 13).

Ever since the contribution of these Caribbean intellectuals, and the wave of postcolonial criticism that has ensued, political readings of *The Tempest* have become, for many, inevitable. In fact, it has become difficult to read *The Tempest* today, especially in the so-called Third World, without thinking of the so-called civilizing mission allegedly carried out by explorers and missionaries, of possession and dispossession, forced labor, economic exploitation, and unbalanced distribution of wealth (Smith and Hudson 1992, 389). The premise now is that such issues can be examined through revisionist readings and analysis of *The Tempest* because Shakespeare's play is a paradigmatic text which encodes, in complex fashion, in Peter Hulme's phrase, "the colonial encounter."

It has been pointed out that appropriation has invariably meant an amplification of the anticolonial voices in a text, and this is clearly verifiable in appropriations of *The Tempest*. However, as Peter Hulme and Francis Barker have demonstrated, categorizing the several links between *The Tempest* and colonialist discourse is no easy task. There is, to begin with, a lack of parameters. Literary history reminds us that in 1611 there were no fictional portrayals in England of New World inhabitants and no fictional examples of colonialist discourse. Thus, to the extent that *The Tempest* is seen to enact an encounter with a New World native, it is the first literary work in English to do so. In Meredith Skura's words: "Shakespeare was the first to show 'us' mistreating a native, the first to represent a native from the inside, the first to allow a native to complain on stage, and the first to make that New-World encounter problematic enough to generate the current attention to the play" (57).

Exaggerated emphasis on Caliban as a pioneering creation in Renaissance literature may reinforce the myth of Shakespeare's transcendental genius, true, but if Caliban can also be construed as a victim of colonialism, such awareness affects the very same notion of Shakespeare, the institution. As is known, for many British subjects, Shakespeare is as much an institution as a corpus of literary texts; he is a symbol of national identity, an exportable commodity, a tourist attraction, the Swan of Avon.[3] Those writers who have taken up *The Tempest* from the standpoint of the colonial subject have depended on a notion of political awareness to revise Shakespeare as an institution, in a complex manner. On the one hand, they hail Caliban and identify themselves with him; on the other, they are "intolerant of the received colonial definitions of the play's values" (Nixon 560). In a word, they seem to find Shakespeare's play compelling—but not untouchable—and want to engage with it on their own terms.

Together, revisionist writers and critics call for a move to counteract some "deeply ahistorical readings of The Tempest" (Hulme 1986; 94), a play that is now seen not simply as an allegory about timelessness, universal experience, or forgiveness and reconciliation, but rather a cultural phenomenon that is grounded on and that impinges upon historical events, specifically English colonialism. What matters now is the whole "ensemble of fictional and lived practices" known as English colonialism, which, it is being claimed, provides the "dominant discursive con-texts" for the play (Barker and Hulme 1985, 198). The revisionist impulse has been salutary in more ways than one, for example, in correcting New Critical "blindness" to history and ideology, in interpreting *The Tempest* as a political act (Skura 43–46).

And the new readings have offered radical views on Sycorax, Miranda, Prospero, and, of course, Caliban. Sycorax is now almost consensually seen as Prospero's other, whom he typically puts down in order to justify his own colonizing attitude (Loomba 152). As a colonialist, Prospero is seen to consolidate a power that is specifically white and male, and his discourse constructs Sycorax as black and wicked in order to legitimize his power. Ultimately, however, Sycorax becomes more than just Prospero's other or the justification for Caliban's territorial rights over the island: she operates as a powerful contrast to Miranda (Loomba 151).

As regards Miranda's new import in the play's ideology, there is an interesting critical controversy. Some believe that even though she holds a position next to Prospero's in the play's hierarchy and enjoys benefits which Caliban, hierarchically inferior, is denied, she herself might be trapped, a victim of her father's oppression and values (Leininger 286). No doubt, not unlike Caliban, Miranda is constantly ordered around: to sleep, awake, come on, see, speak, listen, be quiet, obey, hush, be mute, refrain. As much as Caliban and Ariel, she is Prospero's property, and she will be exchanged between father and husband: "Then, as my gift, and thine own acquisition / Worthily purchas'd, take my daughter" (4.1.13–14), Prospero says, settling the bargain with Ferdinand. Yet, others see Miranda mainly as part of Prospero's colonial project, providing the ideological legitimation of each of his actions (Loomba 153). In this reading, the famous "Abhorred slave" speech (1.2.354 ff), which many an editor has attributed to Prospero, because such vituperation would seem unacceptable coming from Miranda, is definitively restored to her (as per the 1623 Folio).

Prospero is now seen as the epitome of the colonizer. His rhetoric of noble intentions combined with his coercive actions have been recognized as the strategy employed by later colonialists (Loomba 145). Prospero's violent reaction at the end of the betrothal mask is the choice fault line taken by revisionists as strongest evidence of the falseness of his position—the moment when the hidden colonialist agenda emerges openly (Barker and Hulme 191–205, Hulme *Encounters* 133), when Prospero's "political unconscious" is exposed (Brown 69). The disclosure happens when, reminded of the bibulous trio's plot, Prospero suddenly interrupts the magical pageant he is staging for Ferdinand and Miranda. The former Duke of Milan is so worked up that Miranda remarks to a dumbfounded Ferdinand that she has never seen her father so enraged. The revisionist explanation is cogent: Prospero's fury here derives from the unstable politics of colonialism; it reveals the colonizer's disquiet at the irruption onto consciousness of an unconscious anxiety concerning the grounding of his very legitimacy on the island (Barker and Hulme 202).

At such a moment, Prospero must mind Caliban (and his cohorts). And given the revisionists' concern with the cultural context of the New World, it is in regard to Caliban that radical readings have been most germane. Whereas traditional interpretations echoed Prospero's and Miranda's rendering of Caliban as an inherently inferior being, postcolonial readings and appropriations have seized on Caliban to articulate bondage and rebellion (Loomba 144). Caliban—and not Ariel, as Rodó thought—becomes "our" symbol. Famously, Retamar advances the case:

> Our symbol is not then Ariel, as Rodó thought, but rather Caliban. This is something that we, the mestizo inhabitants of these same islands where Caliban lived, see with particular clarity: Prospero invaded the islands, killed our ancestors, enslaved Caliban, and taught him his language to make himself understood. (14)

And in a purple passage, Retamar mentions a list of thirty-seven famous Latin American Calibans, from Tiradentes, Aleijadinho, and Simón Bolivar to Fidel Castro, Ruben Dario, Villa-Lobos, Aimé Césaire, Pablo Neruda, Frantz Fanon, and Violeta Parra. In light of such partisanship and the awareness that Caliban stands clearly in opposition to the strong, colonizing culture, it is small wonder that the character becomes the point of departure for various appropriations of *The Tempest*, as a means for amplifying calls for decolonization within the bounds of the dominant culture (Loomba 144).[4]

Having discussed implications of Shakespeare's *Tempest* for postcolonial appropriations in general, I can now turn to Césaire's *Une Tempête* as a case in point. Initially, a key theoretical consideration will be helpful: according to Hulme, the underlying point of postcolonial theory is a critique of a false claim to universality and essentialism—politically, culturally, historically—a false ahistorical position from which all else is judged. Applied to literature, postcolonial theory denounces the fact that peripheral literatures have been traditionally judged according to ethical and aesthetic standards of a norm that has been unmarked too long: English canonical literature.[5]

Surely, even a cursory anthropological detour from mainstream cultural values will disclose interesting—and valid—mechanisms operating in any given cultural artifact. Lévi-Strauss's notion of *pensée sauvage* comes handy here. Lévi-Strauss sees in the cultural artifact the collective effort of a community to resolve on the imaginary level an intolerable lived contradiction. This imaginary or symbolic resolution is the group's last resort for dealing with explosive forces within it. *Pensée sauvage* becomes the only means of psychological survival in the face of the need for a collective denial of social, historical, or psychic crises (Dash 49). In Michael Dash's proposal, considered as a kind of *pensée sauvage,* "French Caribbean Literature emerges as an example of the formal or symbolic response to a historical nightmare" (49). What underpins the literary imagination are those explosive pressures which are often denied—rootlessness, the aborted revolution, the threat of extinction. Dash concludes that since these crises remain unresolved, the French Caribbean writer dreams (I would suggest, *writes*) about their resolution. Ultimately, exorcising the repressed self would be the impulse that has created such writing (ibid.).

How does *Une Tempête,* a literary cultural artifact, entail *pensée sauvage* and measure up to this process? Let us consider, to begin with, the radical polarization which Césaire produces in relation to *The Tempest*'s traditional themes and interpretation of main characters. Forgiveness and reconciliation give way to irreconcilable differences; the roles of Ferdinand and Miranda dwindle, and the play's social dimension is underscored. Prospero is demythologized and rendered contemporary by being altogether less white magical and more a master of the technology of oppression; he is the "complete totalitarian," but his power is far from inscrutable, embodied in an "arsenal of tricks" (Nixon 571). Most importantly, Caliban is presented as a victim of a colonialism perpetrated in reality by those who come after Shakespeare and Prospero.

Une Tempête is an adaptation (the classification is Césaire's own) of *The Tempest* for a black theater, from the point of view of the colonized world/individual, and, as would be expected, Césaire's demystification of Shakespeare's text has been especially understood and well received in the so-called Third World (Smith and Hudson 393). In *Une Tempête,* typically, the evocation of native culture is crucial. Césaire's Caliban, for instance, is rooted in African religion and culture that draw on traditions uncontaminated by colonialism (Loomba 156).

Césaire's personal indignation at Prospero's totalitarianism in *The Tempest* seems to act as a catalyst for his writing of *Une Tempête.* As Césaire sees it, both Caliban and Ariel were enslaved by Prospero and forced to work for him, under threats or actual punishment. Such acts of coercion are seen as typical of colonization, and they prompt Césaire to say in an interview with Lucien Attoun: "I tried I to take the myth out of The Tempest. . . . In staging the play

I was struck by Prospero's totalitarianism. . . . I rebel when I am told he is a man of pardon ("qtd. in Smith and Hudson 390). Sure enough, near the end of act 2, Prospero brags to a stunned Ariel: "Je suis la Puissance" (2.2).[6] In a mature assessment, Césaire's revision of *The Tempest* must be dealt with in terms of an inquiry into power struggle, entailing a notion that might be qualified as damning reciprocity. Duly problematized, the thesis of this argument is that the real break with Shakespeare's text occurs in the continuing dialogue between Prospero and Caliban. In this light, Césaire's drama would be seen to turn on the two characters' mutuality, their reciprocal recognition (Dayan 131).[7]

Indeed, Césaire presents Prospero and Caliban as though chained to each other. In act 1, scene 2, Prospero asks Caliban: "Sans moi, que serais-tu?" (1.2). To which, Caliban replies right away: "Sans toi? Mais tout simplement le roi! Le roi de l'île! Le roi de mon île, que je tiens de Sycorax, ma mère" (ibid.). Yet, only a couple of exchanges later, it is Caliban's turn to ask Prospero: "Qu'aurais-tu fait sans moi, dans cette contrée inconnu?" (1.2). Dispossessor and dispossessed have inextricable destinies after crossing each other's paths. To be sure, at the end of the play, when Prospero decides to stay on the island, he tells the surprised Europeans, who are about to leave: "Je ne pars plus. Mon destin est ici" (3.5).

Act 3 of *Une Tempête* depicts a strange confrontation. Following the failed attempt to overthrow Prospero with the aid of the conspirators, Caliban blames himself for thinking that "des ventres et des trognes pourraient faire la Révolution!" (3.4). Then, Caliban symbolically toasts Prospero—"à nous deux!"—and, weapon in hand, rushes at Prospero, who responds in a way that could be performed as farce—"Frappe, mais frappe donc! Ton maître! Ton bienfaiteur! Tu ne vas quand même pas l'épargner!" (ibid.). Caliban lifts his arm, hesitates, and does spare him. And Prospero says ". . . tu n'es qu'un animal; tu ne sais pas tuer," to which Caliban replies: ". . . défends-toi! Je ne suis pas un assassin" (ibid.). Caliban cannot kill Prospero.

It has been pointed out that as early as his *Discourse on Colonialism,* in 1955, Césaire recognized how the colonial relationship chains colonizer and colonized in an implacable dependence. "First we must study how colonization works to **decivilize** [sic] the colonizer," Césaire wrote, "to **brutalize** [sic] him in the true sense of the word." And he concluded: "Colonization, I repeat, dehumanizes even the most civilized man" (qtd. in Dayan 132).

It is interesting, however, to explore the ways in which *Une Tempête* can be seen beyond the obvious level of rebellion; in other words, how the play illustrates the complexity of the dependence between colonized and colonizer. Even if we take Césaire at his word and read his play as an adaptation of Shakespeare's—and not as a radical disavowal—we can begin to understand how issues addressed by both texts are complicated through the notion of mutual dependence, or, in Hegel's sense, convertibility. What might have seemed a case of simple rebellion becomes instead an exchange so powerful that it entraps both colonized and colonizer (Dayan 130).

The mutual dependence shared by *Tempests,* Prosperos, and Calibans, however, does not preclude important differences between the two plays. First, *Une Tempête* introduces an important new character—Eshu—a black god-devil who amuses and then outrages the assembled guests, gods, and goddesses during the masque, with his "frankness" and "vulgarity": "Dieu pour les amis, diable pour les ennemis! Et de la rigolade pour toute la compagnie" (3.3). Eshu pops into the masque uninvited and defies Prospero's magic, refusing to obey his order to leave before singing an obscene song.

Second, in *Une Tempête,* Ariel becomes a passive mulatto slave, an Uncle Tom type, who thinks that Caliban is too impetuous, and who implores him to seek to change his condition through peaceful means. Ariel is the idealist intellectual who shuns violence and holds that, faced with Prospero's well-stocked arsenal of tricks, he and Caliban are more likely to win freedom through conciliation than resistance. From Caliban's perspective, of course, Ariel is a collaborationist, a political and cultural sellout who, aspiring both to rid himself nonviolently of Prospero and to emulate his values, is reduced to negotiating for liberty from a powerless position. Surely, Ariel and Caliban are companions in misery, slavery, and hope, but their methods of dealing with Prospero are quite in opposition. They confront each other as a militant who believes in black power and who wants freedom now, and a pacifist who does not believe in violence and who feels that freedom can be achieved through patience, peace, and turning the other cheek (Smith and Hudson 395).[8]

Michael Dash argues that Césaire's reworking of the Prospero-Caliban-Ariel relationship is unique because it introduces yet a new character, a fourth protagonist—the island. In Dash's view, what matters in *Une Tempête* is not only the relationship between the three traditional figures but their attitudes toward the island. For

Dash, we are invited to examine Prospero, Caliban, and Ariel in terms of their responsiveness to the island. In this view, eventually, it is not Caliban who defeats Prospero. Caliban, as we have seen, is too caught up with Prospero to kill him. Prospero is defeated by the island, by the land. True enough, at the end of *Une Tempête,* Prospero's grotto (civilization?) is overgrown by the jungle (Dash 55). The argument is interesting, but diverts attention from the damning reciprocity between Prospero and Caliban, which I see as the crucial problem to be explored in *Une Tempête.*

I prefer to discuss Prospero's defeat in terms of mutual entrapment vis-à-vis Caliban. Close to the end of the play, Caliban predicts that Prospero will allow everyone to return to Milan but will never leave the island himself. Giving Prospero an outspoken dressing-down, Caliban tells him what his true mission has been:

> Ta vocation est de m'emerder!
> Et voilà pourquoi tu resteras,
> Comme ces mecs qui ont fait les colonies
> Et Qui ne peuvent plus vivre ailleurs.
> Un vieil intoxiqué, voilà ce que tu es!
>
> (3.4)

At the end of the play, aged and weary, Prospero is reduced to automatic gestures and failing language. He screams: "Je défendrai la civilisation!" (3.4), to an unresponsive nature, to an unanswering Caliban. Césaire's *Tempête* ends with a powerless Prospero suffering alone in his decrepitude, while Caliban gets the last word. He proclaims his new-found freedom, with the sound of the surf and the chirping of birds as background to his freedom song: "LA LIBERTÉ OHÉ, LA LIBERTÉ!" (ibid.).

For Césaire, Caliban is a trickster, shrewd, keenly aware of Prospero's ploy. When Prospero tells him "tu pourrais au moins me bénir de t'avoir appris à parler" (1.2), Césaire's Caliban instantly replies: "Tu ne m'as rien appris du tout. Sauf, bien sûr à baragouiner ton language pour comprendre tes ordres" (ibid.). And he asks, relentlessly: "Quant à ta science, est-ce que tu me l'as jamais apprise, toi?" (ibid.). Césaire's Caliban is like the militant black who rejects the oppressor's language, the name given to him, and the position of servility (Smith and Hudson 387). Césaire allows Caliban to fight back from the very first appearance. His first word in the play is "*Uhuru!*" (1.2.), which means "freedom" or "independence" in Swahili. And the word announces that a battle for freedom is about to begin. Throughout the play, Caliban curses back at Prospero in relentless verbal confrontation and is supplied, for his defense, with an arsenal of negative epithets: "Vieux vautour" (1.2.); "vieux bouc" (1.2.); "vieux ruffian" (2.1); "mec, écraseur, broyeur" (2.1).

Moreover, Caliban claims his territory as the rightful king of his island. He is very much his mother's son, whom he does not repudiate: "Morte ou vivante, c'est ma mère et je ne la renierai pas" (1.2.). And he will no longer respond to the name Caliban, as Nixon reminds us, "a colonial invention bound anagrammatically to the degrading 'cannibal';" instead, the island's captive king christens himself "X" (1.2.)—clearly a Black-Muslim gesture that commemorates his lost name, buried beneath layers of colonial culture (571). "X" is the right name for a man whose real identity is unknown, having been stolen from him.

Going back to Lévi-Strauss's notion of *pensée sauvage,* we can see that Caliban's defiance is expressed most eloquently through the celebration of the Yoruba gods Eshu and Shango; in fact, two of his four liberation songs celebrate Shango. And the success of Caliban's uncompromising strategies is imminent at the end of the action, as we do see Prospero defeated, be it by the land or by being entrapped in an ongoing psychological battle with his slave. Ultimately, Prospero becomes a victim of his own project. He grows old, tired, and feebleminded, still believing that he is going to defend civilization, even by force—of which he has pitifully little left. In the last analysis, it is not Caliban who cannot do without him, but the other way around. At the end of *Une Tempête,* the incorrigible Caliban continues to sing his song of liberty, which resounds throughout the enchanted island.[9]

The core of my argument, then, is that, after the colonial encounter, Prospero and Caliban depend on each other for better or for worse. Césaire, himself, admits the complexity of the situation:

> Caliban and [Prospero] make an inseparable couple. Just as blacks and whites cannot afford to separate themselves from each other in America, Prospero cannot separate himself from Caliban, and that is the story. It is the indissoluble character of the union which makes the drama. (Qtd. in Smith and Hudson 397)

It is precisely the plays' different endings which draws the most attention. Yet, Césaire's Prospero, I repeat, remains on the island.[10]

Thus, *Une Tempête* ends in a mutually willed (if helpless) confinement that leaves master and servant alone in a profusion of words.

Césaire has radically reassessed *The Tempest* in terms of the historical and cultural circumstances of his region. He values the play because he sees its potential as a vehicle for dramatizing the revolution of colonialism in his land. In an interview with François Beloux, Césaire expresses his realization that there is not much left of Shakespeare in *Une Tempête:*

> My text . . . was greatly influenced by the preoccupations I had at that particular time. As I was thinking very much about a play concerning the United States, inevitably, the points of reference became American. . . . [T]here is the violent and the nonviolent attitude. There are Martin Luter King and Malcolm X and the Black Panthers. (qtd. in Smith and Hudson 393)

Césaire's political engagement as an artist is clear enough. Indeed, he speaks through Caliban, and he shares his Caliban's desire to modify his destiny and that of his people. Césaire himself has said of his dramatic works: "C'ést un peu le drame des négres dans le monde moderne" (qtd. in Smith and Hudson 396).

It is not difficult to demonstrate that Césaire's Caliban is uncontainable. Yet, there remains one final question: is Shakespeare's Caliban necessarily contained? In this respect, David Bevington has reportedly asked: "Is Caliban, in the conclusion of The Tempest, (1) a happy subject once again under Prospero's benign rule, or (2) the victim of a colonialism which Shakespeare, with his usual brilliance, portrayed in his drama before it happened historically? (qtd. in Smith and Hudson 388).

Encomia aside, we are reminded of Prospero's final words about and to Caliban, in *The Tempest:* "This thing of darkness I / Acknowledge mine" (5.1.278–79), as he "introduces" Caliban to the Italians, and "As you look / To have my pardon, trim it handsomely" (5.1.296–97), as he commands Caliban to clean up the grotto. No doubt, Shakespeare's Caliban is harshly dismissed with a promise of a pardon, not with pardon itself. In fact, as Smith and Hudson have submitted, Caliban is the only character in Shakespeare's play who does not receive Prospero's pardon outright. He still has to work for it (392). I find it hard to accept, however, that Shakespeare's Caliban, who has borne so much "wood" (the word-play with "anger," "madness," etc. has long since been pointed out) for Prospero throughout the play, is a candidate for submission at this point. For one thing, at the end of Shakespeare's *Tempest,* it can be assumed that Caliban resumes control of his island, as Prospero, after all, having laid aside his magic, returns to Europe (by the way, with Claribel married to "Tunis," Miranda married to "Naples," and himself now his old "Milan," Prospero's every third thought may indeed be his grave). For another, Caliban's last words and action in the play remain problematic: When he says: "What a thrice-double ass / Was I to take this drunkard for a god, / And worship this dull fool!" (5.1.299–301), partisan resiliency might be suggested in production, for example, simply by directing the actor to make Caliban's last look fall askance on Prospero—and not on Stephano. The idea is less uncanny than it may seem; we are reminded that as early as 1878 Renan understood Caliban as recalcitrant.

In this light, to discuss—or teach—Césaire's *Tempête* as a mere reaction to what is prior or canonical, without challenging the oddly mixed nature of Shakespeare's play, is to continue to marginalize the colonial subject outside the untouchable master narratives of civilization and conquest. What if we were to discuss Shakespeare's *Tempest* by reading Césaire's *Tempête*? We could then pursue the notion of convertibility between classical and new, or revisionary, not in terms of a simple either/or dichotomy, but through a dialogue, a process of continuing complications (Dayan 140).

Given the damning reciprocity in which both Calibans and both Prosperos are caught, is Césaire's Caliban's "Uhuru!" an absolute? Indeed, *mutatis mutandis, The Tempest* and *Une Tempête* can be seen to turn on the question of the relative possibility of freedom. Ultimately, both Shakespeare and Césaire leave the question unresolved, as the end of both plays remain ambiguous. What exactly is Shakespeare's Caliban's future? Why is he made to *appear* contained at the end of *The Tempest*? And why, in his very last declaration of freedom in *Une Tempête,* does Césaire's Caliban change from Swahili to French? Looking back from our twentieth-century perspective, it seems that both authors, separated in time and space as they are, know that the struggle to sustain an ideal of freedom is far more difficult than its mere proclamation. The key issue is not the cry for—or even the attainment of—independence, but what follows, and the point is that, perhaps, both Prosperos are defeated and neither Caliban is contained.

Notes

1. As Annia Loomba has also argued, the distinction drawn by generations of critics between Prospero's always "white" magic and Sycorax's always "black" magic only corroborates Prospero's view of the colonial enterprise (152). For examples of the kind of interpretation Loomba objects to, see Smith's and Kermode's essays cited below.

2. As a reminder of the interest which *The Tempest* has aroused in the center, Norbrook submits that the "libertarian impulse" in the play made it appeal to Milton, who rewrote it in *Comus,* transferring Caliban's less attractive qualities to the aristocratic Comus (w. 1634, pub. 1637), a pagan god with magic power (21–22). Still according to Norbrook, Shelley found in *The Tempest* a central instance of the utopian power in poetry which "makes familiar objects as if they were not familiar" (qtd. from "A Defense of Poetry," in *Shelley's Prose or the Trumpet of Prophecy,* ed. David Lee Clark [London: Fourth State, 1988], 282). Shelley seems to have been alert to Caliban's claim, as can be seen from the parallel he draws in his preface to *Frankenstein,* between Mary's novel and Shakespeare's unassuming application of license to prose fiction. Dryden and Davenant, of course, rewrote Shakespeare's play as *The Tempest or the Enchanted Island: A Comedy* (w. 1667, pub. 1674). A detailed chronicling of English appropriations of *The Tempest* is out of place here, but I want to single out Marina Warner's recent award-winning novel *Indigo* (1992).

3. For an in-depth investigation of the issue, see *The Shakespeare Myth,* a collection of essays edited by Graham Holderness.

4. In the 1970s, Augusto Boal would write his *A Tempestade,* appropriating Shakespeare's in terms of Paulo Freire's "Pedagogy of the Oppressed" and Boal's own "Theater of the Oppressed," all in the context of the oppressive military regime ruling Brazil at the time.

5. The commentary is drawn from my notes on the opening lecture of a course taught by Peter Hulme for the graduate program in English at Universidade Federal de Santa Catarina in August 1994.

6. All references to *Une Tempête* pertain to the Éditions du Seuil cited below.

7. Joan Dayan has done interesting work, grounding this reciprocity on Hegel's notion of "convertibility," Hegel's delineation of the tense bond between he who calls himself master and he who responds as slave. Dayan quotes from *Phenomenology of Mind:* "Just as lordship showed its essential nature to be the reverse of what it wants to be, so, too, bondage will, when completed, pass into the opposite of what it immediately is" (trans. J. B. Baille [New York: 1970], 237).

8. The obvious echoes of contemporary United States race relations history are addressed below.

9. I am here reminded of another incorrigible "Caribbean Caliban," Jamaica Kincaid's Lucy, reminiscing that, at age fourteen, she got up during choir practice and refused to sing: "Rule, Britannia! Britannia, rule the waves; Britons never, never shall be slaves," to which the choir instructor wondered if all her effort, over the years, to "civilize" Lucy had not been in vain (74).

10. Augusto Boal's Prospero, like Shakespeare's, returns to Europe, but not without first leaving surrogates to run his recently established trading company for him.

BIBLIOGRAPHY

Adams, Ian, and Helen Triffin, eds. *Past the Last Post: Theorizing Post-Colonialism and Post-Modernism.* Hemel Hempstead, England: Harvester Wheatsheaf, 1991.

Ahmad, Aijaz. *In Theory: Classes, Nations, Literatures.* London: Verso, 1992.

Aristotle. *The Politics.* Trans. T. A. Sinclair. Harmondsworth, England: Penguin, 1970.

Arnold, James A. "Césaire and Shakespeare: Two Tempests." *Comparative Literature* 30 (1978): 236–48.

Ashcroft, Bill, Gareth Griffiths, and Helen Tiffin. *The Empire Writes Back: Theory and Practice in Post-Colonial Literatures.* London: Routledge, 1989.

Barker, Francis, and Peter Hulme. "Nymphs and Reapers Heavily Vanish: The Discursive Con-texts of *The Tempest.* In *Alternative Shakespeares,* ed. John Drakakis, 191–205. London: Routledge, 1985.

———, Peter Hulme, and Margaret Iversen, eds. *Colonial Discourse/Post-Colonial Theory.* Manchester: Manchester University Press, 1994.

Bellei, Sérgio Luiz Prado. *Nacionalidade e Literatura: Os Caminhos da Alteridade* (Florianópolis: EdUFSC, 1992).

Boal, Augusto. *A Tempestade e Mulheres de Atenas.* Lisbon: Editora Plátano, 1979.

Brown, Paul. " 'This thing of darkness I acknowledge mine': *The Tempest* and the Discourse of Colonialism." In *Political Shakespeare: New Essays in Cultural Materialism,* ed. Jonathan Dollimore and Alan Sinfield, 48–71. Manchester: Manchester University Press, 1985.

Césaire, Aimé. *Discours sur le colonialisme* (1955). Trans. Joan Pinkham. Reprinted in *Discourse on Colonialism.* New York: Monthly Review Press, 1972.

———. *Une Tempête: D'après 'La Tempête' de Shakespeare—Adaptation pour un théâtre nègre.* Paris: Éditions du Seuil, 1969.

Dash, J. Michael. "Ariel's Discourse: French Caribbean Writing after the Storm." *Journal of West Indian Literature* 1 (1986): 49–58.

Dayan, Joan. "Playing Caliban: Césaire's *Tempest.*" *Arizona Quarterly* 4 (1992): 125–45.

Donald, James, and Ali Rattansi, eds. *"Race," Culture, and Difference.* London: Sage/Open University Press, 1992.

Eagleton, Terry. "Nature: *As You Like It, The Winter's Tale, The Tempest.*" In *William Shakespeare: Rereading Literature,* 90–96. Oxford: Blackwell, 1986.

Fanon, Frantz. *Black Skins, White Masks* (1952; reprint, New York: Grove Press, 1967.

———. *The Wretched of the Earth* (1961); reprint, trans. Constance Farrington. Harmondsworth: Penguin, 1967.

Fiedler, Leslie. "The New World Savage as Stranger: Or, 'Tis new to thee.' " *The Stranger in Shakespeare,* 199–253. St. Albans: Paladin, 1974.

Gilroy, Paul. *The Black Atlantic: Modernity and Double Consciousness.* London: Verso, 1993.

Greenblatt, Stephen. "Learning to Curse: Aspects of Linguistic Colonialism in the Sixteenth Century." In *First Images of America: The Impact of the New World on the Old,* ed. Fredi Chiappelli, 2:561–80. Berkeley, 1976.

Griffiths, Trevor R. " 'This island's mine': Caliban and Colonialism." *Yearbook of English Studies* 13 (1983): 159–80.

Hulme, Peter. "Hurricanes in the Caribbees: The Construction of the Discourse of English Colonialism." In *1642: Literature and Power in the Seventeenth Century,* ed. Francis Barker et al., 55–83. Colchester, England: University of Essex, 1981.

———. "Prospero and Caliban." In *Colonial Encounters: Europe and the Native Caribbean, 1492–1797,* 89–134. London: Methuen, 1986.

Kermode, Frank. Introduction to *The Tempest (1954). The Arden Shakespeare,* ed. Frank Kermode, xi–xciii. London: Methuen, 1987.

Kincaid, Jamaica. *Lucy* (1990; reprint, trans. Lia Wyler. Rio de Janeiro: Editora Objetiva, 1994.

Lamming, George E. *The Pleasures of Exile* (1960; reprint, London: Allison and Busby, 1984.

Leininger, Lorie Jerrell. "The Miranda Trap: Sexism and Racism in Shakespeare's *Tempest.*" In *The Woman's Part: Feminist Criticism of Shakespeare,* ed. Carolyn Ruth Swift Lenz, Gayle Greene, Carol Thomas Neely, 285–94. Urbana: University of Illinois Press, 1983.

Loomba, Ania. "Seizing the Book." In *Gender, Race, Renaissance Drama,* 142–58. Manchester: Manchester University Press, 1989.

Mannoni, Octave. *Psychologie de la colonisation.* 1950; reprint, trans. Pamela Powesland, *Prospero and Caliban: The Psychology of Colonization.* New York: Frederick Praeger Publishers, 1964.

McClintock, Anne. "The Angel of Progress: Pitfalls of the Term 'Postcolonialism.' " In *Colonial Discourse/Postcolonial Theory,* ed. Francis Barker, Peter Hulme, and Margaret Iversen, 253–67. Manchester: Manchester University Press, 1994.

Mishra, Vijay, and Bob Hodge. "What is Post(-)colonialism?" In *Colonial Discourse and Postcolonial Theory,* ed. Patrick Williams and Laura Chrisman, 276–90. New York: Columbia University Press, 1993.

Nixon, Rob. "Caribbean and African Appropriations of *The Tempest.*" *Critical Inquiry* 13 (1987): 557–78.

Norbrook, David. " 'What cares these roarers for the name of king?': Language and Utopia in *The Tempest.*" In *The Politics of Tragicomedy,* ed. Gordon McMullan and Jonathan Hope, 21–54. London: Routledge, 1992.

Renan, Ernest. *Caliban, suite de La Tempête (1878).* ed. Colin Smith, Manchester: Manchester University Press, 1954.

Retamar, Roberto Fernández. "Caliban: Notes toward a Discussion of Culture in Our America." In *Caliban and Other Essays,* trans. Edward Baker, 3–45. Minneapolis: University of Minneapolis Press, 1989.

Rodó, José Enrique. *Ariel.* 1900; reprint, trans. Denise Bottmann. Campinas: Editora da UNICAMP, 1991.

Shakespeare, William. *The Tempest. Mr. William Shakespeares Comedies, Histories and Tragedies: A Facsimile Edition of the First Folio.* ed. Helge Kökeritz, 1–19. New Haven: Yale University Press, 1954.

Skura, Meredith Anne. "Discourse and the Individual: The Case of Colonialism in *The Tempest.*" *Shakespeare Quarterly* 40 (1989): 42–69.

Smith, Hallett. *"The Tempest."* In *The Riverside Shakespeare,* 1606–10. Boston: Houghton Mifflin, 1974.

Smith, Robert P., Jr., and Robert J. Hudson. "Evoking Caliban: Césaire's Response to Shakespeare." *College Language Association Journal* 35 (1992): 387–99.

Vaughan, Alden T. "Shakespeare's Indian: The Americanization of Caliban." *Shakespeare Quarterly* 39 (1988): 137–53.

———, and Virginia Mason Vaughan. *Shakespeare's Caliban: A Cultural History.* Cambridge: Cambridge University Press, 1991.

Vaughan, Virginia Mason. " 'Something rich and strange': Caliban's Theatrical Metamorphoses." *Shakespeare Quarterly* 36 (1985): 390–405.

Intertextuality in Shakespeare's *The Tempest* and Cesaire's *Une Tempête*

WILLIAM VALENTINE REDMOND

No poet, no artist of any sort, has his complete meaning alone. His Significance, his appreciation is the appreciation of his relation to the dead poets and artists. You cannot value him alone. You must set him, for contrast and comparison, among the dead.
—T. S. Eliot

IF THE ABOVE STATEMENT IS TRUE, AND, IF "THE EXISTING MONUments form an ideal order among themselves, which is modified by the introduction of the new work of art among them" (Eliot 1975, 38–39), then the publication of *Une Tempête* by the playwright from Martinique Aimé Césaire in 1969 modifies our reading of *The Tempest* of William Shakespeare, setting up an intertextual magnetic field between the two works and opening up new pathways to the understanding of the two texts. The study of the mutual influence of the two autonomous and open texts enriches in complexity and ambiguity the reading of the two plays. Césaire entitles his play *A Tempest* in contrast to Shakespeare's *The Tempest* and subtitles his play "according to *The Tempest* of Shakespeare, an adaptation for a black theatre." The second play inserts the first in the context of black consciousness, of the struggle for true liberty, and the historical reverberations of the relationship between black and white in the subsequent 370 years of history.

This reflection takes place in the year which marks the centenary of the emancipation of the slaves in Brazil. We wisely mark the occasion and avoid all suggestion of festivity though some obviously intend the date to be remembered festively. The black movements refuse to commemorate an emancipation which left them without land and money, without identity and future, and prefer to go back to the memory of Zumbi for commemoration, to rediscover their roots in people who were prepared to die for their ideal of liberty, in people who are mythical heroes like those who founded the identity of other races. The date 1988 for these movements is not a memory to be cherished but a reminder of the still sad music of their reality: a 60 percent minority group who even after the suffering of slavery are still condemned to the difficulties of poverty, seeing their children retarded by subnutrition and themselves refused the honest application of the basic principles of meritocracy. Intertextuality becomes especially strong in this context since Césaire, founder of *Étudiant Noir* in 1934 and inventor of the word *negritude,* used his literary talents in the service of the movement of black consciousness born in the Latin Quarter of Paris among the black students in the thirties.

Into this context comes *The Tempest,* losing its racial innocence. It was after all written in 1610, eight years before the first slaves were taken to the English colonies in America but well after the system of slavery had been implanted in Cabo Verde and some American countries. Palmares was to fall in 1695 and had already been in existence for about fifteen years on the date of the first presentation of the play. Shakespeare knew about slavery and may, in his eternal memorableness on all the subjects he touched, have said something essential on this subject of slavery too.

Shakespeare was always a dramatist interested in communicating with his audience, and most of his plays, although they do not satirize contemporary society, do make references to happenings of the time. In *The Tempest* this is done in various ways. Reference is made to an essay by Montaigne according to the translation of Florio of 1603, "Of Cannibals," in scene 1 of the second act, lines 165-70, where Gonzalo is discussing with the other characters the qualities of an island untouched by civilization:

> All things in common nature should produce
> Without sweat or endeavour. Treason, felony,
> Sword, pike, knife, gun, or need of any engine,
> Would I not have; but nature should bring forth
> Of its own kind all foison, all abundance,
> To feed my innocent people.

Shakespeare speaks of Setebos (1.2.376), a reference to the mythology of Patagonia as related in Robert Eden's *History of Travaile* of 1577. "The still vex'd Bermudas" (1.2.230) recall to the spectators the stories of *Sea Adventure,* a popular booklet at the time about the first pioneers in Virginia. For them, the reference was the same as references to Apollo and the moon to the contemporary person.

Aimé Césaire updates the allusions in his play for his own modern audience. Setebos becomes Shango and Exu, words rich in connotation for his audience, while phrases like "Black Power," "Freedom now," "Uhuru," and "ghetto" appear in the text. The words place Caliban, a servant, in line with the modern mentality of the black movements. Even Ariel becomes "a brother in suffering and in slavery" (1969, 35).[1] Where Shakespeare had quoted Ovid, Césaire quotes Baudelaire's *Les Fleurs du Mal* (40). Césaire makes many references to the history of Christianity with mention of anachoret, and Thebes (20), the rites of the Inquisition (21), the phrase *Vox populi, vox Dei* (63), and to the ritual of exorcism (86). The song "Nearer my God to Thee" recalls the sinking *Titanic.* Consequently, we find that the two plays have a superficial similarity in the use of topicality although it should be pointed out that both dramatists avoid all precise reference to time to allow the plays to have a greater relevance in time and space.

Césaire modernises the references to space in his play. In Shakespeare's play, Alonso and his court are returning from the marriage of his daughter Claribel in Tunis when the shipwreck occurs. Despite the references to the Bermudas, it would seem that Prospero's island is somewhere near Malta in the Mediterranean Sea. In the play of Césaire, the geography of the trip is more explicit. Prospero tells Miranda that he has discovered new lands by precise calculations, and the shipwreck occurs during the voyage they are making to assume control of the new lands. The tropical vegetation would suggest a Caribbean island, and this is confirmed by the group of amateur actors, all black, who are staging a version of *The Tempest* in Martinique.

This version of *The Tempest* was written for a black theater, a term in itself ambiguous, for it can be a play to make the blacks conscious of their own reality or to make the white audience aware of their prejudices.

The play in Césaire's hand becomes considerably shorter: it is reduced from five acts to three, keeping the basic storyline. However, Césaire makes four major changes that make *Une Tempête* a radical adaptation of the Shakespearean play. First, the opening scene is completely new. A group of actors are preparing to rehearse the Shakespearean play. They are all black and they are picking up their masks for the rehearsal. The director is giving them their orders. They go onto the stage and the storm scene begins. But they are wearing masks. Second, two characters of the play are given new identities and one new character is added. Caliban is a "black slave" whereas Shakespeare calls him a "savage and deformed slave." Ariel becomes a "slave ethnically mulato" in place of the Shakespearean characterization of an airy spirit. The God-devil Eshu also appears in the masque for the wedding of Ferdinand and Miranda and causes the artificiality of June, Iris, and Ceres to be confronted with the realism of the black divinity of the fields. In the third place, at the end of the play, Prospero remains on the island: "My destiny is here. I will not go hence" (90), and the final scene is one of an aged and defeated Prospero who has been assimilated to the nature of the island: "Well, Caliban, we are no more than two on the island, no more than you and I. That's all. Me-you then" (92).

In the distance, one hears the roar of the sea and the singing of the birds and Caliban hymning his liberty. The slave considered antinature by his master earlier in the play has made Prospero go native, take on the faithfulness to nature of the black, and live the life of nature. Finally, it is above all in the relationship of Caliban and Prospero that the play has most changed. The relationship is one of explicit hostility. Caliban resists domination:

> Better death than humiliation and injustice. On the day I lose all hope of freedom, let me get hold of those barrels of gun powder and you will see this island go up in the air with the remains of Prospero and myself in the debris. I hope you will enjoy the firework display. It will be signed Caliban. (38)

Caliban refuses the identity Prospero forces on him: "Call me X," he tells Prospero and he is accutely aware of exploitation: "And your science. That you never taught me. You have kept it to yourself. Your science, you have selfishly kept it for yourself, closed up in those big books over there" (25). The hostility between master and slave becomes the central theme of the play, ending symbolically with the victory of the slave. While the action of the play develops, Ariel is the faithful collaborator of Prospero, unaware of his true position, the unenlightened slave working against his own race, lacking in the essential spirit of solidarity. This struggle between master and slave brings the new poetry to the play: the ritual of revolt and the hymning of liberty.

This new version of *The Tempest* forces us back to the original to reread the relationship between Prospero and Caliban, to listen to the rhetoric of silence which tells embryonically of future race relations, and between the lines foresees prophetically the course of later history. The traditional analysis of *The Tempest* is that it is a reconciliation comedy, one of the late comedies. Alonso, after discovering all the evil, is finally able to dominate it and so create a "brave new world:" "*The Tempest* presents a vision of harmony and in this vision, suffering gives way to pardon, misfortune to happiness and reconciliation expressed in a poetic drama which expresses the simple truths of human relations (1966, 6).

Professor Traversi, writing in his work on Shakespeare, sums up this interpretation with the sentence: "a reconciliation born of the bitterness of a tragic experience" (1955, 280). In this interpretation, the strange sadness of the epilogue is seen without reference to the play and is seen as the poetic will of Shakespeare and his farewell to the theater and as "his philosophical and artistic autobiography" (Kott 1962, 210). This *adieu* to theater together with other elements in the text can, however, suggest another meaning to the play. Prospero returns to Milan, fearful of the future: "every third thought shall be my grave" (5. 1.311). His daughter will have to face the same problem of ingratitude and falsehood with a husband who already cheats at chess. "Sweet lord, you play me false" (5. 1.174). Prospero is aware of this and answers rather acidly to her enthusiasm for the brave new world: "Tis new to thee" (5. 1.187). Despite the final reconciliation, the island remains a threat:

> This is as strange a maze as e'er men trod,
> And there is in this business more than nature
> Was ever conduct of. Some oracle
> Must rectify our knowledge.
>
> (5. 1.245–48)

All this with the strange epilogue suggests that the ending of reconciliation leaves room for doubt.

This doubt becomes more serious when we examine the relationship between Prospero and Caliban. While all the hostility between Prospero and the other characters is successfully eliminated at the end, the relationship between Prospero and Caliban continues without a final solution. Caliban is called in Shakespeare's play "a savage and deformed slave" who fights for his liberty: "Freedom, high-day! high-day! freedom! Freedom, high-day, Freedom!" (5.2. 185). After all his efforts to civilize Caliban, Prospero is forced to confess:

> A devil, a born devil, on whose nature
> Nurture can never stick; on whom my pains
> Humanely taken, all, all lost, quite lost,
> And, as with age his body uglier grows,
> So his mind cankers. I will plague them all,
> Even to roaring.
> (4. 1.188–93)

Miranda and Ferdinand see how Prospero is disturbed by the conspiracy of Caliban. Strangely, at the moment when all is reaching a point of perfect solution, Miranda answers Ferdinand's observation "This is strange. Your father's in some passion / That works him strongly" somewhat amazed: "Never till this day / Saw I him touched with anger so distempered (4. 1.142–45).

This is strange: the magician who can do all things foreseen in the poetry of Ovid cannot solve the problem of Caliban. Really, it is this fact and not the controlling, the revenging, and forgiving his former false friends that provoke the deep pessimism about human existence of the lovely lines of Prospero:

> And like the baseless fabric of this vision,
> The cloud-capped towers, the gorgeous palaces,
> The solemn temples, the great globe itself,
> Yea, all which it inherit, shall dissolve;
> And, like this insubstantial pageant faded,
> Leave not a rack behind. We are such stuff
> As dreams are made on, and our little life
> Is rounded with a sleep. Sir. I am vexed.
> Bear with my weakness. My old brain is troubled.
> (4. 1.151–59)

In the final scene, when all is pardon and reconciliation, Caliban goes off to clean the cell without much enthusiasm, without receiving back the island he had inherited from his mother, and complaining about the falseness of his allies in his fight against Prospero:

> Ay, that I will; and I'll be wise hereafter,
> And seek for grace. What a thrice-double ass
> Was I to take this drunkard for a god,
> And worship this dull fool!
>
> (5. 1.298–301)

The epilogue also remains problematic. The King of France in *All's Well That Ends Well* speaks as an actor who has put aside his part in the play and talks as an actor. Prospero speaks as Prospero and unites the time of the play and that of the presentation. He speaks in metaphysical poetry full of doubt and despair; it is the farewell of a Prospero close to failure:

> Now I want
> Spirits to enforce, art to enchant;
> And my ending is despair
> Unless I be relieved by prayer,
> Which pieces so, that it assaults
> Mercy itself, and frees all faults.
>
> (Epilogue 13–18)

In the universal reconciliation, the failure with regard to Caliban causes sadness and is pushed aside and marginalized in the play of Shakespeare: but the failure is there and the tension of the interpersonal relationship continues up to the end.

In the light of *Une Tempête,* this tension between Prospero and Caliban must be reread and many of the abuses of slavery seen between the lines. Caliban, like later slaves, was taught the language of the dominator: "You taught me language and my profit on't / Is I know how to curse (1. 2.366): learning a language not for the acquisition of learning but the obedience to orders. The slave Caliban is dominated by the magic of Prospero but the pain described in the lines of Prospero—"I'll rack thee with old cramps, / Fill all thy bones with aches, make thee roar, / That beasts shall tremble at thy din" (1. 2.371-73)—could as easily describe the domination coming not from magic but from whips, chains, stocks, and superior weaponry. The horror of Prospero expressed in the words of Prospero: "Thou didst seek to violate the honour of my child" (1. 2.350) has echoed terrifyingly down the 370 years in a society permitting all to the master and nothing to the slave when the honor of all the other Mirandas is at stake.

So some of the cruxes of racial tension may be seen in *The Tem-*

pest. But reading *Othello* makes us hesitate to say that in the text of Shakespeare we have an embryonic form of the racial stereotyping of later texts that characterize the black as less competent, more brutish, more lazily dedicated to the enjoyment of leisure. Caliban is indeed one on whom "nurture can never stick," but is Shakespeare stereotyping him? For two reasons, I think not.

In *Othello,* Shakespeare deals with a black man with a certain ambiguity. While telling us in one part that Africans were "canibals that each other eat, / The Anthropophagi, and men whose heads / Do grow beneath their shoulders" (1. 3.142–44) and so showing belief in the gross misconceptions of the Renaissance, Shakespeare presents Othello as majestic, heroic in arms, and magnificent in words: surely one of the most noble of the tragic heroes. It is true that Iago does refer to him in the first act as an "old black ram," a "devil," a "barbary horse," and as a "lascivious Moor," but that is the opinion of the devil Iago. The true vision is given later: "The Moor is of a constant loving and noble nature": an idea confirmed by Desdemona: "My noble Moor is true of mind." The black Moor is an individual sure of his identity and his value to the state, and his hard-won happiness is stolen away by a jealous white man. There is no suggestion of primitiveness or brutishness of lack of control: all inaccuracies of later black stereotyping.

And in *The Tempest* is Caliban the stereotype of the black slave? It would not seem so. Caliban's father is mysterious but seems to be the devil, for he is a demi-devil (5. 1.275). His mother is a "blue-eyed hag from Algiers" left by sailors on the island. She would therefore be probably fair skinned and Arab. Caliban knew his island before Prospero arrived: he showed the master "all the qualities o'th'isle" (1. 2.340). And above all Caliban was deformed. All this would suggest an unique individual and not a type: and if a type, much more an aboriginal than a black slave.

Briefly to conclude: the dramatist is occupied "with the frontiers of consciousness beyond which words fail" (Eliot 1975, 96). For this reason, the stage is more powerful than the page as O'Neill's father used to say. But the page and the stage are more powerful than the platform. The struggling impulses toward the discovery of identity must begin from literature before it is spoken on the platform in language that must be emotionally strong and intellectually clear. If, this year, we become aware of this, then we set out together from this zero year on the true path of liberty through identity in negritude.

Note

1. My translation into English.

Bibliography

Césaire, Aimé. *Une Tempête.* Paris: Seuil, 1969.

Eliot, T. S. *Selected Prose.* New York: Harcourt Brace Javanovich, 1975.

Kott, Jan. *Shakespeare, Notre Contemporain.* Trans. Anna Posner. Paris: Julliard, 1963.

Notes on Shakespeare's *The Tempest.* Study Aid Series. London: Methuen, 1966.

Traversi, D. A. "The Last Plays of Shakespeare." In *The Pelican Guide to English Literature: The age of Shakespeare,* ed. Boris Ford, 2:257–81. 7 vols. (Harmondsworth, England: Penguin, 1955.

Stoppard's and Shakespeare's Views on Metatheater

BERNARDINA DA SILVEIRA PINHEIRO

AN ANALYSIS OF *ROSENCRANTZ AND GUILDENSTERN ARE DEAD* AS A metaplay will show that it reflects both Shakespeare's and Beckett's conceptions of metatheater. When we draw a comparison between Stoppard's play, Shakespeare's *Hamlet,* and Beckett's *Waiting for Godot* and *Endgame,* we are entitled to observe what Stoppard really did in terms of metatheater.

Before discussing some of the metatheatrical aspects of Stoppard's work, we need to define what is metatheater. The expression is rather new, so that the critics have not yet come to a precise definition of what metatheater or metadrama really means. One may say that the word has been probably coined on the analogy of metafiction, metapoetry, and metalanguage. Therefore the most comprehensive definition of metadrama would be the use of a play to discuss some specific elements of the theatrical art, such as the role of actors, performance, dramatic techniques, and the process of composition of the play itself. This kind of procedure may take several forms, expressed by the use of a good many devices.

It is worth considering that the playwright that makes use of metatheater is questioning, in fact, his own work, which proves to be a most significant form of self-evaluation. It is still important to have in mind that metatheater is not an innovation of modern playwrights; Shakespeare himself made use of it in his plays.

What distinguishes, however, Shakespeare from the modern dramatists is that, being perhaps the most consummate representative of the theater of all time, as a character, an actor, a director, a playwright, and a critic, he could and actually did make use of metadrama intuitively.

This is evident in one of his most enthralling plays, *Hamlet.* Its tragic hero, Hamlet, is in reality, simultaneously the leading character in the play, an actor, a director, a critic of theater, and a playwright. As the Elizabethan dramatist's mouthpiece in the play, he is probably the greatest metafictional character, for Shakespeare, being such an accomplished man of theater, may be said to be meta-theater itself.

Hamlet is indeed an actor when, trying to prepare himself for his dreadful task, he puts an "antic disposition" on:

> *Hamlet:* But come,
> Here as before, never, so help you mercy,
> How strange or odd soe'er I bear myself—
> As I perchance hereafter shall think meet
> To put an antic disposition on—
> That you at such time seeing me never shall,
> With arms encumber'd thus, or this head-shake . . .
> (1.5. 169–75)

He is a director when he tells his players how they should perform their parts:

> Speak the speech, I pray you, as I pronounc'd it to you—trippingly on the tongue; but if you mouth it, as many of your players do, I had as lief the town—crier had spoke my lines. Nor do not saw the air too much with your hand thus, but use all gently; for in the very torrent, tempest, and as I may say the wirlwind of passion, you must acquire and beget a temperance that may give it smoothness.
> (3.2. 1–8)

The theatrical critic in him is unveiled when he discusses with Rosencrantz the situation of the theater, concerning the rivalry between his own company and a new one of young actors, or when he ignores Polonius's speech on the current so-called learned classification of drama:

> *Polonius.* The best actors in the world, either for tragedy, comedy, history, pastoral, pastoral-comical, historical-pastoral, tragical-historical, tragical-comical-historical-pastoral, scene individable, or poem unlimited.
> (2.2. 397–400)

Finally, he is the playwright when he adds his own lines to *The Murder of Gonzago,* which will be a decisive element in the disclosure of the true nature of the Ghost and, accordingly, of the part played by the King in his father's death. He is still being a playwright when, stealthily taking Claudius's letter from Rosencrantz and Guildenstern, he replaces it by one of his own, which will seal the messengers' destiny.

Besides all these devices, so typical of metatheater, Shakespeare achieves the climax in *Hamlet* by employing a play-within-a-play—*The Murder of Gonzago*. Such a device, often used by playwrights, is most effective, for it helps to unfold what is sometimes merely suggested in the major play. Most frequently, it even works as an inner comment on the events presented there.

In the specific case of *Hamlet,* its technical aspect is not particularly significant because Shakespeare handles it for the dramatic purposes that he has in mind. *The Murder of Gonzago* with Hamlet's addendum, combined with the dumb-show—the *Mouse Trap,* as Hamlet calls it—will determine the reversal of situation in the play. In fact, at the moment that Hamlet becomes certain that the Ghost was right about Claudius's crime, and Claudius finds out that Hamlet shares his criminal secret, the audience understands things are bound to change. At least one of the two will have to die.

In *Rosencrantz and Guildenstern Are Dead: A Metaplay,* Cesar Brites (1967, 102) says that Stoppard's play is "a drama which takes place in *Hamlet*'s backstage and that every time the Shakespearian text is left behind an entrance in the modern text is automatically implied." In Stoppard's play, the characters' destiny has not been altered. What the modern playwright has done has been to speculate about what might happen to those who, left to themselves, are not able to control their fate.

By juxtaposing the characters, acts, and scenes of his play with passages from *Hamlet,* he devises a particular framework, with unusual refractory effects. One of the outstanding ones is the parody he makes of both the characters and events of Shakespeare's play, which fits one of his metatheatrical purposes. He does not only demote Hamlet from his leading position but he also centers on two of Shakespeare's minor characters, Rosencrantz and Guildenstern, Granville-Barker's (1937, 251) so-called nonentities.

Stoppard starts his play-story at an imaginary moment, previous to his protagonist's meeting with Claudius in Shakespeare's *Hamlet* (H. 2.2) in which Ros and Guil are summoned by the King of Denmark to find out the reason for Hamlet's discontent. From then on,

Stoppard describes the progression of his characters' lives up to the information we are given of their death in England. (5.2.)

In a comparison between Shakespeare's *Hamlet* and Stoppard's *Rosencrantz and Guildenstern Are Dead,* from the point of view of metatheater, something that calls our attention at once is their different approach to the subject, which derives from their distinct and distinctive philosophical and social backgrounds.

Shakespeare's *Hamlet,* classified by H. D. F. Kitto (1960, 251) in his appreciation of the play as a religious tragedy, deals with those ethical values that prevailed in the dramatist's time: love, the precious feeling of friendship, honesty, straightforwardness, all founded upon man's conflicting choice between good and evil. Why are we told from the beginning that "There is something rotten in the state of Denmark," but because such ethical principles have been infringed upon. From the very beginning of the play, we become acquainted with the incestuous marriage of Gertrude and Claudius, who declares himself before the Court that he has taken to wife "our sometime sister." Such information is followed by the fratricide and adultery in the Ghost's confession to Hamlet of the circumstances under which he died. Furthermore, in spite of the fact that the word *spy* is never explicitly mentioned, it is suggested all the time, for spying has become a common practice at that corrupt Danish Court. Claudius and Polonius spy on Hamlet, and Ophelia, besides making use of Ophelia to spy on Hamlet; Rosencrantz and Guildenstern are asked by the King and Queen to spy on Hamlet, which they do without questioning the wickedness of such a betrayal of a friend's confidence; finally, Polonius tells Reynaldo to spy on his son, Laertes. Hamlet is, then, absolutely right to say that "The time is out of joint." This is the rotten world in which Prince Hamlet lives, that young Elizabethan hero whose "cursed spite [was] / That ever I was born to set it right" (1.5. 189–90).

In Stoppard's *Rosencrantz and Guildenstern Are Dead,* a rather different background is to be found. The major characters, modern antiheroes, live in a world deprived of Elizabethan values, that is, one which has lost its central explanation and meaning, its primeval anguish; one in which no conflict remains between good and evil since these two ideas have become relative and vague. In short, theirs is a world in which man's existence "has become trite, mechanical, complacent and deprived of the dignity that comes of awareness" (Esslin 1970, 390).

In such a world Stoppard's modern antiheroes, Ros and Guil, are set. They are indeed prototypes of those depersonalized, mechanical, and alienated individuals who can't even be distinguished one from the other. Having submitted to a higher power, that of the King, they have never stopped for a moment to think about what they are expected to do. They just follow instructions without questioning them, which proves to be not only dangerous but also a terrible mistake:

> *Guil:* . . . A man standing in his saddle in the half-lit half-alive dawn banged on the shutters and called two names. He was just a hat and a coat levitating in the grey plume of his own breath, but when he called we came. That much is certain—we came.
>
> (*R&G*, 29)

Although their alienation spares them the anguish of having to make a decision for the better or for the worse, which is a constant in Shakespeare's plays, they are the victims of their own unconsciousness. As well as their contemporaries, they lack the dignity of the Elizabethan hero, for they are not even aware of their roles of tragic heroes in their everyday lives. Unlike the counterparts in Shakespeare's play, who, being "the indifferent children of the earth" are easily corrupted by the appeal of power, Ros and Guil have not realized the full meaning of the part they are to play. They are merely machines, clocks, which, having been wound up, start working, unable to stop by themselves. Therefore they are not ambitious:

> *Ros.* And then we can go?
> *Guil.* And receive such thanks as fits a king's remembrance.
> *Ros.* I like the sound of that. What do you think he means by remembrance?
> *Guil.* He doesn't forget his friends.
> *Ros.* Would you care to estimate?
> *Guil.* Difficult to say, really—some kings tend to be amnesiac, others I suppose—the opposite, whatever that is . . .
> *Ros.* Yes—but—
> *Guil.* Elephantine?
> *Ros.* Not how long—How much?
> *Guil. Retentive*—he's a very retentive king, a royal retainer. . . .
> *Ros.* What are you playing at?
> *Guil.* Words, words. They're all we have to go on.
>
> (*R&G*, 30–31)

Nor are they consciously disloyal to their friend, for both ambition and disloyalty turn into a game that they are supposed to play:

> *Ros.* I can't remember. . . . What have we got to go on?
> *Guil.* We have been briefed. Hamlet's transformation. What do you recollect?
> *Ros.* Well, he's changed, hasn't he? The exterior and inward man fails to resemble—
> *Guil.* Draw him on to pleasures—glean what afflicts him.
> *Ros.* Something more than his father's death—
> *Guil.* He's always talking about us—there aren't two people living he dotes on more than us.
> *Ros.* We cheer him up—find out what's the matter—
> *Guil.* Exactly, it's a matter of asking the right questions and giving away as little as we can. It's a game.
>
> (R&G, 30)

In his parody of Shakespeare's *Hamlet,* Stoppard is criticizing both the Elizabethan play and his own. When, for instance, the Player, speaking of the characters in his play, Rosencrantz and Guildenstern, calls them spies, he's interpreting Shakespeare's *Hamlet.* Yet, at the same time, he is doing the same in regard to Stoppard's characters, Ros and Guil. In *Hamlet,* the word *spy* is never used explicitly, though, as mentioned above, some of the characters do spy successively on the others, for reasons of their own. Moreover all of them but Ophelia know exactly what they are doing and what they are doing it for.

In *Rosencrantz and Guildenstern Are Dead,* although the Player, describing the inner play *The Murder of Gonzago,* illustrated by the dumb-show, uses the word *spies* as he refers to its two characters, *Hamlet*'s Rosencrantz and Guildenstern, Ros and Guil do not recognize themselves in such a description.

> . . . The King—*(he pushes forward the POISONER/KING) tormented by guilt—haunted by fear—decides to despatch his nephew to England—and entrusts this undertaking to two smiling accomplices—friends—courtiers—to two spies (He has swung around to bring together the POISONER/KING and the two cloaked TRAGEDIANS; the latter kneel and accept a scroll from the KING)*—giving them a letter to present to the English court—!
> And so they depart—on board ship—
>
> (R&G, p. 61)

Not even when Ros comes close to "his spy," dressed in a coat identical to his, does he accept the idea of identifying himself with his mirrored self; what's more, at the end, he goes to the extreme of exchanging position with his counterpart:

> *Ros.* Well, if it isn't—! No, wait a minute, don't tell me—it's a long time since—where was it? Ah, this is taking me back to—when was it? I know you, don't I? I never forget a face—*(he looks into the SPY's face)* . . . not that I know yours that is. For a moment I thought—no, I don't know you, do I? Yes, I'm afraid you're quite wrong. You must have mistaken me for someone else.
>
> (*R&G*, 62)

This reaction of theirs is occasioned either by their total alienation, or by their fear of facing reality, or most probably by both.

If the Elizabethan world is one in which appearance and reality are at stake, our contemporary world is that in which there prevails a tension between illusion and reality. Such a contrast is evidenced in the part played by Hamlet and the Player, respectively, in Shakespeare's and Stoppard's plays. It should be noticed that such a minor character as the First Player in *Hamlet* is turned into a very significant one in *Rosencrantz and Guildenstern Are Dead* for the very reason that he has become Stoppard's spokesman. Not only does he express the modern dramatist's ideas that life, being a stage, is an illusion—

> *Guil.* We only know what we're told and that's little enough. And for all we know it isn't true.
> *Player.* For all anyone knows, nothing is. Everything has to be taken on trust; truth is only that which is taken to be true. It's the currency of living. There may be nothing behind it, but it doesn't make any difference so long as it is honoured. One acts on assumptions.
>
> (*R&G*, 49)

—but he also says that illusion is more convincing than reality, for in a performance people are prepared to believe in it:

> *Guil. (fear, derision):* Actors! The mechanics of cheap melodrama! That isn't *death!* . . . .
> . . . .
> You die so many times; how can you expect them to believe in your death?
> *Player.* On the contrary, it's the only kind they do believe. They're con-

ditioned to it. I had an actor once who was condemned to hang for stealing a sheep—or a lamb, I forget which—so I got permission to have him hanged in the middle of a play—had to change the plot a bit but I thought it would be effective, you know—and you wouldn't believe it, he just wasn't convincing! It was impossible to suspend one's disbelief—and what with the audience jeering and throwing peanuts, the whole thing was a *disaster*!—he did nothing but cry all the time—right out of character—he stood there and cried. . . . Never again.

(*R&G*, 63)

Besides standing for Stoppard in the play, the Player is an actor who describes the players' expertise in creating illusion:

Player. We transport you into a world of intrigue and ilusion . . . clowns, if you like, murderers—we can do you ghosts and battles, on the skirmish level, heroes, villains, tormented lovers—set pieces in the poetic vein; we can do you rapists or rape or both, by all means, faithless wives and ravished virgins.

(*R&G*, 17)

The Player can also express the actors' desolation at the want of an audience, their reason for living:

Player. We're actors. . . . We pledged our identities, secure in the conventions of our trade; that someone would be watching. And then, gradually, no one was. We were caught, high and dry.

(*R&G*, 47)

He is also a drama critic when he describes the mechanics of cheap melodrama:

Guil. (*tense, progressively rattled during the whole mime and commentary*) You!—What do you know about *death*?
Player. It's what the actors do best. They have to exploit whatever talent is given to them, and their talent is dying. They can die heroically, comically, ironically, slowly, suddenly, disgustingly, charmingly, or from a great height. My own talent is more general. I extract significance from melodrama, a significance which it does not in fact contain; but occasionally, from out of the matter, there escapes a thin beam of light that, seen at the right angle, can crack the shell of mortality.
Ros. Is that all they can do—die?
Player. No, no—they kill beautifully. In fact some of them kill even better than they die. The rest die better than they kill. They're a team.

(*R&G*, 63)

He extends his piece of criticism to the Elizabethan drama when he tells Guil:

> *Player.* .... We're more of the blood, love and rhetoric school.
> *Guil.* Well, I'll leave the choice to you, if there is anything to choose between them.
> *Player.* They're hardly divisible, sir—well, I can do you blood and love without the rhetoric, and I can do you blood and rhetoric without the love, and I can do you all three concurrent or consecutive, but I can't do you love and rhetoric without the blood. Blood is compulsory—they're all blood, you see.
>
> (*R&G,* 24)

The most striking metatheatrical device, used quite differently by both playwrights, is the one of a play-within-a-play. In Shakespeare's drama, the play-within-a-play is *The Murder of Gonzago.* It is used by Hamlet as an ultimate dramatic resource to elucidate his doubts about the Ghost's real nature and Claudius's resulting guilt or innocence. In this microplay, Lucianus, who was the King's nephew and the Queen's lover, kills his uncle by poisoning him in the same way the Ghost said he had been poisoned by his brother Claudius. Young Hamlet's psychological need for such a dramatic test results from his hope that the Ghost may not be his father's spirit but the devil, so that such a dreadful and tormenting nightmare—fratricide and adultery—may come to an end. Only Horatio and himself are in on the secret, having agreed to watch the King's reactions throughout the performance. When, finally, the disrupted King leaves the place, on seeing his crime performed, he has condemned himself. Yet Hamlet's knowledge of his criminal deed, also means the Prince's condemnation. At this moment, either the spectator or the reader realizes that something tragic will come of it. The King and Hamlet cannot coexist anymore, at least one of them will have to die: they are too dangerous to each other. Therefore, the turning point or the reversal of situation has been reached. There will forcedly be a change in the hero's fortune.

Stoppard goes further in his handling of this technical device. In *Rosencrantz and Guildenstern Are Dead,* there is *The Murder of Gonzago* within *HAMLET,* which is itself within the major play. The result is, therefore, a play-within-a-play, which is itself within another play. Yet a good many alterations have been made by the modern dramatist for his own theatrical and critical ends. *The Mur-*

der of Gonzago, for instance, instead of being performed at the court, turns into the mere rehearsal of a *"piece of mime."* To Guil's inquiry of its meaning, the Player explains its dramatic function of enlightening a language sometimes obscure:

> *Guil.* What's the dumbshow for?
> *Player.* Well, it's a device, really—it makes the action that follows more or less comprehensible; you understand, we are tied down to a language which makes up in obscurity what it lacks in style.
>
> (*R&G,* 57)

Here, again, with the Player as his spokesman, Stoppard is commenting not only on modern theater but also on his own play.

In Stoppard's play, the dumb-show stands as a kind of backdrop for the Player's explanation of what is going on. It works, so it seems, as a kind of musical background to the Player's words. And it proceeds in this way up to the end of what the Player calls act 1. This part coincides entirely with Shakespeare's own dumb show, which is familiar to both Ros and Guil. However when, without stopping there, the Player announces act 2, Ros, bewildered, asks him whether that hadn't been the end. To the Player it certainly wasn't, for there would be no tragedy for him in an ending without any death. From then on the pantomime, which had revealed only past events, will foretell the future, *Hamlet*'s story, in fact. Then the piece of mime stops being a mere backdrop to the Player's narration. It gains new life, for the Player, becoming a mime himself, assumes a triple role. Besides being the narrator, he is now Lucianus and also, by transposition, Hamlet, Claudius's victim.

> *Player.* Lucianus, nephew to the king . . . usurped by his uncle and shattered by his mother's incestuous marriage . . . loses his reason . . . throwing the court into turmoil and disarray as he alternates between bitter melancholy and unrestricted lunacy . . . staggering from the suicidal (a pose) to the homicidal (there he kills "POLONIUS") . . .
>
> (*R&G,* 61)

At this moment of his narrative, the Player explicitly mentions Hamlet's ambiguous relationship with his mother, the psychoanalytical point of view of Ernest Jones, who detected an oedipal component in the young Prince's conflict:

Player. . . . he at last confronts his mother and in a scene of provocative ambiguity—(a somewhat oedipal embrace) begs her to repent and recant—

(*R&G*, 67)

Accompanied by the Player's words, the dumb-show goes on, summing up scene 3 of Hamlet's act 3 in which Rosencrantz and Guildenstern are ordered by the King to take Prince Hamlet to England. Here Stoppard intentionally inverts the order by making scene 4 precede scene 3. The Player's as well as the playwright's concern is actually with the spies' fate, not with Hamlet's problems.

Stoppard's technical interference in Shakespeare's play fits Ricardou's comments on the *mise en abyme* aspect of Poe's "Fall of the House of Usher": "C'est par le microscopique dévoilement du récit global, donc, que la mise en abyme conteste l'ordonnance préalable de l'histoire. Prophétie, elle perturbe l'avenir en le découvrant avant terme, par anticipation" (1967, 176).

The noncommittal pair is, then, shown arriving in England and being executed there by the King of England's order. Here the dumb-show ends in a most unexpected way, typical of Stoppard. The tragedians performing the spies, Rosencrantz and Guildenstern, lie still, barely visible, covered with their own cloaks by the Player. There is suddenly blackout and, when the light comes on, it does as a sunrise. As the light grows, two figures may be seen lying, covered with those cloaks, where the corpses of the spies had been. They are Ros and Guil, who are resting quite comfortably. Such a coming back in time produces a very special effect on the spectator or reader: a feeling of illusion, of dream. The impression left by these two characters' deaths in Stoppard's play is quite different from the one left by their Elizabethan counterparts. It is not difficult to understand Hamlet's reaction at the death of those two who, having betrayed their friend's confidence, had servilely and ambitiously yielded to the all mighty:

Hamlet. Why, man, they did make love to this employment;
They are not near my conscience; their defeat
Does by their own insinuation grow.
'Tis dangerous when the base nature comes
Between the pass and fell incensed points.

(5.2. 58–62)

Nor is it difficult to agree with the Player's words, in Stoppard's play, when he leaves the judgment of Ros and Guil open to our own conclusions:

> *Player.* Traitors hoist by their own petard?—or victims of the gods?—we shall never know!
>
> (*R&G*, 62)

While the minor play in Shakespeare's *Hamlet* turns back to past events so as to test Claudius's deed and lead him to unfold his criminal secret, Stoppard's *Rosencrantz and Guildenstern Are Dead* projects onto the future, in an attempt to make Ros and Guil become aware not only of their roles at the court but also of their destinies in the play. However, if Hamlet's malicious trick succeeds in awakening the King's conscience, the piece of mime in Stoppard's play is not successful in making the two protagonists recognize themselves in the scene performed before them.

Such contrasting effects make us wonder why Stoppard used passages from Shakespeare's *Hamlet* in his play. That he is an expert in handling metatheatrical devices is unquestionably made clear in his drama. Yet what seems to have appealed to his imagination must have been the possibility of a different perspective on those two characters, Shakespeare's Rosencrantz and Guildenstern, who, after having been disloyal to their friend, die. It should be kept in mind that, enjoying free will, as all of Shakespeare's characters do, they may make their own decisions, which usually implies hesitation and suffering, for fear of making the wrong ones.

Unlike their counterparts, Stoppard's Ros and Guil lack such freedom of choice, for they are circumscribed by the playwright's script. When Guil asks the Player who decides about those who are "marked for death," the appropriation says that nobody does because it is "written":

> *Player.* It never varies—we aim at the point where everyone who is marked for death dies.
> *Guil.* Marked?
> *Player.* Between "just desserts" and "tragic irony" we are given quite a lot of scope for our particular talent. Generally speaking, things have gone about as far as they can possibly go when things have got about as bad as they reasonably get. (*He switches on a smile*)
> *Guil.* Who decides?
> *Player.* (*switching off his smile*) Decides? It is *written*. . . .
>
> (*R&G*, 81)

Later he returns to the same idea, showing the limitation of their actions by what has been decided for them to do:

> *Guil.* .... Free to move, speak, extemporise, and yet. We have not been cut loose. Our truancy is defined by one fixed star, and our drift represents merely a slight change of angle to it: we may seize the moment, toss it around while the moments pass, a short dash here, an exploration there, but we are brought round full circle to face again the single immutable fact—that we, Rosencrantz and Guildenstern, bearing a letter from one king to another, are taking Hamlet to England.
>
> (*R&G*, 76)

And yet, even given the chance to make a decision, they won't take it; they have got used to being led by "scripts," either because they are used to complying, or because they are afraid of defying fortune. Yet above all, to make a decision and act accordingly is too difficult a step:

> *Ros.* .... I could jump over the river. That would put a spoke in their wheel.
> *Guil.* Unless they're counting on it.
> *Ros.* I shall remain on board. That'll put a spoke in their wheel. (*The futility of it, fury*) All right! We don't question, we don't doubt. We perform ...
>
> (*R&G*, 81)

In Ros and Guil, Stoppard has actually portrayed modern men as mere performers in a world deprived of values and beliefs, devoid of certainties, in which there are only questions, but no answers:

> *Ros.* I remember when there were no questions.
> *Guil.* There were always questions. To exchange one set for another is no great matter.
> *Ros.* Answers, yes. There were answers to everything.
> *Guil.* You've forgotten.
> *Ros.* (*flaring*) I haven't forgotten—how I used to remember my own name—and yours, oh *yes!* There were answers everywhere you *looked*. There was no question about it—people knew who I was and if they didn't they asked and I told them.
>
> (*R&G*, 29)

In such a world, these antiheroes, completely unaware of the ultimate realities of their condition, avoid facing the only certainty that has been left them: that, having been born, they will die somehow, somewhere, some day:

> *Ros.* . . . We must be born with an intuition of mortality. Before we know the words for it, before we know that there are words, out we come, bloodied and squalling with the knowledge that for all the compasses in the world, there's only one direction, and time is its only measure.
>
> (*R&G*, 53)

Nevertheless, not being experienced *in life,* death is the only thing that cannot be performed:

> *Guil.* No, no, no . . . you've got it all wrong . . . you can't act death. The *fact* of it is nothing to do with seeing it happen—it's not gasps and blood and falling about—that isn't what makes it death. It's just a man failing to reappear, that's all—now you see him, now you don't that's the only thing that's real; here one minute and gone the next and never coming back—an exit, unobtrusive and unannounced, a disappearance gathering weight as it goes on, until, finally, it is heavy with death.
>
> (*R&G*, 64)

Besides, to the sceptic modern man, there is no glory in dying nobly for one's honor or one's beliefs as the Elizabethans had thought, for as Guil says:

> *Guil.* . . . Dying is not romantic, and death is not a game which will soon be over. . . . Death is not anything . . . , death is not . . . It's absence of presence, nothing more . . . the endless time of never coming back . . . a gap you can't see, and when the wind blows it, it makes no sound . . .

Bibliography

Abel, Lionel. *Metateatro.* Trans. Barbara Heliodora. Rio de Janeiro: Zahar, 1968.

Adler, Thomas P. *Mirror on the Stage.* West Lafayette, Ind.: Purdue University Press, 1987.

Brites, Cesar A. F. "*Rosencrantz and Guildenstern Are Dead:* Uma Metapeça." Master's thesis, Universidade Federal do Rio de Janeiro, Faculdade de Letras, 1980.

Calderwood, James L. *To Be or Not to Be: Negation and Metadrama in Hamlet.* New York: Columbia University Press, 1983.

Camus, Albert. *Le mythe de Sisyphe.* Paris: Gallimard, 1942.

Corballis, Richard. *Stoppard: The Mystery and the Clockwork.* New York: Methuen, 1984.

Esslin, Martin. *The Theatre of the Absurd.* Harmondsworth, England: Penguin, 1968.

Granville-Barker, Harley. *Prefaces to Shakespeare: Hamlet.* 3rd series, vol. 3. London: Sigwig and Jackson, 1937.

Hayman, Ronald. *Tom Stoppard.* London: Heinemann, 1977.

Hunter, Jim. *Tom Stoppard's Plays.* London: Faber and Faber, 1982.

Kitto, H.D.F. *Form and Meaning in Drama: A Study of Six Greek Plays.* London: Methuen, 1984.

Ricardou, Jean. *Problèmes du Nouveau Roman.* Paris: Seuil, 1967.

Robinson, Michael. *The Long Sonata of the Dead.* London: Rupert Hart-Davis, 1969.

Schlueter, Jim. *Metafictional Characters in Modern Drama.* New York: Columbia University Press, 1979.

Stoppard, Tom. *Rosencrantz and Guildenstern Are Dead.* London: Faber and Faber, 1978.

Wilson, Dover. *What Happens in Hamlet.* Cambridge: Cambridge University Press, 1970.

Godard: A Contemporary *King Lear*

Thaís Flores Nogueira Diniz

Humanity has always concerned itself with issues of order, accepted by men as having divine origin. The principles have always been respected and exalted in various ways, including through art. We need only to remember the ceremonies offered to the gods of harvest in ancient Greece, rituals which were the origin of theater. There have, however, always been exceptions and, instead of celebrations, many artists rejected the principles of order, like Euripides, who protested against the religion and ethics of his time. The artist does not always propose something to substitute that which he refuses or against which he protests; very often it is despair itself which comes through in his works, since art and culture may also express a negative view of the world, a view held by the humanist philosophies of the Renaissance and the existentialist philosophies of the twentieth century.

In this chapter I show how the issues of order/disorder, underlying works of art, and certainly Shakespeare's work, have been taken up again in our century, by reference to the translation/adaptation of *King Lear* for the cinema by the French filmmaker Jean-Luc Godard.[1] The aspects that interest me are those relating to changes of interpretation that reflect a cultural trend. They have to do with the nationality of the filmmaker, the cultural context-moment of the production, and reception of the film. In the case of Godard's film, the alterations have to do with the attempt to abolish cultural items as far as is possible. Previous film adaptations of the play show the issue of order at different levels. They make up, as it were, kinds of interpretants by which they can be studied. The issue of social order, for example, is the main concern of the Russian filmmaker Grigori Kozintsev, in his film *Korol Lear,* while the issues of family order in the film *Ran*[2] are taken up again and subverted by Akira Kurosawa, greatly influenced by Japanese culture. The issue of existential order is clear in Peter Brook's film about *King Lear*[3], as well as being a theme of Godard's film, where it is altered to such a point that the film ends up undergoing a change of genre.

Robert Brustein (1967) has argued that the fall of tragic heroes in Shakespeare is evidence of a feeling of futility and despair in European cultures at the end of the Renaissance. This feeling is reflected in later naturalist philosophies, which questioned everything and foresaw the eminent collapse of order. These forecasts took on, in art, the form of myths of defeat and images of decadence and morbidity. Tragedy lost its clear outlines, and good and evil intermingled, while universal order was reviewed. This feeling of despair and futility, of unbelief and skepticism in the face of temporal and spiritual laws that permeated the Renaissance spirit are illustrated in *King Lear* through the idea that "freedom lives hence and banishment is here" (1.1.180) and that "As flies to wanton boys are we to the gods; they kill us for their sport" (4.1.36–37). In spite of still affirming faith in the righteousness of God through punishing weakness, the play presents the world as skeptical, where human nature and the forces of nature are cruel.

In the twentieth century, the idea of order disappears, at least with the meaning of cosmic, universal justice, and there follows a feeling of a lack of meaning to life and the total loss of ideals. Nietzsche declares the death of God and, with it, that of all traditional values. Revolt and protest, born from the spectacle of irrationality, in confrontation with an unjust and incomprehensible condition, become an alternative to nihilism. The playwright adopts an attitude of refusal that places him in conflict with the laws of modern necessity. "Rejecting God, church, community and family—demanding rights against the impositions of government, morality, conventions and norms—the playwright adopts a position of rebel, taunting restrictions, determined to provoke the fall of all barriers" (Brustein, 1976, 23).

The cinema, to a greater or lesser extent, fits these features of the "Theater of Protest," described by Brustein, mainly with regard to existential revolt. This is because the theater—and the cinema, as part of it—does not mix with reality, but runs on a parallel plane. The filmmakers of the twentieth century often adopt a position that is similar to that of playwrights and are often not revolutionaries, but rebels.

With his translation/adaptation of *King Lear,* the French filmmaker seems to adopt this position. He is not concerned with the issue of order, and, on the contrary, seems to subvert it completely.

His film, not at all tragic, is intellectualized and does not offer the spectator the possibility of full understanding. As the filmmaker makes clear in the film, he does not intend to give it a comprehensive treatment, since it is only an approach, a study, which is obviously partial. There is nothing definitive about the text; it is constantly interrupted, discontinuous, a disordered mix of images, a true chaos, which results in a negative view of life.

The film does not present a linear story; rather, diegetically, this nearly does not exist. It is a mass of images, texts, voices without logical sequence. It has dozens of allusions to other works and quotes from famous texts. What is derived from the text are only a few characters, vaguely associated with those of Shakespeare, and some speeches totally out of context.

One of the main elements that make up the film is the pun, the play of words/images, much to the taste of the Renaissance mind and abundant in Shakespeare's works, which Godard uses brilliantly, for example, the word *clearing* which, among other meanings, has that of "making understandable." The work, besides being a study and an approach, also makes things understandable, it insinuates the intertitle. However, as we know, Godard's intention is not making his film understandable, nor making the spectator understand. As a matter of fact, the word *clearing* can also mean an open space in the forest, without the indication of an exit. The clearing, as the film itself, does not lead anywhere. But Godard writes the word in such a way as to provide another clue: C-LEARING. In this way the word *Lear* appears. We can, therefore, read *clearing* as meaning a film about Lear that does not explain anything and leads to a place without a clear exit.

The play of words goes through another expression, *nothing,* a word which recurs in the Renaissance text. The place without an exit is nothing, NO + THING, which Godard shows in another intertitle. One voice states that Cordelia is not silent, and that, instead of not saying anything, she says something, she says "Nothing." The word that she speaks is the NO THING, or rather, NOTHING. Cordelia does not remain silent, she speaks with her voice in the film, but says "nothing." Besides representing a recurring element of the play, this word also refers to the film: a film that is not understood, a nothing. It is not a film, it is only a study, an approach, it is absurd, as Godard anounced at the beginning. This word, meaning *nothing,* permeates all of Shakespeare's text, where Lear symbolizes lack of vision, lack of reason, lack of power. But the idea also permeates the film, where everything is lacking: the plot, the sequence, the order, understanding, comprehension. Therefore, order, which is momentarily broken in the Renaissance play, is translated in the modern world, governed more by the philosophy of the absurd than the relative skepticism of Shakespeare's theater, as total break, disorder, absence of meaning and purpose. In these examples we find what is called transcultural translation, motivated both by the passing of time, as well as by geographical and cultural change from Elizabethan England to the France of our days, or more precisely, to the contemporary Western world.

In the film, Godard plays with the main ideas of the play and ends up with another play on words with *virtue* and *power,* between which he establishes different relations at different moments. He uses "virtue versus power," then he inverts it and uses "power versus virtue," and so on, establishing several oppositions, always making use of the play on words for his translation, until he reaches an identification, "power and virtue" in another intertitle. We might remember here that the two meanings blend in the Latin word *virtus,* a quality belonging to a man who holds power.

The fusion, however, happens at many different levels. First, there is the fusion of voices. Godard begins by making them overlap, leading to total incomprehensibility, which seems to be his objective. The voices of the characters mix. The voices of D. Learo, of William Shakespeare Jr. V, of Godard himself, of George Meredith, and of an unknown woman are heard. They quote lines from *Lear,* but they also remind us of theories about image and word. Shakespeare's sonnets are recited, passages from Virginia Woolf's *The Waves* are read in a loud voice, observations about the mafioso Lansky are dictated by D. Learo to his daughter (who types them), Lear's lines from the play, Joana D'Arc's lines from Breton's film, in a chaotic superimposition of texts and sounds: the recordings of voices, a cry of seagulls, chamber and Renaissance music, as well as other sounds.

The temporal element also blends itself in the film, with a superimposition of different historical moments. Godard, the modern filmmaker, appears dressed up as the Fool, a Renaissance figure. With a difference: the Fool of the film has electric wires and plugs of sound and a telephone on his head, objects which bring to mind the modern world. The Renaissance, the contemporary world, the period after the Chernobyl disaster, are all evoked by words, images, sculptures, and modern paintings, next to Renaissance works which appear without a chronological sequence, leading to a true fusion of the arts. Besides drawing on the resources of the cinema, Godard also uses painting to show his view of the world. This fusion, however, will not lead to a synthesis, since the film does not intend to do this; it represents a chaotic vision, as the initial intertitles suggested: *a study, an approach,* etc.

The characters also blend. Shakespeare is, at the same time, the Renaissance playwright, the descendant William Shakespeare, Jr. V, who tries to recover his works, the voice that recites a sonnet or the lines from *Lear.* On the other hand, George Meredith is Lear, but, at the same time, D. Learo, the Mafia boss, the writer of the book, Cordelia's father. This is the daughter of Norman Mailer, but, at the same time, she is the actress Molly Ringwald, the Joana D'Arc of Bresson's film, and the Cordelia of *King Lear.* This fusion of characters and stars also evokes the instated chaos.

The authors also blend. D. Learo, for example, is writing a book that already exists, whose author is Fried. However, as he dictates, as if he were actually producing the book, he uses, besides the passages from his own work, lines from Shakespeare. William Shakespeare Jr. V, the pseudodescendant of Shakespeare, in turn, copies into a notebook the lines he believes belonged to his supposed ancestor and which he intends to recover. Therefore Shakespeare blends with his false descendant, who intermingles with Lear and, at the same time, with D. Learo, who is George Meredith, but is also Norman Mailer and Godard himself. The authors, therefore, are, at the same time, Fried, D. Learo, Shakespeare and the character William Shakespeare Jr. V. However, through the superimposition of authors, the author is, in a way, descentralizing the idea of author, and emphasizing his "death," declared by currents of contemporary criticism. He establishes paternity in an inverse way. Instead of a Lear and three daughters, there is a Cordelia with three fathers: the true father as star, the father—character of the film—as true father, and the director of the film. Authorship, mainly that of a work of art, is related to the idea of paternity. The film uses father images to speak about creation: it projects portraits of filmmakers and their fathers, of Norman Mailer and his daughter, Kate; and of Chronos, the mythological character who devours his child.

The issue of creation in a work of art takes us back to existentialist theories, where artistic creation is a possible response in the face of the nothingness of existence, in the face of the mysterious grandeur of the universe, which inspires in perplexed men the "fear and trembling,"⁴ the title of Kierkegaard's book. Once again Godard plays with words, altering them to *fear and loathing,* an allusion to Kierkegaard's text, but which expresses fear in the face of something which is loathsome and repugnant. He no longer speaks of fear and trembling, an attitude of terror in the face of divine majesty, a mixture of fear and reverence before the cosmos, something which is recognized as inspiring respect, but of fear and loathing, existential nausea in the face of the absurd, alluding to the title of Sartre's novel *Nausea.* The simple change from trembling to loathing underlines transcultural translation, from Shakespeare's text to the creation of the nouvelle vague. By referring to itself, the film overlays the theme of creation. As in the existentialist theories, the meaning proposed for life, in the film, is the creation, in this case, of the film itself—or, alternatively, the contemplation and appreciation of the work of art through its translation, which is a means of conserving it. By making the film, which is, in a way, a translation of Shakespeare's work, Godard is giving an answer to the nothing of existence; he becomes involved. If this will contribute to improve the life of his peers, we do not know. But the film reminds the spectator of the fact that he, as Lear, is a shadow. This can be taken as a challenge: beginning with this shadow, the human being has to create himself.

Besides the fusion of texts, time, characters, voices, forms of art, and authors, are also fused. They are Renaissance pictures mixed with contemporary pictures and segments from films: portraits of filmmakers mixed with illustrations from a book by Gustave Doré and images of artistic nudes presented to Cordelia in a book she skims indifferently. There are other images of Cordelia, which mix in. Besides the mental image, created by Shakespeare's text, we have the Cordelia represented by Kate Mailer and that represented by Molly Ringwald, two actresses for the same character. These different images lead us to another decentralization: just as there is not a definitive Cordelia, there is no definite text or sound, nor is there, finally, a definitive Lear.

The superimposition also occurs with the *myse-en-abyme* resource, that is, one play within another. The scene of D. Learo, which is initially played by Norman Mailer, who, with his daughter, the artist Kate Mailer, begins the film, fits into the film text, when Mailer is replaced by George Meredith and, the daughter, by Molly Ringwald.

At the beginning, the only clue to Shakespeare's text is the title, which is the same as the text. Next, there appears D. Learo, who is Lear transformed into a powerful Mafia boss. The film has an echo of the words of Shakespeare's Fool, who, answering the question "Who is it that can tell me who I am?" says "Lear's shadow" (1.4:212–13). D. Learo, on the balcony of the hotel, asks the same question, and somebody gives him the same answer: not the Fool, but an unknown character, the Fool's double, who in the film is played by Godard. As he himself tells us, the entire crew left him and he was left alone to make the film and present it before the deadline to the producers. The intertitle suggests the betrayal of the team: "shot in the back." Therefore, indirectly, Godard, by making the film, is playing the Fool. Taken together, the title and the characters, and the recurrence of the Fool and of some lines, return to intertextual links.

All the superimpositions appear to us as absurd, and other absurdities multiply. The initial scenes are repeated several times, without any explanation or reason. In addition, the William Shakespeare Jr. V character, who says he is a descendant of the Bard, is also absurd, because it is well known there are no longer any descendants of Shakespeare.

Each quotation, analogy, demands from the spectator great extratextual knowledge. It is as if Godard concentrated centuries of art and culture in this film, reviewing all of history. He begins labeling the film a study, an approach, and he ends at the same point, showing that nothing is definitive, not even his approach to *King Lear,* which is not a film in a traditional sense, but only insinuates possible transcultural translations.

Using resources of fusion and superimposition, the film shows the total subversion of order at various levels. It exemplifies the rupture of existential order through the lack of sequence and logic between images, the chaotic fusion of elements without an apparent sequence (except to show the subversion of everything) and of the intertitles themselves, which show the film as incomplete and the filmmaker as betrayed. It also presents the rupture of patriarchal order by inverting the issue of paternity/creation of the work of art and coming to a chaotic intertextuality, without any insinuation of the restoration of order, as occurs in the films of Kozintsev, Peter Brook, and Kurosawa.

Since it does not involve the issue of justice or the restoration of order, Godard's film does not portray the tragic view of life, which would demand this restoration. Godard translates Shakespeare's tragedy, in which the view of man is sublime, to a story without importance in a world of banalities. Instead of focusing on the inner conflicts and the search for identity, it deals with the main conflicts of contemporaries, as, for example, a quarrel between Norman Mailer and Godard himself, and other intrigues of the film world. What is implicit is a view of modern culture as trivial and limited, without the least possibility of the grandeur transmitted in Shakespeare's tragic view.

The treatment given to the film is hardly orthodox, in terms of content or form. In this sense, the Renaissance play, belonging to the genre of tragedy, becomes a caricature or travesty, both of literary form and of the theme itself. It may be said that the film is a mock film, in analogy with a mock play. The translation Godard makes of Shakespeare is that of an ironic witness, the product of mediocrity perceived by Godard in the contemporary world. On the other hand, to a greater or lesser degree, it demonstrates what Patrick Cattrysse (1992) calls innovative translation, which is defined as that which, in the film, modifies the literary genre of the work from which it was supposedly taken. Jean-Luc Godard's film, due to the fact that it is the most concrete illustration of this translation defined by Cattrysse, lends itself to specific study on the change of genre resulting from transcultural translation.

Notes

1. Godard, Jean-Luc (dir.) *King Lear* USA/Switzerland: Cannon, 1987.
2. Kurosawa, Akira (dir.). *Ran.* Japan: Greenway Film/Nippon, 1985.
3. Brook, Peter (dir.). *King Lear.* UK: Filmways/Athene, 1971.
4. Kierkegaard, Søren (1939). *Fear and Trembling*: a dialectical lyric by Johannes de Silentio and *The Sickness unto Death.* Tr. with introduction and notes by Walter Lowrie. New Jesey: Princeton University Press, 1953. 6th Printing, 1974.

Bibliography

Benoit, L. "King Lear de Jean-Luc Godard." *Cahiers du Cinema* 399, no. 76 (September 1987): 3.

Bresson, Robert. dir. *The Trial of Joan of Arc.* France, 1962.

Brustein, Robert. *O Teatro de Protesto.* Trans. Alvaro Cabral. Rio de Janeiro: Zahar, 1967.

Canby, Vincent. "Power and Pathos." *The New York Times,* September 7, 1985, sec. C, p. 14.

———. "Godard in his Mafia *King Lear*." *The New York Times,* January 6, 1988, sec. 6, p. 6.
Cattrysse, Patrick. "Film (adaptation) as Translation." *Target* 4, no. 1 (1992): 53–70.
Ciment, M. "King Lear." *Positif.* 3 vols. 1, 317/318 (July/August 1987): 79.
Corliss, Richard. "Mad Monarch as Gang Lord: *King Lear.*" *Time,* February 18, 1988, 71.
Donaldson, Peter S. "Disseminating Shakespeare: Paternity and Text in Jean-Luc Godard's *King Lear.*" *Shakespearean Films/Shakespearean Directors,* 189–225. Boston: Unwin Hynan, 1990.
Dreyer, Carl, dir. *Passion of Joan of Arc.* France, 1928.
Durgnat, R. "King Lear." *Monthly Film Bulletiearn,* 55 (February 1988): 38–39.
Godard, Jean-Luc. "Godard on Godard." In *Godard on Godard,* ed. Jean Leroy and Tom Milne. New York: Viking Press, 1968.
———, dir., *King Lear.* France, 1987.
Hayles, Catherine. ed. *Chaos and Order: A Complex Dynamics in Literature and Science.* Chicago: University of Chicago Press, 1991.
Kierkegaard, Soren. *Fear and Trembling*: a dialectical lyric by Johannes de Silentio and *The Sickness unto Death.* Trans. with intr. and notes by Walter Lowrie. New Jersey: Princeton University Press, 1953. 6th pr., 1974.
Maccabe, Colin. *Godard: Images, Sounds, Politics.* Bloomington. Indiana University Press, 1980.
Martini, E. "Fuori Concorso: re Lear di Jean-Luc Godard." *Cineforum* 27 (June/July 1987): 19.
Nokes, David. "Echoes of Godard." *Times Literary Supplement,* January 29–February 14, 1988, 112.
Philliponi, Alain. "Les Années Lumière." *Cahiers du Cinéma* 404 (February 1988):10–15.
Rich. "King Lear." *Variety* 328 (September 14, 1987): 2.
Robinson, Mark. "Ressurrected Images: Godard's *King Lear.*" *Performing Arts Journal* 11 (1988): 20–25.
Rothwell, Kenneth S., and Annabelle Henkin Melzer. *Shakespeare on Screen.* New York: Neal-Schuman, 1990.
Roud, Richard. *Jean-Luc Godard.* London: British Film Institute, 1968.
Shakespeare, William. *Rei Lear.* Trans. Carlos Alberto Cunha Medeiros e Oscar Mendes, *Obra Completa,* 3 vols. vol. 1. Rio de Janeiro: Nova Aguilar, 1989. 1:621–704.
Wells, Stanley. "Reunion and Death." *Times Literary Supplement,* March 14, 1986, 276.
Wollen, Peter. "Godard and Counter-Cinema: *Vent d'Est.*" In *Readings and Writings: Semiotic Counter-strategies,* 79–91. London: Verso, 1982.
———. "The Two Avant-Gardes." In *Readings and Writings: Semiotic Counter-Strategies,* 92–104. London: Verso, 1982.

Multiple Texts and Performance in the Final Scene of *Henry V*

MARGARIDA GANDARA RAUEN

TWO VERSIONS OF *HENRY V* HAVE PASSED ON TO US FROM SHAKEspeare's time, the First Quarto of 1600 (Q) and the First Folio of 1623 (F). Additional quartos and folios also exist and appear to derive from Q and F. Although Q's origin is unknown and F is generally viewed as the authoritative version, the standard editorial procedure has been to merge words, phrases, and passages otherwise exclusive to each of the playtexts. As scholarship established in the 1980s has demonstrated,[1] however, the conflated or modern "Shakespeare" reshape the dramatic effects of quarto and folio. Even when editors provide extensive footnotes meant to inform where and how they have interfered, the experience of reading each version separately is lost.

By juxtaposing the Q and F versions, we can verify the uniqueness of each playtext, rather than perpetuate the essentialist fallacy of determining the superiority of one of them. My analysis is not focused on changes due to conflation, general editing choices, or adaptations. I do not want to discuss Q and F in order to speculate on Shakespeare's intentions, as orthodox textual scholars have done.[2] My treatment of the playtexts does not address research such as Hinman's, either.[3] The intertextual analysis that follows exposes theatrical possibilities for the roles of Kate and Queen Isabel that are obscure in modern editions of *Henry V* and that have been overlooked by scholarship. This essay demonstrates that different approaches to interpretation emerge as a result of the study of the various versions of *Henry V*.

I would like to stress that all quotations and references are from W. W. Greg's edition of Shakespeare Quarto Facsimiles no. 9 (Oxford 1957) and the facsimile edition of the First Folio per Yale, prepared by H. Kökeritz. It is known that there are discrepancies between the originals and the facsimiles. The Hinman edition of the First Folio is generally more prestigious because it is not a reduced facsimile. Nevertheless, as Blayney has aptly demonstrated, the first folios "differed from one another even as they left the printing house in 1623," so that the idea of a superior copy is misleading.[4] I have used the Yale facsimile and the quarto per Oxford because they do not include pages from various other extant volumes of folios and quartos, such as the Norton facsimile and the Huntington Q facsimiles. Among the available volumes, the Yale and Oxford editions may, therefore, be considered formally complete ones, rather than facsimiles that offer the best available pages from various volumes.[5]

Let us begin considering how Q and F present rather different views of Kate and Queen Isabel. The contrast is striking in what modern editors call act 5, scene 2, the final scene.[6] The variants in the stage direction at the outset of the final scenes in Q and F, and the interaction that follows, are first indications of such difference. Modern editions usually mandate that Queen Isabel and Princess Katherine enter, and assign lines to Queen Isabel right after France speaks. But this is not the case in Q and F:

> *Enter at one doore, the King of England and his Lords. And at the other doore, the King of France, Queene Katherine, the Duke of Burbon, and others.*
>
> *Harry.* Peace to this meeting, wherefore we are met.
> And to our brother *France,* Faire time of day.
> Faire health vnto our louely cousen *Katherine.*
> And as a branch, and member of this stock:
> We do salute you Duke of *Burgondie.*
>   *Fran.* Brother of *England,* right ioyous are we to behold
> Your face, so are we Princes English euery one.
>   *Duk.* With pardon vnto both your mightines.
> Let it not displease you, if I demaund

> *Enter at one doore, King Henry, Exeter, Bedford, Warwicke, and other Lords. At another, Queene Isabel, the King, the Duke of Bourgongne, and other French.*
>   *King.* Peace to this meeting, wherefore we are met;
> Vnto our brother France, and to our Sister
> Health and faire time of day: Ioy and good wishes
> To our most faire and Princely Cofine *Katherine:*

> And as a branch and member of this Royalty,
> By whom this great assembly is contriu'd,
> We do salute you Duke of *Burgogne*,
> And Princes French and Peeres health to you all.
>   *Fra.* Right ioyous are we to behold your face,
> Most worthy brother England, fairely met,
> So are you Princes (English) euery one.
>   *Quee.* So happy be the Issue brother Ireland
> Of this good day, and of this gracious meeting,
> As we are now glad to behold your eyes,
> Your eyes which hitherto haue borne
> In them against the French that met them in their bent,
> The fatall Balls of murthering Basiliskes:
> The venome of such Lookes we fairely hope
> Haue lost their qualitie, and that this day
> Shall change all griefes and quarrels into loue.
>   *Eng.* To cry Amen to that, thus we appeare.
>   *Quee.* You English Princes all, I doe salute you.
>   *Burg.* My dutie to you both, on equall laue.
> Great Kings of France and England: that I haue labour'd

The stage directions in Q do not specifically include Queen Isabel. The word *Queene* is, as in F, meant for Kate (Henry's Queen). Q, in addition, includes no lines for Queen Isabel. In F we are sure both of her entrance and of her participation in dialogue. The theatrical possibilities generated by these differences have several implications for the degree of power associated with gender. A Q production can exclude Queen Isabel and, by doing so, restate the male dominance in a play that is essentially about men in a world of politics and war. Should Queen Isabel be on stage among the "others" mentioned in the stage direction, her business would inevitably suggest a condition of inferiority, whether she weeps, remains mute and acts proudly, or laughs like a madwoman. This presence would be undermined and disrespected further if Henry, whose verbal greeting in Q addresses France, Katherine, and Burgundie, but not Queen Isabel, also ignored her nonverbally.

Queen Isabel's role in F, on the other hand, seems much more dignified, both because Henry greets her ("our Sister") and because she is assigned lines. Her first speech in the last scene actually gives a status of equality to Henry and France, as she, too, expresses appreciation for the meeting between kingdoms: "So happy be the issue brother Ireland / Of this good day, and of this gracious meeting, / As we are now glad to behold your eyes . . ." Spoken seriously, these lines may convey relief at the prospective peace and make the French Queen come across as a sincere pacificator. But they could also be delivered in mockery, in which case Queen Isabel would have a dramatically different role, namely, ironizing Henry. The whole F speech under scrutiny could convey irony. In particular, her mentioning that they came from "the fatall Balls of murthering Basiliskes" but "shall change all griefes and quarrels into love" is sarcastic because the French were not exactly eager to stop fighting. They had no alternative other than settling for peace after losing thousands of soldiers (cf. Q F3 v; F H91). Burgundy's speech exclusive to F accentuates Frances's helplessness further:

> [France's] husbandry doth lye on heapes . . .
> our selves, and children . . . grow like savages,
> as souldiers will, that nothing doe,
> but meditate on blood.
>
> (F H 92)

The response "You English Princes all, I doe salute you" is presumptuous, too, since Queen Isabel is not in a position to be pompous. With sarcasm, the player would not only feign acceptance of Henry's victory, but also come across as a woman who clings to power and to pride.

If Isabel is present at all in Q, her silence generates the opposite effect. Although she could convey pride nonverbally in a performance based on Q, her having no words at all in the final scene could indicate a total loss of control, which becomes more evident if we consider the variations after Burgundy's plea for peace:

> *Duk.* With pardon vnto both your mightines.
> Let it not difpleafe you,if I demaund
> What rub or bar hath thus far hindred you,
> To keepe you from the gentle fpeech of peace?
> *Har.* If Duke of *Burgondy*,you wold haue peace,
> You muſt buy that peace,
> According as we haue drawne our articles..
> *Fran.* We haue but with a curfenary eye,
> Oreviewd them pleafeth your Grace;
> To let fome of) our Counfell fit with vs,
> We fhall returne our peremptory anfwere.
> *Har.* Go Lords,and fit with them,
> And bring vs anfwere backe.
> Yet leaue our coufen *Katherine* here behind.
> *France.* Withall our hearts.
>
> *Exit King and the Lords.Manet,*Hrry*,*Kathe-
> rine,*and the Gentlewoman.*

> You are aſſembled: and my ſpeech entreats,
> That I may know the Let, why gentle Peace
> Should not expell theſe inconueniences,
> And bleſſe vs with her former qualities.
>   *Eng.* If Duke of Burgonie, you would the Peace,
> Whoſe want giues growth to th'imperfections
> Which you haue cited; you muſt buy that Peace
> With full accord to all our iuſt demands,
> Whoſe Tenures and particular effects
> You haue enſchedul'd briefely in your hands.
>   *Burg.* The King hath heard them: to the which, as yet
> There is no Anſwer made.
>   *Eng.* Well then: the Peace which you before ſo vrg'd,
> Lyes in his Anſwer.
>   *France.* I haue but with a curſelarie eye
> O're-glanc't the Articles: Pleaſeth your Grace
> To appoint ſome of your Councell preſently
> To fit with vs once more, with better heed
> To re-ſuruey them; we will ſuddenly
> Paſſe our accept and peremptorie Anſwer.
>   *England.* Brother we ſhall. Goe Vnckle *Exeter,*
> And Brother *Clarence,* and you Brother *Gloucester,*
> *Warwick,* and *Huntington,* goe with the King,
> And take with you free power, to ratifie,
> Augment, or alter, as your Wiſdomes beſt
> Shall ſee aduantageable for our Dignitie,
> Any thing in or out of our Demands,
> And wee'le conſigne thereto. Will you, faire Siſter,
> Goe with the Princes, or ſtay here with vs?
>   *Quee.* Our gracious Brother, I will goe with them:
> Happily a Womans Voyce may doe ſome good,
> When Articles too nicely vrg'd, be ſtood on.
>   *England.* Yet leaue our Couſin *Katherine* here with vs,
> She is our capitall Demand, compris'd
> Within the fore-ranke of our Articles.
>   *Quee.* She hath good leaue.   *Exeunt omnes.*
>
> *Manet King and Katherine.*

The King of France requests, in both versions, that the Council meet. In Q, Henry authoritatively tells the Lords, the men only, to go. F1 emphasizes Queen Isabel's role because, first, Henry turns to her and by asking whether she will "goe with the princes" grants her free choice; second, she bluntly states that she will participate and is not verbally challenged; and finally, Henry accepts her view that "a womans voyce may doe some good, when articles too nicely urg'd be stood on."

In other words, Henry's behavior can shape Queen Isabel's status in at least two different ways. On the one hand, he appears to value her participation in the Council, indirectly undermining male authority. This is true if the scene is played seriously. But Henry could also make Queen Isabel come across as a naive fool if he addressed her with irony. The woman's status would be even worse if she responded to him without irony, though a kind of humiliated dignity could be conveyed if she acted proudly. The same two acting styles would reinforce her status if Henry's imperative "leave our Cousin," at the end of the F speech under consideration, were delivered seriously, or in mockery, since the Queen's reply "Kate hath good leave" would indicate, respectively, either her willingness to approve of a union that is politically important, or her pathetic loss of power, as a Queen and as a mother.

While the Council exits, Henry begins wooing Kate, whose participation in both versions has been silent and, in effect, ornamental. In addition, she has, also in Q and F, been a mere object of negotiation for France and England. But Kate's status differs in each version. A subtle example is her immediate projection in Q, especially if Queen Isabel is absent, or is on stage but not acknowledged by Henry when he greets Kate and the others verbally. In this case, blocking would define the degree of prominence.

The wooing scene has several complex dramatic implications, which I have discussed elsewhere.[1] Overall, Henry is much more dominant and assertive in Q than in F, where his attitude allows Kate to share rhetorical control. This effect is determined both by his reticence in Q as opposed to his eloquence in F1, and by the nature of the interactions:

>   *Har.* Go Lords, and fit with them,
> And bring vs anfwere backe.
> Yet leaue our coufen *Katherine* here behind.
>   *France.* Withall our hearts.
>
>   *Exit King and the Lords. Manet,* Hrry, Kathe-
>   rine, *and the Gentlewoman.*
>
>   *Hate.* Now *Kate,* you haue a blunt wooer here
> Left with you.
> If I could win thee at leapfrog,
> Or with vaunting with my armour on my backe,
> Into m, faddle,
> Without brag be it fpoken,
> Ide make compare with any.
> But leauing that *Kate,*
> If thou takeft me now,
> Thou fhalt haue me at the worft:

And in wearing, thou shalt haue me better and better,
Thou shalt haue a face that is not worth sun-burning.
But doost thou thinke, that thou and I,
Betweene Saint *Denis*,
And Saint *George*, shall get a boy,
That shall goe to *Constantinople*,
And take the great Turke by the beard, ha *Kate*?
  Kate. Is it possible dat me sall
Loue de enemie de *France*.

  England. Yet leaue our Cousin *Katherine* here with vs,
She is our capitall Demand, compris'd
Within the fore-ranke of our Articles.
  Quee. She hath good leaue.   *Exeunt omnes.*

        Admitet King and Katherine.

  King. Faire *Katherine*, and most faire,
Will you vouchsafe to teach a Souldier tearmes,
Such as will enter at a Ladyes eare,
And pleade his Loue-suit to her gentle heart.
  Kath. Your Maiestie shall mock at me, I cannot speake your England.
  King. O faire *Katherine*, if you will loue me soundly with your French heart, I will be glad to heare you confesse it brokenly with your English Tongue Doe you like me, *Kate*?
  Kath. Pardonne moy, I cannot tell wat is like me.
  King. An Angell is like you *Kate*, and you are like an Angell.
  Kath. Que dit il que Ie suis semblable a les Anges?
  Lady. Ouy verayment (sauf vostre Grace) ainsi dit il.
  King. I said so; deare *Katherine*, and I must not blush to affirme it.
  Kath. O bon Dieu, les langues des hommes sont plein de tromperies.
  King. What sayes she, faire one? that the tongues of men are full of deceits?
  Lady. Ouy, dat de tongeus of de mans is be full of deceits: dat is de Princesse.
  King. The Princesse is the better English-woman: yfaith *Kate*, my wooing is fit for thy vnderstanding, I am glad thou canst speake no better English, for if thou could'st, thou would'st finde me such a plaine King, that thou wouldst thinke, I had sold my Farme to buy my Crowne. I know no wayes to mince it in loue, but directly to say, I loue you; then if you vrge me farther, then to say, Doe you in faith? I weare out my suite: Giue me your answer, yfaith doe, and so clap hands, and a bargaine: how say you, Lady?
  Kath. Sanf vostre honeur, me vnderstand well.

In Q Henry truly acts as a *"blunt wooer"* by saving formalities and treating her as Kate, wishing he could "win [her] at leapfrog" or with his armour on his back, and by informing her of his rush to *"get a boy."* He takes intimacy for granted and appears to view Kate as a mere breeder, while she immediately questions the possibility of loving "de enemie de France." Her verbal response implies resistance, but only interpretation will define her status. Kate may express rejection by acting unfriendly and shocked, in which case she would preserve dignity. She may also come across as naive and unaware of her condition as object by acting sensually and/or romantically carried away. The playtext is open to either a tense or a light approach.

The F version also permits a tense or a light approach, but Henry's remark "Katherine . . . is our capitall demand, compris'd within the fore-ranke of our articles" in effect emphasizes Kate's importance before they even begin talking. This attitude could motivate more playfulness, and it gives Kate enough superiority to be ironic towards him during their small talk, an interpretation consistent with the above arguments regarding Queen Isabel. Henry begins by flattering Kate in a formal manner ("Faire Katherine and most faire . . . teach a Souldier . . . [to] pleade his Love-suit to her gentle heart"), which may be played ironically, but also may convey caution and respect. A production based on F could, in any case, raise Kate's status by having her perform intimidating business during their interaction, so that the "warlike Henry" of the prologue would come across as someone fooled by feminine wit, especially when she is modest about her English but then remarks: "Sauf vostre honeur, me understand well"; or when she challenges his honesty in the line "les langues des hommes sont plein de tromperies," a statement about men in general which she never voices in Q. Interestingly, Henry stops flattering her at this point, making some of the remarks that appear in Q:

> *King.* Marry, if you would put me to Verses, or to Dance for your sake, *Kate*, why you vndid me: for the one I haue neither words nor measure; and for the other, I haue no strength in measure, yet a reasonable measure in strength. If I could winne a Lady at Leape-frogge, or by vawting into my Saddle, with my Armour on my backe; vnder the correction of bragging be it spoken, I should quickly leape into a Wife: Or if I might buffet for my Loue, or bound my Horse for her fauours, I could lay on like a Butcher, and sit like a Jack an Apes, neuer off. But

TEXTS AND PERFORMANCE IN THE FINAL SCENE OF *HENRY V* 215

> before God *Kate*, I cannot looke greenely, nor gaspe out my eloquence, nor I haue no cunning in protestation; onely downe-right Oathes, which I neuer vse till vrg'd, nor neuer breake for vrging. If thou canst loue a fellow of this temper, *Kate*, whose face is not worth Sunne-burning? that neuer lookes in his Glasse, for loue of any thing he sees there? let thine Eye be thy Cooke. I speake to thee plaine Souldier: If thou canst loue me for this, take me? if not? to say to thee that I shall dye, is true; but for thy loue, by the L. No: yet I loue thee too. And while thou liu'st, deare *Kate*, take a fellow of plaine and vncoyned Constancie, for he perforce must do thee right, because he hath not the gift to wooe in other places: for these fellowes of infinit tongue, that can ryme themselues into Ladyes fauours, they doe alwayes reason themselues out againe. What? a speaker is but a prater, a Ryme is but a Ballad; a good Legge will fall, a strait Backe will stoope, a blacke Beard will turne white, a curl'd Pate will grow bald, a faire Face will wither, a full Eye will wax hollow: but a good Heart, *Kate*, is the Sunne and the Moone, or rather the Sunne, and not the Moone; for it shines bright, and neuer changes, but keepes his course truly. If thou would haue such a one, take me? and take me; take a Souldier: take a Souldier; take a King. And what say'st thou then to my Loue? speake my faire, and fairely, I pray thee.
>
> *Kath.* Is it possible dat I sould loue de ennemie of Fraunce?

Thus, Henry in F also remarks that "if [he] could win a lady at Leape-frogge, or . . . with [his] armour on [his] backe . . . [he] should quickly leap into a wife." His smooth approach at first, however, makes him vulnerable. And the F Kate can truly fool Henry if she, in addition to being intimidating or distant or formal, is charming and lively, perhaps giggling a few times while Henry delivers his long wooing speech, but suddenly becomes serious by the time of "Is it possible dat I should love de ennemie de Fraunce?" Acting thus, Kate would achieve a considerably higher condition than that of Q, accentuating the rhetorical control which she takes when she ignores his words of love and abruptly shifts the conversation to a political dimension. In Q, the placement of "Is it possible dat me shall love de enemie de France?" strikes me as less unsettling, both because his speech is short and because she does not entertain his wooing with small talk before asking the question. A naive and/or mellow Kate would obscure these dramatic possiblities.

The above relationships make it very difficult, in both versions, to determine the extent to which Henry and Kate love each other. As the dialogue continues, several other variations occur, but Henry claims to love Kate in Q and in F, trying to persuade her that she loves him, too. Her final reaction to him is, in both versions, "That is as it shall please the king my father," which further obscures her feelings and accentuates her condition of instrument in a political game.

It is, nevertheless, plausible to argue that Kate achieves a higher status in F, where Henry promises that she will be the "Queene of all" (F H 94), England, Ireland, France, and Henry Plantaginet, something he does not say in Q. Henry indicates, in F, a disposition to receive Kate as a Queen and to allow her a voice in political matters, just as he did with Isabel moments before. In Q he imposes his dominance and does not seem to view her as more than the breeder of the boy who "shall goe to Constantinople and take the great Turke by the beard" (Q G r/v). Henry's attitude is clear if we consider additional differences:

> Therefore tell me *Kate*, wilt thou haue me?
> *Kate.* Dat is as pleafe the King my father.
> *Harry.* Nay it will pleafe him:
> Nay it fhall pleafe him *Kate.*
> And vpon that condition *Kate* Ile kiffe you.
> *Ka.* O mon du Ie ne voudroy faire queike choffe
> Pour toute le monde,
> Ce ne poynt votree fachion en fouor,
> *Harry.* What faies fhe Lady?
> *Lady.* Dat it is not de fafion en *Frannce*,
> For de maides, before da be married to
> May foy ie oblye, what is to baffie?
> *Har.* To kis, to kis. O that us not the
> Fafhion in *Frannce*, for the mayees to kis
> Before they are married.
> *Lady.* O wye fee vetree grace.
> *Har.* Well, weele breake that cuftome.
> Therefore *Kate* patience perforce and yeeld.
> Before God *Kate*, you haue witchcraft
> In your kiiies:
> And may perfwade with me more,
> Then all the French Councell.
> Your father is returned.
>
> *Enter the King of France, and the Lordes.*

TEXTS AND PERFORMANCE IN THE FINAL SCENE OF *HENRY V* 217

> thy English broken : Therefore Queene of all, *Katherine,*
> breake thy minde to me in broken English; wilt thou
> haue me?
> *Kath.* Dat is as it shall pleafe *de Roy mon pere.*
> *King.* Nay, it will pleafe him well, *Kate*; it shall pleafe
> him, *Kate.*
> *Kath.* Den it fall alfo content me.
> *King.* Vpon that I kiffe your Hand, and I call you my
> Queene.
> *Kath. Laiffe mon Seigneur, laiffe, laiffe, may foy: Ie ne
> veux point que vous abbaiffe voftre grandeus, en baifant le
> main d'une noftre Seigneur indignie feruiteur excufe moy. Ie
> vous fupplie mon tref-puiffant Seigneur.*
> *King.* Then I will kiffe your Lippes, *Kate.*
> *Kath. Les Dames & Damoifels pour eftre baifee deuant
> leur nopcefe il net pas le coftume de Fraunce.*
> *King.* Madame, my Interpreter, what fayes fhee?
> *Lady.* Dat it is not be de fafhion pour le Ladies of
> Fraunce; I cannot tell wat is buiffe en Anglifh.
> *King.* To kiffe.
> *Lady.* Your Maieftee *entendre bettre que moy.*
> *King.* It is not a fafhion for the Maids in Fraunce to
> kiffe before they are marryed, would fhe fay?
> *Lady. Ouy verayment.*
> *King.* O *Kate,* nice Cuftomes curfie to great Kings.
> Deare *Kate,* you and I cannot bee confin'd within the
> weake Lyft of a Countreyes fafhion : wee are the ma-
> kers of Manners, *Kate*; and the libertie that followes
> our Places, ftoppes the mouth of all finde-faults, as I
> will doe yours, for vpholding the nice fafhion of your
> Countrey, in denying me a Kiffe : therefore patiently,
> and yeelding. You haue Witch-craft in your Lippes,
> *Kate :* there is more eloquence in a Sugar touch of
> them, then in the Tongues of the French Councell; and
> they fhould fooner perfwade *Harry* of England, then a
> generall Petition of Monarchs. Heere comes your
> Father.
>
> *Enter the French Power, and the Englifh
> Lords.*

The issue revolves around the kiss. In Q, Henry insists on kissing Kate as soon as he has the cue "Dat is as please the king my father." He seemingly disrespects Kate in at least two ways: by wanting to break a cultural custom, and by forcing her to do so ("... perforce and yeeld"). His verbal forcefulness almost naturally mandates a similar physical effect, such as a struggle during which Kate pulls away and rejects the kiss.

Henry's remark "you have witchcraft in your kisses" might suggest that their lips do touch, but it may also express what he imagines her kisses would be like. Whether or not they kiss, Henry comes across as a male disturbed by desire and is assertive both physically and verbally about Kate's power over him: "... [she] may persuade with [him] more, than all the French Council." But probably not as much more than a prospective sexual partner.

In F, Henry, less aggressive, does not pursue this desire to kiss so roughly. He begins by wanting to kiss Kate's hand, while stressing that he views her as his Queen. When she protests, he threatens to kiss her lips. Then, he describes the custom of not kissing before marriage as "nice," aptly arguing that they, as King and Queen, "are the makers of manners" and may, therefore, change the custom. F is open to a patient, gentle Henry, with better chances of persuading the woman before the King of France's return, than the rude, macho-type Q man. Whether Henry's gentleness in F is hypocritical or not, his willingness to persuade Kate places her in a status superior to that of Q, where her motives are ignored and she must simply "yieeld perforce," rather than "patiently." Kate's status continues to be different after the Council returns.

In Q (G3 v), Henry greets the Lords, and the King of France immediately remarks that he agrees with all the articles. France does not ask about Harry's conversation with Kate, and their marriage remains as taken-for-granted. A long exchange between Henry and Burgundy in F1 (H94), on the other hand, tells us that Kate has been unyielding and suspicious, so far resisting Henry's wooing. Burgundy speculates as to why Kate resists, and we learn that Henry "cannot so conjure up the spirit of love in her." Henry does not seem to care whether he and Kate are truly in love. He'd rather have her "wink," close her eyes, and yield to him perforce, like the "maiden walls that warre hath entred."

The fact that Kate's feelings are brought up in F defines her role as a woman who struggles with male authority, even though she complies with her father's will in both versions. Such a struggle may be true, and perhaps more oppressive and ironic in Q, but it never emerges as an impediment, which domineering Henry must overcome.

It would be perfect to conclude that, despite having a more dignified status in F1, Kate essentially emerges, in both versions, as a helpless war prisoner, a personification of France's defeat at Agincourt, like the "maiden cities [that] shall shew [Henry] the way to [his] will (F1 H94). But she actually rises above the status of prisoner if we consider that Henry ultimately reveals an obsession for her, settling for a lot less than what he had intended, when he and France agree, in both versions, on the terms of the following article:

> ... the King of France ... shall name your highness
> in this form and with this addition, in French,
> "Nostre très-cher fils Henri, Roi dÁngleterre, Héritier de
> France"; and thus in Latin, "Praeclarissimus filius noster
> Henricus, Rex Angliae
> et Haeres Franciae."
>
> (F H95; Q G3v)

Henry becomes the heir, and not the King of France. Kate's influence upon his decision appears to have been even greater in F, which contains, in the conventional act I, scene 2, an exclusive speech about his determination to take over France:

> now we are resolv'd, and ... France being ours,
> wee'l bend it to our Awe, Or breake it all to
> peeces, or there wee'l sit, (Ruling in large and
> ample Emperie, Ore France, and all her (almost)
> Kingly Dukedomes ...
>
> (F H 72)

What the ending of the play presents is a Henry who is quite far from sitting on the throne of France!

An additional textual evidence of Henry's fascination with Kate is that he, already knowing that the French had granted all the articles, requests her hand again in both versions when he is settled as France's heir:

> Why then let this among the rest,
> Have his full course And withall,
> Your daughter Katherine in marriage.
>
> (Q-G4 r)

> I pray you then, in love and dear allyance,
> Let that one Article ranke with the rest,
> And thereupon give me your Daughter.
>
> (F1-H 95)

Henry's speaking of "love and dear allyance" in F could be played romantically, so that Kate would emerge as the woman who tamed the aggressive warrior. This interpretation is further supported if we consider what happens in the final moments of action:

> *Har.* Why then faire *Katherine,*
> Come giue me thy hand:
> Our mariage will we present solemnise,
> And end our hatred by a bond of loue.
> Then will I sweare to *Kate,* and *Kate* to mee:
> And may our vowes once made, vnbroken bee.

FINIS.

> *King.* Now welcome *Kate:* and beare me witnesse all,
> That here I kisse her as my Soueraigne Queene.
> *Flourish.*
> *Quee.* God, the best maker of all Marriages,
> Combine your hearts in one, your Realmes in one:
> As Man and Wife being two, are one in loue,
> So be there 'twixt your Kingdomes such a Spousall,
> That neuer may ill Office, or fell Iealousie,
> Which troubles oft the Bed of blessed Marriage,
> Thrust in betweene the Pation of these Kingdomes,
> To make diuorce of their incorporate League:
> That English may as French, French Englishmen,
> Receiue each other. God speake this Amen.
> *All.* Amen.
> *King.* Prepare we for our Marriage: on which day,
> My Lord of Burgundy wee'le take your Oath
> And all the Peeres, for suretie of our Leagues.
> Then shall I sweare to *Kate,* and you to me,
> And may our Oathes well kept and prosp'rous be.
> *Senet.* *Exeunt.*
>
> *Enter Chorus.*

In Q their "bond of love" is represented by the holding of hands, as Henry asks Kate to "come and give [him her] hand." But what if she refused to approach him? The play would end with a nonverbal statement of her resistance to an imposed marriage. A peaceful atmosphere is almost inevitable in F, with a Henry who kisses his "Soveraigne Queene," a solemn flourish, and Queen Isabel's speech bringing concord into focus. A pathetic effect could be achieved, nevertheless, if Kate rejected the kiss, in which case Queen Isabel's final words would probably sound preposterous.

The Q version of the final scene of *Henry V* ultimately allows women, therefore, a lower status: Queen Isabel is either silent or totally absent, and Kate does not emerge as more than a breeder. Unless Henry's attitude in F is ironic, on the other hand, Isabel and Kate achieve a higher status in that version as participants in Court politics: Isabel uses power actively in the Council episode, while Kate's power is Henry's promise that she will act as his "Soveraigne Queene."

I believe, in light of the above, that the extent to which Queen Isabel and Kate can rise to prominence in Q and F will depend on the theatrical exploitation of irony, the playtext being open, as I have suggested, to at least five approaches: one in which Q is played without irony, to portray submissive women; one in which Q is used to portray nonverbally ironic and/or rebellious women; one in which F is played seriously and the man-woman relationship emerges as harmonious; an F interpretation in which Henry uses irony to mock the women; an F interpretation in which the women use intense irony to expose Henry's obsession with Kate.

One might argue that these possibilities are an obvious result of Isabel's having speeches in F and of F's wooing passages being longer than Q's. But this would be to reason in terms of quantity rather than quality, and worse, to confound plot with story line, since the textual differences do alter characterization and the arrangements of events. If Isabel is present at all in Q, it is as a flat character, whereas in F her speeches, physical appearance, and actions cause us both to perceive her more roundly and to notice additional effects regarding the use of power. Likewise, variations in the courting scene do not simply generate a Kate who uses more time in F and less time in Q, but one whose thoughts are developed differently in each version, with implications on the dramatic representation of power. One would simply fail to discover these relationships by viewing variants as cuts or additions, missing, or complementary parts of the scripts.

Of course, no one has been trying to decide which versions of Shakespeare's multiple-text plays to produce, and I do not intend to persuade anyone in this sense. My point is that not only directors, but also editors, critics, teachers, and general readers, including those who are primarily concerned with Shakespeare's intentions, should experience texts which, rather than literary pieces, were meant for theatrical use. *Play* is, therefore, a continuum of playtext, conceptualization, and performance.

The *Henry V* scripts available in bookstores today, just as the scripts of any other multiple-text play, are recreations of editors that offer additional examples of the unstable nature of texts. On the one hand, we can try to envision performance back in Elizabethan and Jacobean times by studying quartos and folios. It should be clear, however, that these different versions are not sources of immanent meanings. This paper has indirectly emphasized the point that the ultimate effects of a play are a result of choices in casting and interpretation. If we also consider that audience responses are historically particular, the dramaturgical information provided above would be especially useful for directors in trying to decide which playtext would be more coherent with particular staging choices and conditions.

NOTES

1. For representative reformist and performance criticism, see M. Warren, "Quarto and Folio 'King Lear' and the interpretation of Edgar and Albany," in *Shakespeare: Pattern of Excelling Nature,* ed. D. Bevington and J. L. Halio (Newark: 1978); G. Taylor and M. Warren, *The Division of the Kingdoms* (Oxford, 1983); P. McGuire, *Speechless Dialect* (Berkeley, 1985); S. Urkowitz, " 'Wellsayd olde Mole"—burying Three Hamlets in Modern Editions," in *Shakespeare Study Today,* ed. H. Furness and G. Ziegler (New York, 1986), 37–70; M. G. Rauen, "Shakespeare's Endings and Effects: A Study of Quarto and Folio Versions of *The Merry Wives of Windsor, Henry V,* and *Hamlet* (Ph.D. diss., Michigan State University, 1987); Paul Werstine, "The Textual Mystery of Hamlet," *Shakespeare Quarterly* 39, no. 1 (1988): 1–26.

2. For orthodox textual studies see H. Craig, *A New Look at Shakespeare's Quartos* (Stanford, 1961); H. Craig, "The Relation of the First Quarto Version and the First Folio Version of Shakespeare's *Henry V, Philological Quarterly* 6 (1927): 225–34; A. W. Pollard, *Shakespeare's Fight with the Pirates and the Problem of the Transmission of His Text* (Cambridge, 1920); H. T. Price, *The Text of* 'Henry V' (Newcastle-under-Lyme, 1921); W. W. Greg, ed., introduction to William Shakespeare's *Henry V,* Shakespeare Quarto Facsimiles, no. 9 (Oxford, 1957).

3. C. Hinman, *The Printing and Proofreading of the First Folio of Shakespeare* (Oxford, 1963); *The First Folio of Shakespeare* (New York, 1968).

4. W. Gundersheimer, foreword to *The First Folio of Shakespeare,* by P. W. M. Blayney (Washington, D.C., 1991). I have also verified that the passages which have been quoted from the Yale facsimile do not differ from those in the Norton facsimile: William Shakespeare, *The First Folio of Shakespeare,* 2 ed. (New York: W. W. Norton, 1996). This second edition of the Norton facsimile was used, in which Peter W. M. Blayney provides a thorough critical review of preparator Charlton Hinman's methods and procedures.

5. The modern edition I used was A. Harbage's *William Shakespeare, the Complete Works,* the Pelican text revised (New York, 1969).

6. The core ideas in this essay originate in my discussion of irony in *Henry V*

Q1 and F1, the subject of a chapter in my doctoral dissertation (q.v. Rauen, note 1). The following methodological choices are important: (a) When I use the phrase "final scene," I refer to the unit of dramatic action which we now call act 5, scene 2 in *Henry V.* I have discussed endings because they reshape the previous action and our understanding of it. I do not employ orthodox act, scene, and line numbering because they are based on conflated versions and on methods which I could not adopt in order to continue my research; (b) My references to the playtexts correspond to the quire numbering found at the bottom of the page in Q, and to the numbers found at the top of each F page. I add "H," which stands for Histories before the F page numbers, in order to identify the section of the volume, since the same numbers are repeated for comedies and tragedies. I add either an "r" (recto) or a "v" (verso) to specify the side of the page in Q; (c) I include photocopies of passages from actual quarto and folio playtexts both to provide a clear sense of the variations and to avoid the confusion that extensive quotations on the basis of a modern edition would cause.

7. For a full treatment of differences in the wooing scene, which I won't develop here for the sake of brevity, see *"Henry V"* in Raen, "Shakespeare's Endings."

Notes on Contributors

THOMAS LABORIE BURNS, Ph.D. in literary studies from the Federal University of Santa Catarina, has lived in Brazil since 1970 and is an associate professor of English and American literature at the Federal University of Minas Gerais. He has published poetry, literary translations, and criticism in Brazil and the United States. His principal research area is contemporary fiction and history.

ANNA STEGH CAMATI is an assistant professor of English literature and drama studies at the Federal University of Paraná. She obtained her Ph.D. in English language and Anglo-American literature from the University of São Paulo. She has published articles on Shakespeare and British drama and is currently working on an open course entitled "Shakespeare, our Contemporary."

SILVIA MUSSI DA SILVA CLARO is an assistant professor of Comparative Literature at the State University of São Paulo, Marília, where she works in the Department of Philosophy. She obtained her Ph.D. from the University of São Paulo and has published various articles on English and Brazilian literature, especially Machado de Assis. She is now researching the short stories of Machado de Assis in her post-doctorate work.

THAÍS FLORES NOGUEIRA DINIZ is an Associate professor of English Literature at the Federal University of Minas Gerais. She got her Ph.D. in Comparative Literature from the Federal University of Minas Gerais. She has several articles on Intersemiotic Translation and Film Adaptation. She is mainly interested in literature and the other arts, myth as translation, and intersemiotic translation.

MARIA CLARA GALERY, Ph.D. from the University of Toronto, wrote her dissertation on Shakespeare in South America, whose title is "Identifying Strategies for the Production and Reception of Shakespeare in Brazil and Argentina." She obtained her M.A. in English at the Federal University of Minas Gerais, Brazil, after having pursued research at the University of London, England, on a British Council Fellowship.

MARIA LÚCIA MILLÉO MARTINS is an associate professor of literatures in English at Universidade Federal de Santa Catarina. She obtained her Ph.D. from the University of Massachusetts. While a student there, she participated in a special seminar on Shakespeare, "Shakespeare and Cultural History" that gathered scholars from different institutions. The course resulted in the essay published in this collection. In addition to articles and translations, she published *Antologia de Poesia Norte-Americana Contemporânea.* She is also a contributor to *Metamorphoses,* the journal of the five-college seminar on literary translation. Currently she is working on an adaptation of her dissertation, a study on Elizabeth Bishop and Carlos Drummond de Andrade, to be published in Brazil. She was twice awarded Fulbright Scholarships.

ADELAINE LA GUARDIA NOGUEIRA is an associate professor of literatures in English at Fundação de São João del Rei, Minas Gerais. She has an M.A. degree in English from the Federal University of Minas Gerais and is currently working on her Ph.D. dissertation in comparative literature at the same university.

SOLANGE RIBEIRO DE OLIVEIRA is Professor Emerita of the Federal University of Minas Gerais. Associate of the University of London Institute of Education, Fulbright Scholar (1980–82) and former associate professor of English of the Federal University of Ouro Preto, de Oliveira cites as her main interests cultural studies and literature and the other arts. She has published extensively, including *A Barata e a Crisálida: o Romance de Clarisse Lispector* (1984), *Stylistic Markers in William Golding's Early Novels* (1985), *Literatura e Artes Plásticas* (1993), *Abgar Renault* (1996), and *De Mendigos e Malandros: Chico Buarque, Bertold Brecht, John Gay* (1999).

JOSÉ ROBERTO O'SHEA is professor of English and American literature at Universidade Federal de Santa Catarina. He received his Ph.D. in English from the University of North Carolina, Chapel Hill. He has published Portuguese translations of fiction by Flannery O'Connor, Christopher Isherwood, and James Joyce; poetry by W. H. Auden and various contemporary American poets, and annotated, verse translations of Shakespearean drama, for example, *Antônio e Cleópatra*. He has just completed an annotated translation of *Cymbeline, King of Britain* (forthcoming). He spent all of 1997 at the Shakespeare Institute, in Stratford-upon-Avon, as an Honorary Fellow, researching performance translation.

BERNARDINA DA SILVEIRA PINHEIRO is Professor Emeritus of English Literature at the Federal University of Rio de Janeiro. She has published several articles on English Literature. She translated James Joyce's *A Portrait of the Artist as a Young Man,* is a researcher of Joyce's work, and is currently translating *Ulysses.* She has also translated Laurence Sterne's *A Sentimental Journey.*

MARGARIDA GANDARA RAUEN has a Ph.D. in English from Michigan State University and was a postdoctoral fellow at the Folger Shakespeare Library in 1992 and 1997. Professor of Drama at the Faculdade de Artes of Paraná, she has published theater reviews in various Brazilian newspapers and academic articles in *The Modern Language Journal, Shakespeare Quarterly,* and *Allegorica.* As a guest editor, she organized an issue about English Renaissance poetry and drama for *Ilha do Desterro,* a journal of the Federal University of Santa Catarina. Rauen is the author of *Richard II: Playtexts, Promptbooks, and History: 1597–1857* (1988), and has edited the entry about Shakespeare in Latin America for the Oxford University Press Companion to Shakespeare. Her current research interests include genders and the use of counterdiscourse in theater.

WILLIAM VALENTINE REDMOND is a retired professor from the Federal University of Juiz de Fora, Minas Gerais, and is at present working at the Centro de Ensino Superior de Juiz de Fora. Vice-president of Centro de Estudo Shakespeareanos, in Brazil, he got his Ph.D. in literary theory from the Federal University of Rio de Janeiro. He is at present engaged in research on the intertextuality of authors from Minas Gerais and those of the literatures of the English language. He has published on authors of the modernist movement of English literature.

AIMARA DA CUNHA RESENDE is a retired professor of English literature from the Catholic University of Minas Gerais and a retired associate professor of English literature from the Federal University of Minas Gerais. She is now Professor of English Literature at the University of the State of Minas Gerais. She got her Ph.D. in comparative literature from the University of São Paulo. Founder and president of the Shakespeare Studies Center (Centro de Estudos Shakespeareanos), in Brazil, she has published several articles on Shakespeare, including some on Shakespeare in Brazil and Shakespeare and cultural studies. She is currently researching in Shakespeare on the Brazilian TV and finishing a book on Shakespeare for the Brazilian reader/spectator. She has been working as a dramaturg for different theater companies for the performance of Shakespeare's plays.

MARLENE SOARES DOS SANTOS, M.A. in English from the University of California, Los Angeles, and Ph.D. in English literature from the University of Birmingham, UK, is professor of English literature at the Federal University of Rio de Janeiro. She has published several articles on English literature in general and Shakespeare and Elizabethan theater in particular. Among them are "Ritual in Shakespearean Drama," in *Myth: Yesterday and Today,* edited by Donald Schüler and Miriam Barcellos Gomes, "The Elizabethan Theater," in *Theatre through History,* edited by Tânia Brandão, "Introduction to *Antony and Cleopatra* by William Shakespeare, translated by José Roberto O'Shea.

Index

Abujamra, Antônio. *See* Brazilian actors and actresses
Abyssinian maid, 60
Adaptation: concept, 30
All's Well That Ends Well, 180
Appropriation: concept, 30, 43
Arena Conta Zumbi, 48
Ariel, 157. See also Latin American thinkers: Rodó, José Enrique
Aristotle, 155. *See also* Slave: "natural"
Tempestade, A, 17–19, 33, 49, 170n. 10. *See also* Brazilian directors
Auden, W. H., 42
Warning for Fair Women, A, 104

Baker, Paul, 63
Bakhtin, Mikhail, 36, 141
Black Skins, White Masks, 158–59
Boal, Augusto. *See* Brazilian directors
Borges, Jorge Luis, 151
Braithwaite, Edward, 43, 159
Brazilian actors and actresses: Abujamra, Antônio, 63; Almeida, César. *See* Brazilian directors; Caetano, João, 13, 34, 76; Fernanda, Maria, 55; Guarnieri, Gianfrancesco, 46, 48; Pagu, 66; Stocklos, Denise, 63, 72, 74
Brazilian companies: Arena Theater, 33, 46–48; Grupo Galpão, 23–24, 30; Teatro Brasileiro de Comédia (TBC), 45–46
Brazilian critics: César Brites, 185; Eugênio Gomes, 13; Maria Lúcia Pallares-Burke, 62; Silviano Santiago. *See also* Latin American thinkers
Brazilian directors: César Almeida, 34, 63–72; Augusto Boal, 17–19, 30, 33, 43, 46–53; José Celso Martinez Corrêa, 27, 39, 63–64; Paulo Alfonso Grisolli, 19–21, 39; Felipe Hirsch, 27, 39, 64; Marcelo Marchioro, 67; Chico Pelúcio, 30, 32; William Pereira, 63; Gerald Thomas, 63, 72, 74; Gabriel Vilela, 23, 24, 26, 27, 39
Brazilian folklore: religious, 20, 21; songs from, 24–25, 30, 32; types in, 30
Brazilian translators: Jerônimo Aquino, 55; Augusto Campos, 55; Haroldo Campos, 55; Antônio Houaiss, 55; Ivan Junqueira, 55; Oscar Mendes, 55; Décio Pignatari, 55; Péricles Eugênio Ramos, 33, 55–61
Brazilian writers: José Alencar, 11, 12; Jorge Amado, 39; Carlos Dummond de Andrade, 39, 68; Mário de Andrade, 11, 16. *See also Macunaíma;* Oswald Andrade, 45. See also *Manifesto Antropófago* and *Manifesto Pau Brasil*; Assis, Machado, 15, 34, 39, 76–99, 151; Azevedo, Álvares, 12; Barreto, Lima, 29; Camargo, Joracy, 45; Dias, Gonçalves, 14; Rodrigues, Nelson, 39, 45; Rosa, Guimarães, 23, 25, 26
Brook, Peter, 198, 204
Browning, Robert, 42

Caetano, João. *See* Brazilian actors and actresses
Caliban: Apuntes sobre la Cultura en nuestra America, 43. *See also* Latin American thinkers
Caliban by the Yellow Sands, 42
Caliban: suite de la Tempête, 37, 43, 156–57. *See also* Renan, Ernest

INDEX

Caliban upon Setebos, 42
Carnivalization, 26–28, 36–37, 140–52
Celso, Zé. *See* Brazilian directors
Certain Hamlet, A, 63
Césaire, Aimé, 37, 43, 159–81
Cinema Novo, 44
Cuba hasta Fidel, 159. *See* Latin American thinkers
Cultural industry, 69–72
Curtain Theater, The, 102

Dark Lady, 57, 59–61, 145
Davenant, William, 42
Deleuze, Gilles, 132, 135
Denise Stoclos Unearths Hamlet in Irati, 63
Deus lhe Pague, 45
Dias, Gonçalves. *See* Brazilian writers
Doctor Faustus, 104
Dogg's Hamlet, 63
Dryden, John, 42

200 Exercícios para o Ator e o Não Ator com Ganas de Dizer Algo Através do Teatro, 48. *See also* Brazilian directors
East, West, 139, 140, 142, 149
eau de Jouvence, L', 43
Eles Não Usam Black Tie, 46
Eliot, T. S., 139, 141, 151, 174, 181
Elizabethan theaters: costumes: 110–11; setting, 101–5
Elsinore, 63
Estou Te Escrevendo De Um Lugar Distante, 27–29, 64

Fanon, Frantz, 158. *See also Black Skins, White Masks*
Fera Ferida, 29. *See also* TV appropriations
Film adaptations: Godard's *King Lear*, 38, 198–205
Fletcher, John, 36, 42, 130–32, 135

Godard, Jean-Luc, 38, 198–205
Gomes, Eugênio. *See* Brazilian critics
Guarnieri, Gianfrancesco. *See* Brazilian actors and actresses

Hamlet, 13, 27–28, 29, 34–35, 36, 38, 63, 67, 76–97, 140, 183–96. *See also* Parody

Hamlet ESP, 63
Ham-let, 27, 63–64
Hamlet Machine, The, 63
Hamletrash, 34, 64–75. *See also* Parody, of *Hamlet*
Haunted House Hamlet, 63
Henry V, 39, 207–23
Hulme, Peter, 162. *See also* Postcolonial theory

Imaginary Homelands, 139, 151
Interpretation. See *Henry V*
Islands, 43

King Lear, 38, 198–205
Kozintsev, Grigori, 198, 204
Kubla Khan. *See* Abyssinian maid
Kurosawa, Akira, 198, 204

Lamming, George. *See* Latin American thinkers
Language: use of, 36, 129–30, 148–49
Latin American thinkers: Sérgio Bellei, 11, 12, 13, 14, 32, 56; Antônio Cândido, 52; George Lamming, 43, 157; Roberto Fernández Retamar, 11, 16, 17, 32, 43, 49–50, 159, 162; José Enrique Rodó, 11, 15, 156, 162; Silviano Santiago, 11, 16, 24, 52; Vasconcelos, 11
Leonor de Mendonça, 14
Lobo, Edu, 48
Loomba, Ania, 43
Lotman, Iuri, 14

Macbeth, 13, 35, 114–25
MacKaye, Percy, 42
Macunaíma, 16
Mambembe theater, 24
Manifesto Antropófago, 15–17, 26, 45
Manifesto Pau Brasil, 15
Mannoni, Octave, 158
Marovitz's Hamlet, The, 63
Marowitz, Charles, 36, 63, 132, 134
Metatheater, 28, 38, 183–96
Military dictatorship (1964–1984), 43–45, 48
M.O.R.T.E., 63
Müeller, Heiner, 63

Myse-en-abyme, 203
Nineteenth-century Brazil, 11–15

O Rei da Vela, 45
Otelo de Oliveira, 19, 21
Othello, 13, 14, 58–59, 181. See also *Otelo de Oliveira*

Palmares, 175. *See also* Slave
Papp, Joseph, 63
Parody, 65–66; of *Hamlet*: 62–99, 140–53, 188, 199–205. *See also* Social satire
Paz, Octavio, 150
Performance, 39
Pleasures of Exile, 157
Political readings, 21, 67–68
Political theater, 46–47, 48
Postcolonial theory, 162
Psychologie de la Colonization, 158

Racial issues, 33–34, 37, 58–61, 180–81
Renan, Ernest, 37, 43, 156–57
Retamar, Roberto Fernández. *See* Latin American thinkers
Revolução na América do Sul, 49. *See also* Boal, Augusto
Rodó, José Enrique. *See* Latin American thinkers
Romeo and Juliet, 13, 24, 29. See also *Romeu e Julieta*
Romeu e Julieta, 19–21
Rose Theater, The, 100–01, 103, 104, 106, 108–11, 113n. 24
Rosencrantz and Guildenstern are Dead, 38, 63, 183–96
Rossi, Ernesto, 11, 13, 34, 76
Rushdie, Salman, 36, 138

Said, Edward, 43, 50
Salvini, Tomaso, 11, 13, 34, 76
Sea and the Mirror, The, 42
Sentimental Journey, 142
Serious comedy, 66, 73n. 11
Sir Thomas More, 103

Slave: "natural," 155–56; in Brazil, 174–75
Social readings, 21–23, 29, 68
Social satire, 78–99
Sonnets, 33, 55–61
Sterne, Laurence, 142–43, 152
Stoppard, Tom, 28, 38, 63, 183–96
Swan Theater, The, 103–5, 112n. 14, 113n. 32

Taming of the Shrew, The, 36, 126–36
Teatro do Oprimido, 48. *See also* Brazilian directors
Técnicas Latino-Americanas de Teatro Popular, 48
Tempest, The, 33, 37, 42, 43, 50, 154–181; revisionist readings of, 156–162 ; traditional readings of, 154–56, 178
Textual study, 39, 207–23
Theater: of Protest, 199; of Repetition, 36, 132, 135–36
Titus Andronicus, 35, 104–113
Tristram Shandy, 142–43
Tamburlaine, 103
TV appropriations, 19–23, 29
Twelfth Night, 30–32, 103

Tempête, Une: D'après La Têmpete de Shakespeare—adaptation pour un théâtre nègre, 37, 43, 154, 162–181

Vasconcelos. See Latin American thinkers
Vestido de Noiva, 45. *See also* Brazilian writers: Rodrigues, Nelson
Vilela, Gabriel. *See* Brazilian directors
Virgin Queen, The, 42

Woman's Prize or the Tamer Tamed, The, 36, 126, 130–32
Weiss, Peter, 63
William Shakespeare's "Naked" Hamlet, 63

Yorick, 36, 138

Zefirelli, Franco, 36, 132–34, 135
Zumbi, 174